In Pursuit of Clouds:

The Journey of Oswego's Weatherman Bob Sykes

Jim Farfaglia

ISBN-10:151519020X
ISBN-13:978-1515190202

Also by Jim Farfaglia

<u>Poetry</u>

Country Boy

People, Places & Things: The Powerful Nouns of My Life

Reach Out in the Darkness: How Pop Music Saved My Mortal Soul

<u>Local History</u>

Voices in the Storm: Stories From The Blizzard of '66

Of the Earth: Stories From Oswego County's Muck Farms

Camp Hollis: The Origins of Oswego County's Children's Camp
(co-written by Jane Spellman and Alysa Koloms)

DEDICATION

To Bob's children:
Barbara, Bruce and Fred.
Thank you for the opportunity
to tell this weatherman's story.

CONTENTS

Foreword by Al Roker

FOREWORD

I was a kid from Queens, looking to major in cinematography; I loved movies, radio and TV. Since I was putting myself through college, I knew I could not afford a private school like Syracuse University, so I turned to the state schools. While looking through the SUNY catalogue, I saw that Oswego State met my career objectives and I said, "You know what, why not?" I applied and was accepted; any school that would have me, I was willing to go to. So in 1972, I started at the State University College at Oswego, New York, where Professor of Meteorology Bob Sykes taught from 1961 to 1983.

It turned out to be a great move. After my first meteorology course, which I took to fulfill a science requirement, my department chair, Lew O'Donnell, who was Mr. Trolley on "The Magic Toy Shop" at WHEN-TV in Syracuse, told me the station was looking for a weekend weatherman. Andy Brigham, who was the News Director for WHEN, had asked Lew, "Have you got any students up at Oswego who will work for little money? I can only afford to pay for a drunk or a college student." And that was my start in TV weather forecasting.

Oswego, New York was and still is a great place for meteorology teachers and students. When the weather is beautiful, it is one of the most sublime places on earth. You're sitting there on a warm summer day and see that green flash just as the sun sets into Lake Ontario, and you're thinking, *Man, it cannot get any better than this.* Then winter comes and you're in a howling snowstorm, hearing thunder. Thunder? In winter? Sure enough, one night when going from the Oswego campus radio station to my dorm, I got to experience "thundersnow," and I remember thinking, *What the hell?*

From a meteorology standpoint, Oswego presents many such challenges and opportunities. And because of its location on that Great Lake, it attracts a certain individual who isn't interested in

1

being in a major city or in the center of the universe, but likes being where they are for its own sake. Oswego has always attracted a certain type of teacher – and I mean that as a compliment; all the professors I had the good fortune to learn from were terrific people.

Bob Sykes encompasses what I think is a hallmark of the professors at Oswego State. He was a military guy, and though he would never brag about his role forecasting the weather in Arctic conditions during World War II, that ruggedness really made him suited for SUNY Oswego and its famous winter weather. Professor Sykes had this presence about him and you could just see that he knew what he was talking about. The times that I chatted with him, I was always impressed. Here's this guy that runs meteorology programs and yet he takes the time to talk with you.

I remember once going into his office and being surprised that he was listening to a classical music piece, a movement from Beethoven, I think, and I said to myself, *I didn't see that coming!* Then I looked around his office and saw all these pieces of fine exotic wood. When you're a kid in college, you don't think of your teachers as full people, you think of them just being up in front of the classroom. I was always surprised at the fullness of who Bob Sykes was.

I got to experience one of Bob's famous meteorology classes taught on the roof of Oswego's science building, Piez Hall. One of my suitemates was a meteorology major and he convinced me to go. It was freezing when we got up there, with the wind blowing at about 25 miles per hour. And Bob was just like a kid in a candy store, pointing out the winds and such. After about 10 minutes, I thought, *This is crazy*, so I slowly sidled back toward the door and slipped into the backend of the stairs. I was sure I could never do that for a living.

Today, of course, I find myself standing in the middle of blizzards and hurricanes a lot. If only I had known and stayed on that roof with Bob a little longer, I would have been much more prepared for what my career has become.

When I consider the great advancements in meteorology since my years at SUNY Oswego, I think things like supercomputers would have fascinated Bob Sykes. But then again, he was very much a guy about gut. You can have all the technical expertise, but sometimes you just have to go on your own experience, which is exactly what Bob did. Coupled with all of today's science, Bob Sykes would have been great at helping today's meteorology students keep that human touch.

Al Roker
March 2015

PART ONE

A WEATHERMAN IS BORN

"Hath the rain a father?
Or who hath begotten the drops of dew?
Out of whose womb came the ice?
And though for hoary frost of heaven,
who hath gendered it?"

– Job 38:28-29

From Bob's opening remarks at his May 20, 1969
program for the Oswego County Historical Society.

Prologue

Inklings

The noonday sky over New York City is thick with clouds. All morning, they have been driven inland by a stiff winter wind off the Atlantic. Filling the heavens as far as the eye can see, they cast a gray probability to the day. Sure enough, by early afternoon, snow begins to fall, and drifts start forming, swirling at the wind's beck and call. Most people would have looked out on that cold December scene in 1924 and sighed. Most people, but not everyone.

Sitting at his desk in Public School # 21's second grade classroom, seven-year-old Bob Sykes is trying hard to pay attention to his teacher's lesson. But something keeps drawing his eyes from the blackboard to an eastern-facing window. Across Lee Avenue, where PS 21 is situated in Yonkers, there is a hill devoid of buildings. On blustery winter days, the wind meets that hill and carries fallen snow up and over it, creating intriguing drifts.

Like the wind churning that snowy landscape young Sykes is so intently studying, so does a curiosity stir in his mind. Nearly 75 years later, compiling the important challenges and achievements of his life, Bob would remember the view from that classroom window as the first time the weather commanded his attention.

The questions stirring in Bob on that windswept day guided him through his life. They would nudge him out of that classroom chair and into the outdoors, where he could not only see the phenomenon of turbulent weather, but also hear it, taste it, smell it and feel it. What his senses ignited in him would influence his academic choices, directing him down a career path that took him, first, to the top of the world, where he would serve his country with meteorological prowess, and later, to the top of college campus buildings, where he shared his passion for the weather with hundreds of like-minded students. Eventually, word about this unique and inspiring college professor spread to a local radio station, and soon Bob Sykes would daily be unlocking the sky's mysteries for his loyal listeners, including a particularly spectacular blizzard that made 1966 so memorable.

That second grade classroom window would be, you might say, Bob's porthole to our world's unpredictable weather; one he gladly entered, devoting his life to making it even a measure more predictable. Beginning with that day in 1924, no matter what he was doing or who he was with, when something amazing was happening in the sky, Bob Sykes stopped to notice.

Chapter 1

Learning to Look Up

Robert Brown Sykes, Jr. was born June 29, 1917 in New York City's Bronx borough. Twenty-nine years earlier, the devastating Blizzard of 1888 caught what was then thought of as the most sophisticated city in the world by surprise, claiming the lives of hundreds of ill-prepared citizens. And though the meteorologists who witnessed that storm's destruction vowed to advance their science in order to avoid such a tragic loss in the future, on the day Sykes began his journey toward joining his fellow weathermen in that quest, the tools of their science had hardly changed. Indeed, the radar and computer models that would intrigue Bob in his later years, were more than a half century away.

The forecaster announcing weather conditions on Bob's day of birth still relied on little more than a thermometer, air pressure gauge and wind meter to predict what people found when stepping outside their New York City apartments. His report on that June day promised a few gentle summer showers, making the day different enough from a recent string of summer-in-the-city scorchers to cause a curious person to pause and take notice. Had Bob been old enough, he would have surely set aside what he was involved with to find a better vantage point for observing the sky. Cloudy days had a way of doing that to him.

Young Sykes had lots of opportunities to take note of the weather in various New York City locations. When he was a toddler, Bob moved with his parents, Robert Brown, Sr. and Isabelle Tolemie Sykes, into an apartment on 134th Street in the Bronx. It would be one more move after many made by his parents and their families. After Robert Sr.'s kin had emigrated from Wales and Isabelle's from Scotland, both families settled in the Scranton, Pennsylvania area. There Robert and Isabelle met, courted and married. They headed north to New York City, where Robert found work in the meat market business on the west side of Manhattan. Their wish to start a family came true with Bob. He would be their only child.

At age five, Bob and his family moved to DeVoe Avenue, in Yonkers, in the northernmost part of New York City. Situated between the metropolis' bustling life and the rural areas just beyond it, DeVoe would be home to Bob until his adulthood. Growing up in such a major city wouldn't seem like an ideal place for a youngster who was curious about the complexities of the weather. But the New York City of Sykes' childhood was markedly different from what one sees today. Looking back on the neighborhood of his youth, Bob remembered it almost country-like:

"As a matter of fact, about 1,200 feet toward the north beyond our house, there were woods. To the east was a short road, part of what was known as Hall Place. If you went east of the intersection of Hall Place and DeVoe, you went right into farmland. Cows would come down into the our area occasionally."

This pastoral setting gave Bob plenty of room to explore his growing interest in the weather. In his younger years, the gravel streets of his neighborhood were unlit, offering a sky of stars majestically visible on cloudless nights. What those luminary displays stirred in Bob's imagination matched the wonder he found in falling snowflakes. Of course, he was not alone in his fascination

10

with heavenly bodies. Night skies can become a storyboard for the legends we hear as children. And when the right story comes along, it can often turn that curiosity into a lifelong quest.

Just such a metamorphosis would take place for Bob when, sometime during his eighth year, Isabelle Sykes sat her son down and shared stories she had learned about her family's history. It seems that Isabelle's surname, Tolemie, was derived from the name of one of science's early great thinkers: Ptolemy. Born in AD 90, the Greco-Egyptian writer was known for his advanced theories as a mathematician, geographer, astrologer, and particularly interesting to Bob, an astronomer. Ptolemy's assertion that Earth was the center of the universe was widely accepted for nearly 1500 years, and while this and most of his other theories would eventually be disproven, his outstanding abilities in mathematics are still highly regarded.

Isabelle and the rest of the Tolemies learned of their supposed link with Ptolemy through research done by her brother, Alfred. The study of his ancestors led Alfred to believe that when the Tolemies left Scotland, they Americanized their last name. This was common practice for immigrants, who hoped that a name's easier pronunciation would provide for a smooth assimilation into United States culture. But Alfred's research did not stop there. Though his methods were not particularly scientific and he took many liberties with the information he was uncovering, Alfred determined that Ptolemy, and thus Tolemie, could be traced back even further, not ending until his family roots showed up in man's earliest records of civilization.

Tolemie, Alfred surmised, was also a variation of Tolemaekis, a name found in fourth century BC, during the time of Aristotle and Alexander the Great. Adding more support for his historically-rich theory, Alfred learned that one of Alexander's generals who ruled part of the Alexandrine Empire was, in fact, named Tolemie.

With her brother's research considered to be factual by the

Pennsylvania Tolemies, Isabelle did not hesitate to share this version of her family's heritage when Bob became old enough to appreciate it. As he progressed through his school studies, when history lessons focused on the world's greatest minds, his family ties to Alexander the Great's empire sparked young Sykes' imagination. For those history lessons were to reveal that both Alexander and his General Tolemie were purportedly students of Aristotle, whom Sykes came to consider as one of the greatest thinkers that ever lived.

"Matters that he wrote about and taught lasted for perhaps 2,000 years," Bob would one day deduct. "He is credited, though it may not be true, with [coining the word] meteorology, which is from the Greek words meteor: things above the earth and logy: the study of."

How exciting it must have been for Bob to hear of his family's link to the legacy of Aristotle. Did his fascination with what he saw in the heavens flourish when his mother shared her beliefs? Or was he merely encouraged to learn that his interest in celestial observation was in the same league as those ancient Greeks? One thing for sure: Bob embraced his mother's story and passed on the proposed Tolemie/Ptolemy lineage to future generations of Sykes, starting with his children.

Bob's son, Fred, thinks that his father's family connection to Egyptian and Greek history was "tenuous," but he also acknowledged that "it held my father's interest." Later in life, Bob enjoyed traveling and he made sure to include in his destinations a visit to sites of early Egyptian civilization. "While there," Fred notes, "my father acquired papyrus [vegetation used by Egyptians and other Mediterranean cultures to record sacred documents] and brought it back to the United States."

Two of Bob's grandchildren, Sarah Sorensen and Kathleen Sykes, remember listening to stories about their family's possible connection to Egyptian culture. "Grandpa was certain that his mother was related to Cleopatra," Sarah says. "And so he had a love for all things Egyptian." "He was a bit of a collector," Kathleen adds. "After he had passed, we were admiring his collection of beautiful relics, jewelry and such. In particular, I remember that he had this Egyptian gold ring." "He wore it all the time," Sarah recalls.

When his career path led him to State University of Oswego meteorology classrooms, Sykes shared with his students the proposed link from his family to those ancient, wise minds. One of those students, Tom Moore, still remembers how his professor began the first day of each class: "Bob was telling us about his background: where he went to school, the military, etc. Then he wrote the word 'Ptolemy' on the board. 'Before I was ever interested in meteorology,' Bob told us, 'my initial interest was astronomy.'

"Professor Sykes claimed that he was a direct descendent of the Ptolemies," Tom continues. "I didn't challenge what he said, although, as time went on, I would learn that he would say things that were kind of 'out there.' But then they would end up being true, so it was like he was in touch with the way things are beyond this world."

Bob's claim that an interest in astronomy actually preceded his immersion in the weather was accurate, for right around the time that Isabelle Sykes shared her thought-provoking history with him, an astronomical event took place right in the Sykes' backyard. In January 1925, word spread throughout New York City and all of the northeastern United States of a rare opportunity to witness what few people ever do: a total eclipse of the sun. The projected date of January 24 was excitedly anticipated by young and old; among them Bob Sykes.

In early 20th century America, an eclipse was a great mystery to most people, not only because science was just beginning to understand the phenomenon, but also from their rareness. The probability of a total solar eclipse occurring on a given spot in the world is once every 400 years. Annually, Earth will never play host to more than seven eclipses, and in some years that number can be as little as four. Added to the slim chance of witnessing one, there's the frustrating fact that an eclipse is rarely observable for more than two minutes; none, in fact, will ever last longer than seven. The odds of being in the right place in the right year – if not the right century – are few indeed.

But, humanity's fascination with eclipses goes beyond their rarity; their mystique during Bob Sykes' youth had also resulted from all that was unknown. Primitive civilizations dating as far back as 2100 BC tried in vain to understand the meaning behind these awe-inspiring events. From this fear, early cultures created rituals to keep what they perceived as the gods' fury from harming them. It took thousands of years before people would be able to trust that these unexplained shifts in the heavens were actually based in reason and not to be dreaded. Still, even today, an eclipse holds many in awe.

And so, when Bob's introduction to the thrill of observing an eclipse took place, it became as memorable as that snowy landscape outside his classroom window. In his autobiographical notes, Sykes described that first eclipse: "The January day was cold and virtually cloudless; a perfect day for viewing. It had been one of the more snowy winters in our part of the state, but, fortunately, by the day of the event, the weather was very good." Bob explained the 90-second showing taking place in mid- to late morning, with his family among the dozens in their neighborhood to witness it. "My father smoked some glass," he noted, "which was the recommended viewing method at the time."

The experience of watching the amazing display in the sky, Bob later wrote, "marked me forever," and for the inquisitive seven-year-old, a passion was born. That passion eventually matured into an understanding of the proper science of an eclipse, but Bob would forever balance those facts with the wonderment such a celestial show cast over people. In many ways, an eclipse's mysteries were as intriguing as the story of his family's lineage to the great minds of long ago. Throughout his life, his pursuit of ideal viewing conditions never waned, with Sykes traveling the world in order to bear witness to 13 more eclipses. Looking back, his children suggest why.

"I suspect that Dad's fascination with eclipses had to do with the historical aspect of the distant past," his daughter, Barbara, offers. "Long ago, when people saw an eclipse, they thought the world was ending and all kinds of horrible things might happen. There were so many things that people didn't understand that, in fact, some of them went crazy. That was part of Dad's interest, but, of course, an eclipse takes place in the sky, just like the clouds, and he probably wondered how this affected the weather."

Eclipses and weather certainly do interrelate: A random cloud drifting overhead at the wrong time can ruin this once-in-several-lifetimes event. In fact, as Fred points out, "my father's whole interest in clouds stemmed from that first eclipse he saw as a child. It got him interested in the atmosphere and looking up – and that is what got him interested in weather."

All too soon, young Bob experienced how clouds could easily interrupt an opportunity to witness the majesty of an eclipse. His next viewing, during his teen years, would be thwarted by bad weather. But that disappointment did not slow down the budding weather-watcher. At some point between his first and second encounters with an eclipse, Sykes acquired some important tools that could address his ever-expanding questions hovering above.

Like any budding astronomer, Bob was anxious to begin investigating this rapidly-advancing science for probing the skies. But he would only be able to do so through the kindness of a family friend, something that the Sykes family would have to rely on more and more as the United States entered a disturbing financial chapter of its history.

Robert and Isabelle Sykes struggled throughout Bob's early life to provide for their eager-to-learn child. When the stock market crashed and in the hard times that followed, like many trying to provide for their families, Robert Sr. was periodically out of work. Eventually, he was employed by Tupman Thurlow, an English company whose main business was the purchase and sale of meat in large quantities. "My father worked for this firm until the Depression got so bad that his business trailed off," Bob recalled. "Being extremely honorable, he could not see being kept on if there was not enough work. My father offered to resign, even though he had two or three more years on a contract which was not breakable unless he chose to break it." It was a stirring lesson in integrity that, years later, Bob referenced when he was faced with his own career-altering decisions.

Things did not improve for the Sykes family throughout Bob's impressionable teen and early-adult years, and he would thereafter refer to himself as a "Depression kid." Images of the long lines of people begging for scraps of food and cigarettes never faded for him. "In my own family, my parents lost almost everything except the house," Bob revealed in his later writings. "This included my father's job, some property that they had bought and investments they had made, which were primarily for their old age and for my college. They lost all that money."

After the Depression ended and into the 1940s, Bob's father struggled to maintain steady employment. He bought a truck and printed "Robert B. Sykes" on its side and then acted "as a 'jobber,'" Bob explained, "someone who buys and sells on a daily basis." This business, too, would fail. In his adulthood, Bob would relate an experience to his daughter, Barbara, that vividly and painfully illustrates those lean years for the Sykes family. "One year at Christmas, there was only one present," Barbara recalls her father telling her. "Maybe it was something like an orange, which would have been a huge gift at that time, since they weren't readily available. But he only got the one gift, and later that day when he took the dog out for a walk, he cried the whole time."

Every Christmas after she heard that story, Barbara made sure her father had lots of little things to open.

Perhaps it was this lack of possessions early in life that later influenced the decisions Bob made about his own material wealth and how he shared it with others. Though he became a collector of sorts and surrounded himself with examples of nature's beauty, he made these things available to those less fortunate in life. Doing so must have given him great satisfaction, as did how he ultimately chose to reflect on his youth.

Rather than focus on the melancholy aspects of his childhood, he chose, instead, to frame those years and his parents in their best light: "My great fortune was in having the parents that I did. [With] their support and, of course, the many sacrifices that they made on my behalf, I could go to college and pursue my interest in weather."

When they could, Bob's parents found ways to engage in some pleasurable experiences as a family. During his elementary school years, the Sykes joined a yacht club. (Bob would refer to it as a "swimming club," though, since his parents had no way of purchasing such luxuries as a boat.) A family by the name of Kincaid also had membership at this club and the family's father, Eric, worked with Robert Sr. Through their conversations, Mr. Kincaid learned about the enthusiasm Bob had for astronomy after his first encounter with an eclipse, and something that he saw in the youngster inspired Kincaid to offer him several books on the subject.

"Some of them were pretty good because of their illustrations," Bob gratefully recalled. One book, *Splendour of the Heavens,* would have a lifelong place in Bob's library. Another, *Norton's Star Atlas,* included in its glossary the plans for building a telescope support known as equatorial mounting. If properly set, the mounting provided a viewer the ability to follow astronomical bodies across the sky. Bob's intense interest in studying the heavens prompted his father to have a carpenter construct the special mounting. The elder Sykes then fastened it to a telescope and surprised his son with it.

Bob was never sure where the telescope came from: Was it something his father already owned? Did he acquire it from the Kincaids? Did his father spend what little extra money the family had for its purchase? However it came to be in his possession, Bob noted his appreciation for such a sophisticated method of celestial exploration.

After seven years of closely examining the skies, 15-year-old Bob Sykes and his family took off for Lancaster, New Hampshire, where the Mt. Washington Observatory* had planned a program centered around the August 1932 total solar eclipse. Young Sykes was eager to put his growing astronomical knowledge to use, hopefully enhancing his viewing experience.

But Bob's excitement quickly faded when the late summer sky turned cloudy, preventing the group from seeing the sun's total eclipse. Though he remembered that trip as "a failure," he also saw it as a turning point in his life. Noting how the timing of the cloud cover so decidedly altered his plans, Bob's disappointment led to a "very rapid [switch] from astronomy to being interested in the weather."

And not just any kind of weather. Though he would also enjoy the challenge of exploring thunderstorms and extreme windstorms, it was winter's weather systems, with their variety seem-

---

*Since 1932, the Observatory has been dedicated to advancing the understanding of weather and climate, and has regularly sponsored expeditions and educational events, both on and off Mount Washington.

ingly as limitless as a snowflake's, which commanded Sykes' attention. His partiality to a good snowstorm would begin as it does for any active child. Along with books to be read and observatory instruments to master, there was also the joy of experiencing winter weather. Bob and his friends found that the hills of DeVoe Avenue – he would later determine that they were drumlins formed in the Ice Age – made perfect landscapes for long rides on their Flexible Flyer sleds.

Young Bob Sykes exploring one of the many complexities of winter weather.

But Bob couldn't help noticing how those sled rides could either be enhanced or impeded by the type of snow accumulating on those hills. Especially during snowstorms, Sykes' attention was rapt. He recalled that a western-facing window of his childhood home was perfect for observing a valley which the Hudson River passed through: "I could not see the Palisades from the window, but I could see the effects of the winds coming from the west and northwest blowing snow across DeVoe Avenue. This snow and the clouds related to snow conditions activated my interest, [much as they had] in second grade at PS 21."

Over time, Bob's attention to the particularities of winter weather led to his curiosity of cloud variations. Wondering what the elements were that could produce a good storm, he also began differentiating snowflake composition based on whether storm systems traveled over land or ocean. With each observation of a storm, a cloud or a snowflake, Bob uncovered new questions and he enjoyed pondering each winter weather mystery. In time, he would discover that he was not alone in his intrigue.

Chapter 2

The World as Small as a Snowflake

Snowflakes photographed by Bob Sykes during his research on lake-effect snow at SUNY Oswego.

Around the time that Bob's interest in snow matured beyond striving for the best sledding conditions, another dedicated weather enthusiast published a book that invited readers into the very essence of a winter storm. In 1931, Wilson "Snowflake" Bentley, who had devoted a lifetime to perfecting an innovative art technique known as photomicrography, collected his work into a volume named simply *Snow Crystals*. The book contained 2,300 snowflake images, each one painstakingly captured by Bentley through the magnification of crystals with his high-powered microscope. Shortly after its publication, *Snow Crystals* became a popular resource for winter weather observers like Sykes, providing them with their first comprehensive collection of snow-flake variations.

It's unclear when Sykes first discovered Bentley's work; he was 14 when *Snow Crystals* was published. Could a copy of it have been among the books shared by the Kincaids? Or did he have to wait until one of his college meteorology classes to learn of it? Whenever it finally became a reference book for his studies, it proved to be an apt guide for a detail-oriented weather observer like Bob Sykes. As his interest in the weather grew, not only was Bob looking for answers in the expanse above him, but he also began searching at a microscopic level. In Wilson Bentley, Bob found his first mentor in the art of observational precision.

Bentley was a perfect role model for Bob. The artful collection of flake formations displayed in *Snow Crystals* was a culmination of 40 years of the photographer's work. As the first person to successfully capture a snow crystal's composition, Bentley provided tangible proof that, indeed, no two snowflakes are alike. As a result of his groundbreaking work, his biographer described Bentley as a "tireless observer," the very phrase that those who had worked alongside Bob would use to describe him.

No matter when or how Bentley and Bob's work crossed paths, Sykes had found a kindred spirit, and he made sure that those who loved the study of weather as much as he did would be introduced to such an important contributor to the science. This included sharing Bentley's microscopic world of snowflakes with his family. As soon as his oldest child, Barbara, could hold a book in her hands, she was given a copy of *Snow Crystals* to explore.

"It is my earliest memory of a book," says Barbara, a lifelong reader who worked for many years as a librarian. "It was how I learned about books; *Snow Crystals* was where I learned how to turn the pages of a book."

Bob's intrigue with the world as small as an ice crystal didn't stop with snowflakes. On those winter days of his childhood, one of the boys sledding alongside Bob was a neighborhood friend, Billy Browne. When snow conditions weren't good enough for winter games or it was just too cold to be outside, the boys would look for indoor activities, and it was Billy who introduced Bob to yet another new interest, this one drawing him deeper into the world of precise detail and order. Billy Browne was a stamp collector, and once Bob Sykes learned the intricacies of the hobby, he exuberantly became one as well.

Stamp collecting would have been a logical hobby to pursue for bright young boys and girls in the 1930s. During the Depression, Americans of all ages were looking for an inexpensive form of entertainment. When the nation's leader, Franklin Roosevelt, proclaimed his enjoyment of stamp collecting, people took notice. Since every stamp told a story, Roosevelt promoted them as a useful teaching device, and soon, having a well-organized stamp collection was seen as an important facet of a meaningful education. So it would have made sense for Billy's parents (his father was a college professor) to foster this activity in their son and, in turn, for Billy to pass it on to Bob.

Soon, Sykes had his own collection, which quickly grew once he discovered a good source for stamps in the unlikely place of his parents' Baptist church. Located in lower New York's bookselling and bookbinding district, the church had a bookstore owner among its congregation. "A Mr. Schulte," Bob recalled "who played organ at the church. My father took me to his store and Mr. Schulte gave me some stamps he'd received from many parts of the world."

Stamps from across the globe have a way of transporting a youngster's imagination, and Bob found himself immediately drawn to the Cape of Good Hope of South Africa. With its colorful history of Dutch and British colonization before achieving independence in 1910, the Cape issued attractive stamps that were unique in design. Bob and Billy found a particular interest in their triangular shape, but after the boys realized their extra cost (neither ever had much money to spend on their hobby), they looked elsewhere in the world.

Soon their focus shifted to Rhodesia, which the boys had been hearing about in radio broadcasts. The South African country had been long fighting to free itself from colonization under British rule, and its calls for freedom and the courageous fights that led to its eventual success produced some emotionally-stirring, expressive stamps.

As a new collector, Bob soon learned that there was an art to presenting such important history in an effective manner. A properly displayed and thought-provoking collection demanded that Sykes look at the minute details of his subject. Every element of a stamp, just as with a snowflake, had to be examined. His findings then needed order, structure and reference points to support his work – all important skills for a future weatherman.

Bob honed this ability to study and perfect details at a remarkably young age; he would not yet be in his teens when his stamp collection began to garner attention. But focusing on detail would have seemed natural to someone who always had an eye for life's intricacies. Here is Sykes describing his earliest memory:

"The first thing I remember in my life is being in the hospital. It was after I had my tonsils and adenoids out. As I was coming out of the ether, everything was all white, including the bed and the nurses' uniforms, of course, and I had the impression of being stepped on by an elephant."

Quite a disturbing image for a first memory. His second, though much gentler, was just as descriptive. Recalled at the end of his life, Bob shared a boyhood memory of the landmark in his front yard. Something that many of us can remember, perhaps, but it is within the details of his home's sugar maple – last seen by him 70 years earlier – where Sykes' gift is realized: "It was about 55 to 60 feet tall, and around two and a half to three feet in diameter near the base of the tree. It was a good-sized maple, with small leaves."

Years later, when discussing persistent weather patterns with fellow Oswego meteorologist Elmer Loveridge, Bob was able to relate his memory of severe winter flooding in New York City throughout the mid-1930s:

"There was ice around The Battery on the southern tip of Manhattan, thick ice chunks in the lower Hudson River, and also in the Bay beyond. And there was Arctic 'sea smoke.'" Not one to leave unique weather conditions unexamined, Sykes goes on to explore the misleading term 'sea smoke':

"It is a conglomeration of three misnomers: this 'smoke' is not smoke, but condensed water due to evaporation from a warm surface and immediate condensation in cold air above; the phenomenon is not limited to the sea, but can occur over one's swimming pool; and, of course, [it] is not limited to the Arctic."

Before he ever took a meteorology class, Bob's career as a weatherman was already taking shape with his inherent attention to detail and ability for recall. His instinct for considering and comprehending complex subjects in his youth were an early introduction to the still-evolving science of weather he would one day encounter.

Other youth-oriented activities, such as the Boy Scouts, taught him the value of continual striving toward achievement despite the obstacles, as well as elements of teamwork, goal-planning and successful leadership. His attainment of these skills earned Sykes his Eagle Scout Award in 1931, at the unusually young age of 14.

Some might look at all these activities – the stamp collecting, amateur astronomy and pursuit of eclipses – as the fleeting hobbies of a youngster. But what is a hobby, if not an opportunity to consider and explore the full range of life's possibilities? For many, hobbies come and go, but for Bob they were the opening doors to his life's work. As he grew from a child to a young man, he began to more clearly envision where life could take him, and as he advanced through his school years, Bob Sykes aptly chose the tools he would need to successfully get there.

Proud Boy Scout Bob Sykes.

Chapter 3

School Successes and Struggles

When not being distracted by winter storms outside classroom windows, Bob Sykes was an attentive and bright student. PS 21, where Bob began his formal education, was one of the hundreds of New York City learning institutions distinguished only by their number, and despite the implication of its commonplace name, 21's neighborhood-school environment was nonetheless an exciting setting for Sykes to develop his scholastic skills. A succession of report cards reflected his academic abilities, as did his class's seating chart, which Bob could vividly reconstruct in his mind years later:

"The class size, as I remember, was around 25 or 30. In those days in grammar school, you were seated according to your academic placement from front to back. The first row started to the teacher's right, going down that row, then the next row, and so forth. There were three of us who generally alternated in the first three seats." As assuredly as Sykes shared this detail of his class position, he quickly added: "I hope my memory isn't colored by my own personal enthusiasm."

Like every young person, adept at his studies or not, Bob

found some subjects more to his liking than others. For every social studies, English or writing class he enjoyed, there were others he would not look forward to. He dreaded his music class, which required all students to perform a song in front of their peers. Sykes couldn't read music and remembered "shivering and shaking until, finally, the teacher took pity and had me sit down. She never called upon me again."

Not exceling in playing or performing music was something Bob learned to live with. The same could be said for his lack of interest in competitive sports, which he would later attribute to an inferiority complex that overshadowed his youth and continued into his college years. But one subject he encountered at PS 21 caused him strife in such a way that it had profound consequences for the future weatherman.

It wasn't that Bob disliked mathematics; he appreciated and understood the subject's basic concepts. But, as he continued through his grammar school years, math's progression into more advanced theories proved challenging for Sykes. Though he could not have known it with those first struggles, when his problems with the subject persisted into his college years, Bob was all too aware of the concern for someone heading toward a career in meteorology. In retrospect, he would concur, a bit of tutoring in his primary grades would have helped. Instead, Bob would later regretfully admit, "I swept it under the carpet."

Besides his academic weaknesses in math, the emergence of Bob's helpful and caring personality during these years also became a challenge for him. This is evident when reading his description of how hard he tried to please his teachers: "I used to go get things at a nearby delicatessen for [them] before I would go home for lunch. That wasn't such a good idea because we only had a three-quarter-hour period to do so."

Again referencing his tendency towards feelings of inferiority, Bob struggled trying to stand up for himself. It was his mother who finally protested the use of his lunchtime to appease his teachers, and Bob wrote about his memory of her help by admitting: "I was relieved." It was a lesson, though, in finding the balance between altruistic behaviors and letting people take advantage of him. Much later in life, others would try.

Strong friendships were also formed in his elementary years, the first of many that would add a meaningful and satisfying aspect to his life. Among those joining him in his classes' front row seats were Helen Cohen and Paula Astle. These were friends he easily recalled years later, perhaps because of their loyalty when it came time to vote for class offices Bob campaigned for, such as president.

Friends would also cheer him on during extracurricular activities like school plays. One performance, a historical piece in which he portrayed Abraham Lincoln, required this first-time actor to memorize and recite the Gettysburg Address. Bob studied it word for word, relying on his superior ability for recall and detail to deliver his lines with near-perfection.

Billy Browne, Bob's stamp collecting and sledding neighbor, was another early influential friend, and their close bond proved instrumental in the progression of young Sykes' education. As his elementary school years were ending, Bob's parents considered their options in what would come next for their only child. It was 1931, and though the grips of the Depression remained tight on the country, Robert Sr. and Isabelle were determined to provide Bob with the best education they could provide for him. It was Billy Browne's parents who offered the concerned Sykes a glimmer of hope.

During his college days, Billy's father, William, had formed a friendship with a fellow student who would end up as the headmaster of Horace Mann. The all-boys school in Yonkers was developed as an extension of Columbia University's Teachers College. It was founded so that all who desired, regardless of their background, could receive a public education based on the principles and practices of a free society. When Billy Browne came of age to consider a preparatory school, his father remembered his college classmate and made arrangements for Billy to attend Horace Mann.*

Bob, a year younger than Billy, got reports from his friend about his new school and the boys' parents talked about the merits of such a school for young Sykes. Bob would remember Horace Mann as much like "the English schools, not of the same category as the New England prep schools that prepare students for Harvard, Yale, etc., but it still was a prep school." Though established as a public pay school, scholarship support to families in need was always part of Horace Mann's recruitment strategy; important news for William Browne to share with the Sykes. Application was made, and shortly after graduating from PS 21, Bob was accepted with full benefit from the scholarship.

This gift of financial support would not rest easily on Bob's mind. It was the first time the Sykes asked for help toward Bob's education and he remembered it with a degree of remorse. Bob's daughter, Barbara, reflects on what receiving scholarship money meant to her father: "He was an extremely proud man and Horace Mann was a fairly high level, exclusive sort of prep school. It pained him terribly that he didn't have the same level of economic security as many of the students he was around."

Indeed, many who attended Horace Mann had no reason to worry about money. From his fourth-floor classroom on the sprawling campus, Bob observed his new classmates with lifestyles quite

---

*There were actually six Horace Mann college preparatory schools throughout New York City. After the first was established in 1887, the schools fluctuated between serving as co-ed or boys-only institutions until 1968, when all six began welcoming boys and girls.

different from him. "I can remember standing at the school windows in the afternoon, looking at the cars parked on the street alongside the main building," Sykes remembered. "In those days there would be eight-, twelve- and maybe even sixteen-cylinder cars parked outside waiting for students. These were Depression times, but there would be these huge Cadillacs, Packards, and some Rolls."

His own transportation was in sharp contrast to what Sykes observed from his classroom. 14-year-old Bob would rely on Mr. Browne, a teacher at the City College of New York City, for his morning commute, and he and Billy traveled the 15-mile distance home by trolley car.

Unfortunately, once entering Horace Mann, Bob would lose the top-three-seat status he held at PS 21. "I didn't particularly shine out among students," he said, more often remembering himself in the upper half to upper third of the class. He continued to determine which his best classes were and which most challenged him. Despite his ongoing struggle with mathematics, his developing interest in the weather kept him motivated to strive for success in the sciences. He joined the school's tennis team and managed to successfully complete a swimming class, though only because it was a required sport.

Outside of classes at Horace Mann, Bob recalled an occasional social evening hosted by his parents for some of his teachers. This practice actually began when Bob attended PS 21. "It was not unusual for us to invite teachers to the house for dinner," Bob explained. "I don't know that this is done anymore, but in our day it was an act of respect. So, I can remember when I was in grammar school having the principal and several teachers at the house to eat. While we didn't have much money, my mother was an excellent cook and we had excellent meat from my father's job in that industry.

"When I was in Horace Mann we did the same thing. I can remember inviting my English teacher, William Blake, who also led the choir. (Though in the choir, Sykes maintained that he "couldn't, and still can't, read music – so all I could do was follow.") I remember having the Blakes and others to our house. It was not out of the ordinary to do that and you did not feel like you were currying special favor." This relaxed relationship between student and teacher, and the comfortable conversations outside academia were remembered by Bob years later. When the roles were reversed and he was a college professor hosting students in his home, there were similar spirited conversations on a variety of topics. But they never were too far removed from what was foremost on the teacher and his students' minds: the weather.

The arrival of spring 1935 brought to an end Bob's schooling at Horace Mann. For 18-year-old Sykes, his ongoing interests in the weather pointed to career options that involved that science. His parents agreed, but they and Bob soon found that every school offering a degree in meteorology also expected students to complete a substantial course load in mathematics, and by the end of high school, Bob's command of the subject had not improved. Throughout the college selection process, discussions with his parents always ended with Bob having to make a decision between his passion for weather and what course of study he could successfully complete. After much debate, the decision was to enroll as a student of chemical engineering. It seemed like a course of study that could benefit from Bob's attention to detail and structure, but would not be reliant on math competency.

Bob applied to several colleges in the northeastern United States, including Dartmouth, Swarthmore, MIT and Brown University. All were schools with a reputation for graduating students with a strong knowledge base in the sciences, preparing them for careers in those areas. Though he was also accepted at Dartmouth and Swarthmore, Brown would be his choice, and several factors would influence Bob and his parents' decision. First,

William Browne, so helpful in getting young Sykes a good start at Horace Mann, was a graduate of Brown University. When Billy followed his father's educational path and entered the Providence, Rhode Island school in 1934, he reported to his friend about freshman college studies and campus life. Advocacy for the university was also made by Horace Mann's headmaster, Dr. Charles Tillinghast, another Brown alumnus.

But the major reason to opt for Brown again came down to financial support. When the university offered the Sykes a generous scholarship assistance, their decision was made, and in the fall of 1935, Bob headed to Providence, resigned to become a chemical engineer.

Bob on the campus of Brown University .

Once on campus, Bob was not happy to find on his fall semester schedule an introductory class in mathematics. Though he would also have trouble in his other classes (including in his major of chemistry) as he tried to adjust to college study standards, the course in math resulted in a situation Sykes described as "catastrophic." It was time to face the truth: he lacked, and could not seem to acquire on his own, a working basis of mathematical theory. While he was certainly not destined (nor inclined to want) to be a mathematician, he could not hide from the fact that his deficiencies in this area were holding him back from *any* career path he thought might be even somewhat interesting.

A tutor, of course, would have been a logical solution, but tutors cost money and Bob knew all too well that there were not resources for such support. Years later, as a college professor, Bob acknowledged the great value of tutoring, but even at the 1930s' rate of 50 cents per hour, providing a tutor was too much to expect of his parents. Once again, he regretted not addressing his math deficiencies earlier, acknowledging that "30 to 50 hours during my 9th through 11th academic years would have accommodated my adjustment to the then modern developments in meteorology." It even would have helped him in his current course of study, chemical engineering.

But, perhaps there was a silver lining to what seemed like a hazy future for Bob. In a serendipitous fashion, the failures he endured grappling with math theory – which had *not* managed to dampen his interest in the weather – somehow challenged him to find other ways to interpret meteorology. For every shortcoming Bob faced in his math coursework, he found success when calculating the real world's numbers. Confidence in his weather-interpreting ability surfaced when Sykes began paying attention to the meteorological patterns of his college town. By comparing the weather systems of this New England coastal location with his hometown of New York City, he began developing his own theories of why this was. In time, he would prove and disprove them, and unconventional as it was, Bob Sykes was beginning to formulate his own methods of meteorology.

Sykes realized competency in other areas while at Brown, but they were far removed from the university's academic expectations. One such activity, which dated back to his grade school years, had been packed with his belongings when Bob left for college: his cherished stamp collection. At Brown, the still-enthusiastic collector found others at the school with a similar passion. College-sponsored stamp clubs had steadily gained popularity during the 1930s, as United States postal delivery methods advanced and interesting stamps from around the world became readily available. Meeting informally at first, Bob and his fellow classmates eventually formed the Brown University Stamp Club, and for much of his time in college, he served as its president.

Though not the only stamp club on Brown's campus, it quickly rose to prominence and became affiliated with the prestigious Rhode Island Stamp Club. At its meetings, Sykes got to know the Club's secretary, who regularly informed members about stamp exhibitions both locally and beyond. One in New York City featured the collections of college students, and after seeing Bob's professionally-crafted Rhodesian collection, which he began compiling while in grade school, fellow club members encouraged him to enter the exhibition. Enthusiastically, he did so.

Once the goal had been set, Bob found out that such an endeavor required a good deal of work. Collections were judged not only on a well-organized visual display, but also by the accompanying documentation detailing the collection's subject. In Sykes' case, correspondence with the British-South African Company, which oversaw Rhodesian stamp issuances, was necessary to validate his work. Additionally, sketches of the errors a collector found in stamps were taken into the judge's consideration. Only after completing each of these steps, could exhibitors organize their work for submission.

All this took extra time, and Sykes chose to find it by forgoing his studies. But his efforts paid off when Bob won the Nicholas Murray Butler Permanent Intercollegiate Philatelic Trophy at Columbia University's Filatelikus Stamp Society Exhibition. To win such an award as an undergraduate (Bob was a junior at Brown) was indeed quite an honor.

"I received a telegraph and letter that I had won first prize," Bob remembered, "and was invited to a dinner at a New York City hotel. The Rhode Island Club helped with my travel costs. I was [the recipient of] a 'permanent' trophy, which means your

Bob works on his award-winning stamp collection.

name goes on it, but you don't get to keep it. [At the dinner], I was introduced and presented the trophy. In those days, I was bashful and really not much into public speaking. I had little to say."

But he was both proud and determined to build upon this initial win. In 1939, during his final year at Brown, Bob again entered and won the contest, this time for his collection of Spanish Civil War issues. While the second win equally pleased him, this was the last stamp collecting exhibit Bob entered. He was, by then, well aware of what the time and energy he devoted to collecting had done to his academics. This, and the additional impact of the money needed to maintain a winning stamp collection, drained his enthusiasm for continuing. The resources were just not available; they never were.

Throughout college, whatever spending money Bob had came from his parents. To save on finances, Isabelle Sykes worked out a system with her son. Bob would mail his dirty laundry home on a weekly basis, and once cleaned, it was returned to him, sometimes with what little money they could offer slipped into a shirt pocket. To supplement this support, in a misguided plan to cover his expenses, Bob used money that should have been spent on his food coupons. Soon, he realized that this only caused further problems, not the least of which would be poor health. Next, he tried to earn spending cash offering his services in typing. Charging ten cents a page, it was slow-going, and in the end, he made a paltry $10.00. On top of such a small financial reward, Bob later admitted, "I hated typing then and I hate typing now."

Early on in his academic challenges and floundering study habits, Bob's grades were so poor that, at the end of freshman year, he and his parents were informed that the scholarship from Brown was being rescinded. A frank discussion between Bob and his parents transpired, and even without considering those persistent math difficulties, he had to admit that he just wasn't motivated to pursue a career in chemical engineering. At no surprise to his parents, Bob talked about his steadfast interest in the weather, and discussions on how to achieve success in the study of meteorology were revived. There had been one class, Bob told them, where he saw a glimmer of hope.

The science of weather, still in its infancy in the first decades of the 1900s, was relegated to the geology department on many college campuses. Bob had experienced some degree of success in two geology classes during his freshman year. The first, an introductory class, included a sampling of weather activities and experiments. Sykes worked hard in those sections and was rewarded with a solid B in the class. Encouraged, he immediately registered for his next science elective in Geology II, which he was happy to find out was also known as Introduction to Weather. In sharp contrast to the math and chemistry classes where he faltered, this subject was of no difficulty to Sykes. In fact, he excelled, earning his first A in college.

Though geology focused on the study of Earth's solid ground, through it Bob Sykes found himself on a pathway to exploring the skies.

Sykes' success with his new course of study was due to more than his particular interests in the subject matter; it was also aided by having some inspiring teachers. Introduction to Weather's professor, Dr. W. O. (Jack) Roberts, was a dynamic instructor and Bob was captivated by both his teaching methods and choice of course material. Dr. Roberts was discussing the very concepts and theories Bob had been pondering while pursuing an understanding of the weather on his own.

Soon, the reinvigorated Sykes found that class time with Roberts was not enough and he offered his services as an assistant for a basic meteorology course. Sykes asked for no compensation and his generous offer was accepted. The casualness with which Bob offered his time may have seemed unwise to some, but soon after his volunteering began, Sykes found himself in a position to alleviate some of his family's longstanding financial concerns. Bob's intense interest in weather and willingness to work beyond class expectations came to the attention of Brown's geology department chairperson, Professor Charles "Brickyard" Brown.*

A Harvard graduate, Brown was remembered by Bob as "a chap of the old school and quite proper." But Bob also had a high regard for Brickyard's passion for the weather, and 40+ years later, at the end of his Oswego State teaching career, Sykes reflected that "Brickyard Charlie was my first academic role model," noting how his professor took the study of weather outside the classroom. Bob was especially impressed that Brown loved to encourage his students to do the same.

Early in Bob's association with his newly-found mentor, he learned that the professor's interest in the weather had been enhanced by joining the American Meteorological Society. Founded in 1919, the AMS was originally an organization for members of the United States Signal Corps, a predecessor of the National Weather Bureau. By the time Bob first learned of the AMS from Professor Brown, its membership had grown to include not only practicing meteorologists, but also weather hobbyists and enthusiasts. When Brown recognized Bob's genuine passion for weather, he invited him to join. With that apt suggestion, Sykes began a lifelong membership in an organization that embodied his love of weather.

Professor Brown's regard for Bob's volunteerism at the university also led to more immediate and tangible rewards for Sykes. Not one to let a student's interest sit idle, in Bob's junior year

---

*Brown's nickname came from a prank his students pulled on him. When they submitted a mysterious "rock sample" for identifying, Professor Brown delighted in seeing students invested in their studies. Upon closer examination, though, the rock turned out to be a piece of fused brick.

Brown offered him a paid assistantship in the geology department through The National Youth Administration. The NYA program, a component of Franklin Roosevelt's New Deal, offered eligible students work study projects. Like its "sister" program, the Work Progress Administration, which created many parks and trails systems in the United States, NYA put youth whose families were in need back to work. In Bob's case, Brown University's geology department was able to offer him an assistantship with a payment of $12.50 per semester – a welcome contribution to the Sykes family's finances.

NYA guidelines offered students the option for a second assistantship per semester. Bob readily acted on this financial bonus by securing an additional position in the university's music department. In an Introduction to Music Appreciation class, where he also achieved good grades, he discovered a fondness for great operas and symphonies. Sykes' own shortcomings in singing and music performance did not quell his enjoyment of composers such as Beethoven, Dvorak and Chopin. Enthused by this exposure to classical talent, Bob proposed his help to the head of the music department and was granted the second assistantship.

Combined, the extracurricular projects earned Bob $50 a year. With a switch in his major, an improvement in his academic standing and his willingness to help beyond regular course requirements, Bob was back in the upper third of his class ranking. By his final year of study at Brown, his original scholarship had been reinstated.

All of this was good news to Sykes and his parents, but perhaps the most rewarding for Bob's future was the geology assistantship. Though he was working under the sponsorship of that science's department, through his agreement with Professor Brown, Bob was able to narrow his subjects of study to those that particularly interested him. Topics eagerly suggested by Bob and approved by Brown included the little-researched Arctic snow systems, the life cycle of a blizzard, hurricanes, and East Coast cyclogenesis, a cyclonic circulation often associated with nor'easter winter storms. Clearly identifying the facets of weather Sykes was anxious to explore, these topics foreshadowed his groundbreaking work in Upstate New York's Snowbelt area.

Aside from advancing his interest in subjects that he felt passionate about, Sykes learned how to work independently as he completed the assistantship requirements. The NYA program guidelines only required Bob to meet with his advisor two or three times a semester to consult on his progress. It was an opportunity for Sykes to prove his abilities while relying on himself. Freed to learn how and where he deemed best, the curious student began sifting through the documents and weather-study materials that had been accumulating in the geology department, and in its basement storage room, Bob hit the jackpot.

Wisely preserved by the college, Bob found and was able to review United States Weather Bureau daily weather maps, some dated as far back as the mid-1800s. Among those records were evaluative reports of severe cold-weather outbreaks that had occurred throughout the northeastern United States in late 1933 and early 1934. Though Bob would have only been in his teens when this took place, his keen attention to unusual weather conditions had logged the frigid event in his memory. Wanting to compare his recall with the data, he studied the records endlessly.

It was the first time Sykes had access to such a comprehensive collection of information about a notable weather event, and from those records he began to understand the value of properly recording precise observations. After interpreting the report's information, Bob took his study project one step further. Comparing the recorder's somewhat antiquated observation methods with what he was learning in his classes and independent studies, Sykes began to develop his own strategies to better understand – and perhaps advance – the science. And though he would not have known it as he poured over those records, his ideas on how *he* would go about studying weather phenomenon were about to get their first test.

It came in the form of a hurricane – the New England Hurricane, as it became known – and it hit the northeastern United States in September 1938. The major storm system passed dangerously close to Providence and Brown University, giving Bob an eyewitness vantage point to watch, learn and analyze its impact. And the timing for the budding weatherman couldn't have been better: Bob had recently landed a position reporting the weather for Brown University's newspaper.

Becoming *The Brown Daily Herald's* weatherman was a natural outcome of Bob's assistantship. Once he began applying his growing meteorological knowledge to what he had been observing for years, he began searching for ways to share it with others. With its popularity among students looking for news about university life, *The Daily Herald* was a perfect vehicle for Bob to apply his unique approach to weather, and he soon became a regular contributor with a six-day-a-week column he called "Weather Wise."*

As a regular contributor to *The Herald,* Bob was given its all-important front page for his story following the New England Hurricane's rampage through the region. His account of its impact on the campus and nearby community made good copy for the college paper's special edition. Readers could feel their weatherman's enthusiasm for this powerhouse of a storm, as Bob's

---

*Sykes would also broadcast similar reports on the campus radio using the same "Weather Wise" banner. Years later, he would contribute to a nationally distributed magazine with the same name and Bob was certain that he had coined the phrase prior to the magazine's inaugural issue. He regretted not copyrighting it.

report on the hurricane featured precise details of its destructive course and colorful language describing the damage it had on several campus buildings and grounds. It was like Sykes had discovered a golden key to a future career: he was avidly following the weather *and* reporting it to those who needed to know.

A sample of Bob's' column in his Brown University's newspaper, *The Herald*.

Students and faculty at Brown did need to know how the weather would influence their day. But the question for the newspaper and for Sykes was *how much* they needed to know. In Bob's zeal for reporting what he was seeing and learning, his column began embellishing on what *The Herald's* readers expected to see in their weather forecasts. A sample of Sykes' column illustrates what a typical Brown University student – including those not particularly engaged in the sciences – found when they opened up their paper:

"Today should prove to be quite cold, with the lowest temperature around 18°. Toward the end of the day, do not be surprised if you see some cirrus clouds moving in from the southwest, followed still later by a thicker cloud level. There is a possibility of some snow late tonight and early tomorrow, perhaps turning to rain Saturday morning when the temperature rises under the influence of easterly winds. Sunday will probably be partly cloudy with moderate temperature."

Most weathermen would have stopped there. But not Sykes.

"This morning's low temperature was due to the clear skies last night," his column continued, "which permitted the earth to radiate heat to space. The concept of radiation is important to weather study, because it is upon the adjustments between incoming and outgoing radiation that meteorology as a science is based."

One can almost feel Bob's pleasure as he blended what a student might experience when they stepped outside their dorm with why it was all happening. How many of his fellow students actually appreciated his thoroughness is unknown.

Despite an improved grade-point average in the later part of his college career and two successful assistantships, Sykes considered his graduation from Brown in May 1939 as carrying "no particular distinction." His geology degree, though it had allowed him to study weather, offered him little in regards to a clear career path. He was beginning to develop a sense of what he could accomplish within the field of meteorology, but a column in the school newspaper and some independent studies just weren't enough to garner him job opportunities. Unsure of his future, Bob and his parents decided that he should continue his studies in graduate school, this time finding a university that would welcome him as a full-fledged student of meteorology. His aversion to math aside, Sykes was determined to make weather his life work.

The Massachusetts Institute of Technology was Bob's first choice for graduate school. Its reputation as a top-notch institution for the sciences was partly due to their stellar meteorology course of study. Bob had applied to MIT upon his graduation from Horace Mann, but was not accepted. In retrospect, he saw this denial as in his best interest, given his struggles with math.

Once graduated from Brown, MIT was again at the top of Bob's list of schools, in part because of what he'd heard about its meteorology department chair, Carl Gustaf Rossby. While at Brown, Bob kept hearing Rossby's name associated with some exciting scientific advancements in the study of weather.

As MIT's top meteorological professor, Rossby was credited with a number of climate-related discoveries, including the understanding of upper air flow – 'waves' they were initially called – which controls what happens in the higher atmospheric ranges. Through his isolation and study of these waves, Rossby was able to mathematically chart them and develop theories about their influence on the weather. Eventually, these theories were accepted, and these waves – now known as jet streams – greatly advanced the science. Bob was in awe of Rossby's accomplishments, admiring how he "worked hard, played hard, and lived hard." By the time he graduated from Brown, Sykes had determined that Rossby was "the century's top meteorologist; a weather enthusiast who tended to live life at both ends." Sykes set up an interview with him seeking graduate school acceptance.

But Bob's hope for MIT was denied a second time. Math, again, was the culprit: He just didn't have the numbers on paper to prove his worthiness for the esteemed program at the university. Though he was now uncertain where to continue his search for a good graduate study match, his admiration for Rossby would not die with his dreams for MIT – the two men's paths, in fact, would cross in the future, providing Sykes with an even more important career opportunity. For now, though, Bob was out of ideas. He returned to his parents' home in New York City to consider his options. Once he had returned, he didn't have to look far for an answer.

New York University's campus, located in Sykes' borough of the Bronx, seemed like a logical choice to explore. Founded in 1832 as an undergraduate school, NYU established a graduate studies program in the 1920s, partly to offset the declining enrollment realized when the United States began its financial slide into the Depression. The college's restructuring would prove a boom to Bob when, in 1929, they added meteorology to their graduate degree programs. Further research gave Sykes even more reason to be hopeful: within NYU's meteorology graduate program, students could specialize in a division simply titled "Weather."

NYU certainly made financial sense, with its close proximity to the Sykes' home. There would be no room and board fees for Bob and his parents, and he could use public transportation to and from school ("for 20¢ per day!" Bob recalled). The university also offered the all-important scholarship assistance to the Sykes and Bob would pursue it, applying for the Charles Hayden scholarship.* By late summer 1939, Bob was notified that both his scholarship request and application for admission had been accepted.

Finally, at 22 years of age and after spending nearly three-quarters of his life engrossed in the weather, Sykes was enrolled in a program with a full course load of meteorology classes. Though he was ready for the challenge, Bob also was aware that his weather-related studies at Brown were primarily comprised of his independent projects. Those were "in the caliber of honors work," as Bob would later consider them, but that type of learning had been random and self-directed. At NYU, Bob would be required to follow a prescribed course of study. Under his professors' guidance, he would be learning the more traditional and accepted methods of plotting daily weather charts, proper analysis, and then some prediction: the essence of forecasting.

This time, Sykes was ready. He was able to complete his assignments and meet the school's requirements, earning good grades in his classes. His problems with math did not disappear, but Sykes found ways to work through them. When he earned an A in synoptic meteorology – the comprehensive understanding of weather conditions over a wide geographic area – he would remember it as an especially proud moment. Such achievement made his career goals, having once seemed so distant, now appear reachable.

---

*Hayden was an ardent supporter of NYU, also providing money for the school's planetarium.

Two professors at NYU had a tremendous impact on Bob's development as a weatherman. The first was Gardner Emmons, who taught the synoptic meteorology class he had excelled in. Bob described Emmons as "from a Boston 'blue-blood' family who did not need to work." Despite that, Sykes found his teacher devoted to the subject of weather, and under Emmons' influence, the impressionable student would discover yet another passion (some would call it an obsession): weather charting. The process of drawing and plotting weather maps and recording atmospheric details would become a key component of Bob's work, and in his career-reflective writing made later in life, he made sure to thank Professor Emmons for his guidance in learning the skill.

Bob's other influential NYU instructor was the head of its meteorology department, Athelstan Spilhaus. Aside from ably introducing pertinent meteorological theory to his students and engaging them in spirited conversations about weather, Spilhaus spent his summers working and teaching at locations around the world. One such place was the Woods Hole Oceanographic Institute at Cape Cod. The Institute was a Harvard University program that employed college professors and students to conduct current weather theory studies and research. In the spring of 1940, Spilhaus asked Bob if he would like to spend his summer at the Institute. Sykes didn't hesitate to accept.

With the Institute's focus on oceanography, Bob's summer on the Massachusetts shores would not be spent on his beloved cold-climate weather study. But it would still provide him with another opportunity to explore meteorology career options. His daily duties were twofold: time would be spent out in the Atlantic on the research raft, where thermograph instruments were monitored to research and record ocean temperatures. Equal worktime took place on land, where slides used with these instruments were prepared and analyzed, and their information decoded and filed.

For Sykes, it was a taste of a dedicated weather observer's life: balancing the execution of rote duties with riding the waves of an exciting natural world. Though Bob clearly had his preference, he concluded both were important, and with each new experience, he narrowed his vision of the ideal career. It turns out his career was closer than he thought, but it didn't look like anything the emerging weatherman could have imagined.

Chapter 4

A Call to Duty

By 1940, as Bob Sykes was completing his final year at NYU, the United States found itself in a tenuous situation. On the other side of the Atlantic Ocean, an undeclared war was being fought. England, France and others were trying to stop the onslaught of Adolph Hitler's regime, and while the United States sympathized with the efforts to keep his plans for world domination at bay, it was determined to maintain neutrality. With memories of WWI's bloodshed fresh in America's collective mind and the financial sting of the Depression still felt by many, the White House and its military counterparts were reluctant to enter into battle.

But too soon it became clear that Hitler's destructive plans were threatening the whole world. It was only a matter of time before the United States would need to pledge military support. Young men and women would be called to help their country, and some of them answering that call would come to the fight armed with the science of meteorology.

Meteorology to win a war?

The images of battles fought in World War II, or in any war, that most readily come to mind don't include weathermen engaged in forecasting precipitation or noting fluctuations in wind velocity. But actually, in some form, meteorology and the military have been linked as far back as the United States' first struggles for its freedom. To understand why Bob Sykes' weather observation skills would be destined to play such a vital role in World War II, one needs to turn the pages of history back to the early 19th century, when weathermen and war heroes first stood side by side.

The earliest records of United States' armed forces using weather intelligence are found in 1802, when Army Captain Meriwether Lewis was assigned to assist William Clark on an expedition to and from America's largely-unexplored Pacific coast. In his orders to Lewis, President Thomas Jefferson specified that regular weather observations were to be noted and recorded. Later in U.S. history, atmospheric recordkeeping also became important when doctors at Army hospitals were attempting to discover the causes of a suspected link between bad weather and disease. By the mid-1800s, these hospitals, now with their own "weather stations," used the new Morse telegraph system to send reports to Washington, D.C., where the country's first comprehensive overview of weather was compiled as military information.

During the late 1800s conflicts fought in Europe, the United States observed how destructive weather played as much of a role in a country's success in war as the actual battle strategies. France noted the relevancy of providing accurate forecasts to military intelligence by establishing the first national weather service in the world. Commanders on U.S. soil convinced government officials to follow France's lead, and on February 9, 1870, President Ulysses S. Grant signed into law a proclamation:

"Be it resolved by the Senate and House of Representatives of the United States of America in Congress assembled, that the Secretary of War be, and he hereby is, authorized and required to provide for taking meteorological observations at the military stations in the interior of the continent and at other points in the states and territories of the United States."

To accommodate this change, the Army created a new department: the Signal Corps. Aside from organizing military communication systems and collecting pertinent information, the Corps began operating an official United States Weather Bureau*, which performed regular observing, forecasting and data collection. During its first year, the Signal Corps' 22 stations each maintained an "observing-sergeant" – the United States' first professional weathermen.

The late 1800s to early 1900s, a relatively peaceful time for U.S. military, resulted in the deemphasizing of meteorological reporting. Their weathermen's duties were sharply curtailed. Weather Bureau meteorologists returned to their posts at the onset of World War I, as the United States began testing its first versions of battle aircraft. Forecasters stationed at key locations around the globe provided necessary weather information and predictions for military aviators. When WWI's conclusion again returned the United States to a period of peace, meteorological expertise, no longer considered critical to national safety, was assigned to a department that seemed more appropriate for weather concerns: The Department of Agriculture. Trained weather observers were now relegated to advising farmers.

But the world was rapidly changing in the 1920s and '30s; advances in aviation among its swift transformation. Long-distance travel captured the imaginations of Americans when heroes such as Charles Lindbergh broke records while attempting risky expeditions and headlines proclaimed Amelia Earhart's disappearance in the Pacific and the *Hindenburg's* burning while moored at Lakehurst, New Jersey. Air travel's successes and failures were being strongly correlated to the accuracy of weather interpretation. Soon, domestic

---

*The Weather Bureau underwent a name change in 1970, when it became known as the National Weather Service.

airlines were launched, giving non-military Americans access to this streamlined method of transportation. By the late 1920s, airlines were offering more than 250 flights across the country and beyond.

But it was during a six-month period between 1936 and '37, when five of the six major aerial crashes were attributed to the weather, that it became clear: meteorology was essential to successful air travel. Safety in the air became a prime concern, just as the concern of America and other peace-loving countries could no longer ignore what was happening in late-1930s' Europe.

With immediacy, expert prediction of weather conditions became a top priority for the Army. Major Arthur F. Merewether, the newly-appointed Chief of the U.S. Army Air Corps Weather Service *, tapped NYU's Athelstan Spilhaus and other professors of meteorology to create a first-of-its-kind, weather-specific military cadet program. Merewether's committee was also instructed to handpick meteorologists to complete the program and serve in upcoming battle strategies. Major Merewether was wise to appoint college professors for his committee. Not only would they create a training using the most current weather evaluation systems, but they would know the best and brightest of the spring 1941 graduating class of meteorologists. Bob Sykes would be among them.

These newly-trained meteorologists would have some catching up to do. By spring of 1940, the Air Corps had established its goal of training 7,000 pilots and 3,600 bombardiers a year. While they knew that an expansive airborne fighting team would be needed (the plan also called for 50,000 military aircraft to be built), they also knew that these pilots and their crews would be traveling in un-

---

*The Air Corps was the forerunner of the United States Air Force. Formed in 1926 as the U.S Air Service, it was a division of the Army until after World War II, when military air fortitude was deemed essential enough to merit its own branch of the service.

unfamiliar territory. The original order to Merewether was to train 40 officers who were well-versed in meteorology. But with the war expanding into areas with greatly diverse weather conditions, military intelligence knew they needed meteorologists who could specialize in unique climates, including Arctic conditions. Military brass reconsidered their plan and increased the need to 175 meteorologists.

While military intelligence was developing their weather program and strategies, Bob Sykes was facing the final requirement for his graduate work at NYU: the successful completion of his master's degree project. Designed to incorporate all of a degree candidate's training while at the university, it was a major last step for the hopeful students. Professors lectured in graduate classes about the importance of selecting a topic that would truly motivate and inspire the candidates. Bob didn't have to look too far to find just such a topic. Once again, a major weather system would power into Sykes' world at the opportune time.

It became known as the Armistice Day Storm, a November 1940 blizzard that held much of the United States in its grip. The mammoth storm, which carried with it a particularly strong cold snap (temperatures would fall to the single digits as far south as the Mississippi Valley), had not been well forecast, catching many off guard.* Those uninformed would include hunters ready to enjoy their day off – Armistice Day was the precursor to Veteran's Day – many who were in fields and forests far from home when heavy snow and high winds hit. Over 160 people perished in the Southern

---

*Flu had broken out in many parts of the United States that November and one explanation for the poor forecasting and communications during the storm was a result of little or no staff at weather stations.

Plains and Midwest regions.

The storm was an ideal master's degree topic for Bob, with its unpredictable cold-weather twists and turns. He dove into a thorough analysis of the Armistice Day Storm, compiled weather statistics and snowfall data, and analyzed his findings. Confident of his work, he developed his thesis and scheduled an oral presentation. Bob felt certain he had demonstrated a command of his topic, and those reviewing his data would agree. But they had one problem with his work. One final time, Bob Sykes was at odds with his nemesis: math.

"When I gave my first oral report to the class," Bob recalled, "Spilhaus criticized my presentation because it lacked sufficient mathematical formulas. Consequently, my faculty mentor had to work with me to add math concepts and material into the final production." The project was resubmitted, and with his second presentation, it was accepted.

It was May 1941 and Sykes had finally reached a pinnacle of his own personal success by earning a master's degree in weather and meteorology. The world of academia, which had proved so challenging as he moved toward his career goal, had finally been satisfied. With a career in the military clearly in sight, Bob Sykes may have doubted he would ever step foot in a college classroom again.

As Bob completed his graduate studies, U.S. government and military administration were completing negotiations with the countries already battling German's depraved leader. Great Britain, the USSR, the Republic of China, France and others spelled out the details of their request to the United States, and their answer came in the form of The Lend-Lease Act, signed into effect on March 11, 1941. In it, America promised its Allies much needed supplies such as weaponry, ammunition and tanks – even assistance in railroad construction. But perhaps most importantly, the United States pledged assistance via its airborne forces.

America's military had come a long way in its aviation knowhow as they headed into World War II. Great advances had been made in transatlantic flight, including the development of more powerful motors that enabled aircraft to reach higher speeds and altitudes. There had been more sophisticated design of U.S. military aircraft, allowing for improved surveillance, bombing runs and aerial battles.

All this was good news for the fight against Germany's occupation efforts, but there was one roadblock in America's mission to help its European counterparts, a roadblock that couldn't even be tackled on solid ground. In order for the United States to reach Europe with its help, it had to travel over the treacherous waters of the North Atlantic Ocean.

In the mid-20th century, there were three main air routes across the Atlantic and each passed through some of the world's most dangerous weather. The most northern route, spanning 2,000 miles of frigid, turbulent water, stretched over the Arctic between North America's Newfoundland stations and Great Britain. Crossing over Greenland and Iceland, pilots would be flying through what meteorologists were starting to call "Arctic weather factories." Due to its unpredictable weather, this route generated a high rate of aircraft casualties, and because of this, at the time of U.S.'s entry into the war the route had not been considered a viable option. But the Allies knew the airway was important and that American military's recent pledge to help could play a vital role in opening it.

The request from Europe was clear: Could the United States provide a series of weather airbases connecting Newfoundland, Labrador, Greenland, Iceland, and Europe? Could these stations, manned by properly trained meteorologists, accommodate important weather studies and radio connections on both sides of the Atlantic, as well as serve as safe landing zones for warplanes?

People in the United States knew little of such negotiations taking place as their country inched closer to war. Robert Sr. and Isabelle Sykes certainly weren't aware how strategies to develop an Arctic air route might involve their soon-to-graduate son. Matters much closer to home had their attention and, for this reason, the 1940 Armistice Day Storm would remain more than an important topic for Bob's graduate work.

While the massive weather system did not bring the extensive damage to the Northeast that it did to the Midwest, it still tampered with plans Bob and his parents had made to entertain NYU faculty and students. Slated to be an opportunity for the Sykes to share a meal and conversation with Bob's colleagues, the less-than-ideal weather threatened to spoil the event.

But Sykes was not one to let a storm deter his plans. While heavy winds and rain resounded outside the Sykes home, a fellow student and two faculty members carried on a riveting conversation about the merits of the storm with an exuberant weather observer.

Beyond dinners with faculty and friends, Bob's college years would be marked by other social engagements. While at Brown and NYU, Sykes began dating more frequently and more seriously. (His first girlfriends back at PS 21 and Horace Mann, were, as he described it, "really more friends and acquaintances.") His first steady girlfriend was the sister of a friend, Preston Kodak. Alice Kodak and her family lived on the next street over from the Sykes and Bob had made acquaintances with her at PS 21. An accomplished singer, Alice was a part of the neighborhood's Episcopal Church choir. With her encouragement, Bob joined, and before long, he and Alice were spending time strolling through their neighborhood, holding hands and talking; "an early and warm romance," he called it, one that lasted into his graduate school years.

But Bob's relationship with Alice would take a turn for the

worse when his demands of college study and extracurricular projects kept them apart. When he finally found time to free himself, he made a point to visit her. "I could look in a window in the lower part of her house," Bob recalled, "and she was with a boyfriend of hers and they were romancing. My romance with Alice ended then, and although I can remember several other contacts [with her], the 'thread' was broken and even talking was difficult."

There were other girlfriends of short duration, until Bob initiated a serious relationship with someone he remembered from his childhood. Marie Lips and Sykes had met through their mothers when the two women were members of the Yonkers Garden Club. When the mothers realized that their families lived near each other – the Lips family was on the next drumlin over from the Sykes – the families started socializing while Bob and Marie were quite young. The two remained friends through high school, although Marie was two years younger than Bob.

Marie's parents, like the Sykes, were not well off, and early in life she learned the thrifty skill of designing and sewing her own clothes. This interest blossomed into a career goal in Home Economics, and after graduating high school in 1937, she entered Syracuse University to study it. With Bob in Rhode Island at Brown, and Marie in Upstate New York, the two could only manage to stay in touch as friends. When Bob began his graduate work at NYU and Marie took a teaching job on Long Island, their relationship had the opportunity to develop by more frequent visits.

Though its importance would grow over time, initially Bob and Marie's relationship remained a friendship. For Bob, there were important reasons for it being so. He knew that upon his graduation from NYU, his involvement in the Air Corps weather cadet program would surely require him to serve his country somewhere beyond the United States, and he had no idea where. Furthermore, he couldn't imagine what those travels might have in store for him. He was, after all, heading into war. Any possibility of a deepening romance with Marie would have to wait.

PART TWO:

A WEATHERMAN'S THREE CAREERS

MILITARY
OFFICER
(1941 – 1961)

"I never saw a moor,
I never saw the sea;
Yet now I know how the heather looks,
And what a wave must be.

I never spoke with God,
Nor visited in Heaven;
Yet certain am I of the spot
As if the chart were given. "

   - Chartless, by Emily Dickinson,
   read at the celebration of Bob's life,
   February 3, 1999.

Chapter 5

Greenland's Endless Winter

A 1940s photo of Greenland. Though the picture was taken in September, it appears that winter had already arrived.

In order for Bob Sykes to answer his country's call to service, he first had to complete the special training developed for newly-appointed meteorological servicemen. Anxious to get started, immediately after finishing his NYU coursework, Bob forewent his graduation ceremony and reported to Mitchel Field on the Hempstead Plains of Long Island, New York. To reward cadets for this mandatory "crash course" in military protocol, Bob and the others in the program were promised an immediate promotion to lieutenant upon its completion.

While in training, the servicemen filled out paperwork to be used in determining where each would be assigned their first tour of duty. Included was a question asking for the soldier's assignment preferences. "That was really interesting," Bob recalled, "because, generally speaking, one did not get much choice in the military in regards to selection of one's place of duty." Perhaps this unexpected leniency was offered because of the equally unexpected military duties awaiting the new meteorologists. Giving these new recruits, who were weather smart, but war ignorant, input on where they would endure the hardships ahead seemed like the least the military could do.

It should come as no surprise that Bob chose "cold weather" as his preference, quite confident this would result in his assignment to an established weather station in Alaska. Sykes was eager and hopeful, and in his words, "green-behind-the-ears" to explore the climate and weather systems in this largely-uncharted, new United States territory to the north. And head north he did, but not in the direction of Alaska. Instead, Sykes' commanding officer informed him that his military career would begin in Greenland.

Though Germany had invaded Denmark in April of 1940, Greenland, a commonwealth of the Danish government, wasn't seen as an area potent for battle. Nearly 3,000 miles from its mother country, for centuries the largely-undeveloped island had only been reachable through ice-packed Arctic waters; by the 1940s, few had managed to arrive there by aircraft.

But, although Greenland had been considered a neutral space by the time the United States entered the war, Hitler's army had shown interest in establishing control of it. German submarines began patrolling its rough Atlantic waters, and the Danes, fearing the worst, looked to the United States for help. Shortly after The Lend-Lease Act was passed, the Danish Minister arrived in Washington with word from the King of Denmark granting the United States the right to build airfields and weather stations in Greenland.

Bob learned of his Arctic assignment in a face-to-face meeting with the newly-appointed Major Merewether. Mereweather's predecessor, Capt. Robert Moffat Losey, had just become the first American military officer to be killed in World War II's hostile action and Merewether was swiftly moved into the position. Handed his first assignment from Washington – build a weather-savvy division of the military and do it fast – he would soon show his superiors that they had chosen the right man for the challenge.

Like Sykes, Merewether was a graduate of Brown University. After several career mismatches (including a season playing for the Pittsburgh Pirates), Merewether entered the Army Air Corps in 1929 and completed flying school. While training as a pilot, he noted the Corps' inadequacies regarding weather forecasting and advised the Army to revamp its schooling. Directed by the Corps to do so, he toured several well-established weather stations in Europe, and when the call came for the U.S. Army Air Corps to upgrade and prepare for World War II's airborne battle across the ocean, Merewether had the knowhow to make it happen.

Standing before his commander to receive his orders, Bob had no way of knowing that Major Merewether would one day be included at the top of the list of leaders he admired and aspired to emulate.* Not only did the training he designed for Bob and the other meteorologists prove instrumental to the eventual success of the United States and its allies, but the Major also became a mentor who guided him through the Greenland experience that forever changed how Sykes conducted weather study.

During his first visits to Europe to learn its weather patterns, Merewether had realized the secret of Greenland's significance in World War II. Time and again, he saw how the Arctic country had

---

*Arthur Merewether would retire from the military as a Colonel in August 1946, having been promoted to that rank in March of 1942. He had a successful second career working as a meteorologist in commercial flight for American Airlines. Bob would maintain a lifelong friendship with him.

notoriously become known as "the birthplace of Europe's weather." With Merewether's understanding of how weather was hitting battle zones, Allied commanders knew that to better predict the storm systems that might hamper their war strategies, they would also have to be aware of what was happening far north and east of Europe. Greenland, it was determined, would be the ideal home for much-needed weather study stations, and word got to Merewether that Bob Sykes was already "right at home" with the study of such weather.

Army Air Corps Lieutenant Robert Sykes

On July 16, 1941, Bob Sykes, a new "brown bar,*" Bob in uniform) arrived at Bolling Air Force Base, the final stop before his departure to Greenland. After cadet training, Sykes had a month to prepare himself for what lay ahead. He had read and reread his orders: "Build an effective weather service," Sykes remembered. "Merewether suggested that I should use the remaining 1941 calendar year to get started. My instructions were, more or less

---

*A lieutenant ranked far below those with brass and denoted by a single bar of that color on his sleeve.

along the lines of 'You'll have a base weather station where you are located in South Greenland and then some few scattered Danish-Greenlandic stations. That's enough to get started. You'll have to develop what else is needed.' "

Two days later, Bob boarded the *Siboney** in Brooklyn, beginning an eight-day journey to his new Greenland home. Sykes knew he was heading into primitive territory, but if he was honest with himself, he wasn't even sure what that meant. Merewether had informed him he would find little in terms of a United States presence when he stepped off the boat at Narsarssuaq, a village on the southern tip of Greenland, where the Danes had positioned a structure that they were calling a weather station. Bob had been forewarned that he would find it either inoperable or functioning poorly.

Narsarssuaq was already serving as a refueling destination for aircraft traveling the North Atlantic route across the ocean, making it a logical place to establish a more effective weather station presence in the Arctic. While onboard the *Siboney,* Bob developed his strategy: Once arrived in Greenland, he and his troop of ten men would first create some semblance of a residency (they would live in tents until more permanent housing could be constructed) and then he would begin leading the work of installing weather equipment, establishing reliable radio contact, and eventually expanding the number of stations in Greenland. But before that could begin, Sykes had to orient himself to his new home.

---

*This would not have been Sykes' first time on the *Siboney.* Back in his grammar school days, Robert Sykes, Sr. was on an extended trip to Cuba as part of his work in the meat distribution business, and Bob and his mother boarded the *Siboney* to visit him. Years later it would be converted for wartime use. What a different voyage his second trip on the *Siboney* would be for 24-year-old Sykes.

Aerial photo shows the site where Bob was stationed during his Greenland assignment. The photo accompanied paperwork Bob was issued prior to his departure for the Arctic.

The military had been wise to schedule Bob's arrival in Greenland during the Arctic's summer, though they couldn't have planned the unseasonably warm temperatures Sykes and his men found when they pulled close to Greenland shores. Temperature gauges on *Siboney's* arrival day, July 26, had climbed into the 60s. A light rain was falling. From their boat, the men could even see some vegetation along the shoreline and into the glacially-made Green Fjord of Narsarssuaq. "There were many areas, near sea level at least," Bob remembered, "that did have bushes, and hence, a greenish hue to them, certainly as viewed at a distance." It *was* summer, after all, and its long sunny days gave these first-timers the idea that Greenland might be somewhat inhabitable.

That first view of their new home would not last long, though. Once on shore and their belongings unloaded, Sykes and his men explored the area inland. Within an hour of travel time by jeep, away from the shoreline and its ocean-influenced climate, Bob could look in all directions and see nothing but ice and snow. "It was a weird feeling," Sykes recalled in his first impressions of the area. "I knew that four-fifths of the land was covered with ice, but I still kept thinking it can't be. There just isn't that much ice! But there was."

The newly-arrived troops were not only observing these frozen conditions on the countryside's jagged peaks, and Bob knew that the surface his jeep was traveling on was more than a thin covering of ice with a promise of rich soil beneath it. Years before Sykes and his men stood on the surface of Greenland, German meteorologist and Arctic explorer Alfred L. Wegener had used reflected sound from explosions to estimate the depth of ice, finding thicknesses ranging from 5,600 to 8,850 feet. Maybe Sykes was on a solid foundation, but it was not like anything he had ever tried to dig his heels into.

By the end of his first day, what Bob had seen eerily matched what he had been told: Greenland, such a deceiving name, was a landmass nearly devoid of greenery. Moving over the endless mass of rock formations covered with thick ice where he would spend the next four years, Sykes might have wondered how a person could ever acclimate to such an environment. In fact, how had anyone ever seen this mass of floating ice as inhabitable?

Greenland, legend tells, was given its unlikely name in the tenth century by Eric the Red. A Norse explorer, Eric voyaged to the uninhabited island from Iceland, where he had successfully managed colonization. Looking to entice others into joining him in this even newer territory, the Viking leader chose the name Grönland, hoping to recall the lush homeland of those brave enough to follow him. Once the curious arrived, however, they realized it was even more desolate than its more aptly named neighbor, Iceland. Inhabitants of Eric's Greenland colonies eventually died off, leaving only hearty Inuit, who had emigrated from Eskimo villages and lived in the northern parts of Greenland. Norsemen, now known as Danes and Norwegians, revisited the area in the 1700s and established control, eventually making Greenland a colony of Norway/Denmark.

Like Eric and his followers, Sykes and his ten men found little in terms of resources to establish the weather stations he had been charged with creating throughout Greenland. Traveling even a short ways from its southern tip meant adverse weather conditions year round. Bob had been duly advised that Greenland's winter season, which begins in October and lasts until February, meant a long string of 24 hour days in almost total darkness. He and his men would have to disregard any semblance of a normal daily schedule, ultimately establishing their own regimen of work, meals and free time; all accomplished without the benefit of natural light. And in that darkness came some of the most brutal snowstorms known to man.

Severe winter temperatures were not the only frigid presence the U.S. weather station team would find when they reached Greenland's shore. The men were also greeted with much apprehension by their new home's inhabitants, most who had never laid eyes on Americans before. Though Greenlanders and the Inuit found a way to live in cold climates, their life had primarily been one of isolation which began when a "mini Ice Age" fell upon the Arctic shortly after Greenland's original colonization. With travel to and from them severely inhibited due to the ice-packed waters, Greenlanders were cut off, not only from Europe's goods and services, but also its cultural and social advancements.

Greenland's cold shoulder toward Americans may have been due to the fact that its people, the Inuit in particular, had no concept of war or its purpose. The idea of strangers coming to their land to protect it from battle seemed oddly foreign and pointless to the natives. This inability to understand war could very well have been a central reason why Bob was not the first weatherman who had been stationed at Greenland; in fact, he was the seventh. A combination of cold weather, an icy reception and the struggle to establish a weather station while keeping the Germans at bay may have felt like a losing battle to Bob's predecessors. Though the natives of Greenland never warmed up to Sykes's team, he did not shy aware from the work entrusted to him by his superiors.

The first order of business was to establish radio contact in Narsarssuaq.* Immediately, Sykes ran into a roadblock: Building a weather station could hardly be accomplished when adequate materials and supplies weren't available. Bob's men were often forced to work with what they had at hand, often waiting weeks or months for shipments to arrive. Then, barely at the point of beginning to achieve some success in construction, Bob and his crew's first summer quickly turned to winter.

Not much could be accomplished during the days of 100 mph winds the new season ushered in. A "more manageable" 60 mph might have fooled the men into thinking conditions had improved, only to have it gust to double or triple that speed. Weather station structures, once they did get built, had to be bolted to rocks so the winds wouldn't carry them out to sea. The frigid air, sand and small stones battering the men in those winds made them feel as if they'd been swept onto the war's battlefield.

Even when the winds did stop, Sykes' men were left with significant snow accumulations that had craftily used their buildings to create drifts 25 feet high. In order to keep them from being buried under the heavy snow, instrument shelters were built on stilts. The mountains of snow also made various shelter doorways

---

* There was also work that needed to be done on the station's airfield. While this task was tackled by both military and civilian contractors, Sykes was still seen as in charge of that component of the project.

71

useless, forcing Sykes and his men to build plywood shafts extending through roofs. These "escape routes" were the only way for them to maneuver their way outdoors to maintain the required daily weather observations.

In time, the meteorological military division from the United States managed their first success. Once radio connections were made, contact from Sykes' command station in Greenland to both America and Europe were among the first transatlantic messages to be successfully conveyed. Another goal achieved within their first months in Greenland was to increase the number of reports per day (prior to Bob's command, stations were only reporting once in 24 hours), assuring war strategists up-to-date weather data to inform their planning.

While working on this myriad of projects, Bob's abilities as an official meteorologist got its first tests. "When I arrived in Greenland, I was pretty much on my own," Sykes stated. "Data was sparse, and historical material was fragmentary and of doubtful reliability." But less than a month after his Greenland work began, Bob was able to prove his forecasting capability. Anticipating the arrival of a second team of officers, Sykes successfully predicted a major storm blocking their plane's attempt to land, avoiding a potential disaster.

Once winter set in, those forecasting challenges would come in rapid succession. A January 1942 Arctic storm, which Sykes remembered as "two days of weather conditions ranging from rain through what we might call a frontal passage, with major changes in wind direction and resulting effects on local personnel and their activities." Bob had posted his forecast for this event nearly 24 hours prior to its occurrence, with accuracy within a half hour of the storm's arrival. Though originally ignored by the U.S. Naval captains who had received his predictions, thus causing them countless problems, once Sykes' superiors were made aware of his astute forecasting, commendations were made.

Earning a reputation as a reliable weatherman well in control of a successfully-functioning observation station, Sykes could next turn his efforts to establishing similar sites further inland and north of their home base. This work would be even more isolated and dangerous than what Bob's men had already undertaken. How would he be able to find soldiers willing to live and perform job duties in such a treacherous environment?

After consulting with his superiors, Sykes decided that the heightened risks involved might be considered in a more favorable light if those being asked to work in them could be offered some incentive. As fresh troops arrived in Greenland from the cadet training program, the new servicemen were informed that they could either elect to work at the newly-named District Weather Control Office in Narsarssuaq or choose to be assigned to a more isolated area. The choice of staying close to their home base seemed logical until the recruits learned that the tradeoff for the more desolate work assured them of a shorter tour of duty in Greenland. Bob found no shortage of men willing to sacrifice the "comforts" of Narsarssuaq for an earlier ticket off the island.

No matter on the shores of their new home or inland, loneliness was a part of every serviceman's experience and Bob was not absolved from it simply because he was in command. Like everyone who came to Greenland with memories of home and loved ones, Bob missed his parents, but he also missed the opportunity to become better acquainted with Marie. His growing affection for his childhood friend had been kept alive through newsy letters from her. Sykes responded, but was allowed to reveal little of his life in writing, due to the delicate details of his wartime work.

Like those under his leadership, Bob kept a keen eye skyward at the start of each day. Would conditions allow for a plane to travel and land at their icy home? Sunshine offered the chance for correspondence; snow and clouds meant another day alone.

Servicemen who felt the desolation of these conditions began to refer to their Arctic home as "Groanland."

But there was opportunity in that isolation. Bob Sykes' keen interest in observing and understanding weather phenomenon was richly rewarded in his Arctic home. In fact, his appreciation of it had grown with each breathtaking storm. On those overpowering high-wind days, with little more to do than witness spectacular storm systems play out on a stark landscape, Bob spent hours in observation.

He taught himself to estimate snowfall amounts using landmarks as visual cues. He learned to identify and categorize each storm based on their unique snowflake consistency. When breaks in the weather allowed, he ventured outside and taught himself to measure snow in adverse conditions, differentiating between fallen snow and drifted snow accumulations. He relied on his finely-tuned organizational skills to catalogue his observations. By astutely observing the unique weather systems in Greenland's expanse of uncharted territory, Bob Sykes spent those lonely days mapping out a journey that would lead him to his own definition of a weatherman.

Chapter 6

Life and Death in the Arctic

Though Bob never lived in those isolated Greenland locations where his troops were working under adverse conditions to set up weather stations – being commander required him to remain at his District Weather Control Office – periodically he made official visits to review their development. Travel to those remote areas could be as harrowing as the work being performed there, and on one tour of a newly-established station, Bob experienced his first brush with death. While traveling an ocean route to his home base from a wilderness outpost, Sykes spent two weeks aboard ship to cover the 150-mile distance, a trip that should have taken less than a week. It wasn't Arctic weather that threatened Bob and his shipmates, but what frigid temperatures create in northern waters: icebergs.

While on route down the coast of Greenland, Bob's boat became helplessly snarled in an ice jam. "The vessel was completely out of control when I suddenly spotted three icebergs coming toward us," Sykes recalled. "The middle one was headed straight for the boat, and there seemed little chance, even if it should miss us, that one of the others wouldn't crush our boat against the pack ice.

At the last moment, however, the strong current created by the moving icebergs whirled us into a narrow, ice-free lane between two of the bergs and deposited us safely past them." Slowly, with an eye out for further danger, the boat made it back to Narsarssuaq.

The ocean produced a second life-threatening boat ride for Sykes, this one perhaps the most serious during his four years in Greenland. In mid-December 1942, after commanding the Greenland post continually for a year and a half, Bob was granted his first furlough to the United States. Though the trip would primarily consist of meetings with Major Merewether and other military supervisors, it also included a much-needed reunion with family and a measure of time to become better acquainted with Marie.

In a twist of fate, on the day of Bob's scheduled departure from Greenland, he made a decision to attend the showing of a movie with friends, letting his intended ship sail. Another vessel headed for home, due to leave the following day, included Sykes among its passengers. The decision to wait an additional day most certainly saved his life.

Both ships were headed for Boston and both ended up in the middle of a major Atlantic storm which had an impact so far-reaching that it gave New England areas their lowest temperatures recorded to that date. From aboard his ship, a 110-foot trawler, Bob observed 40-foot waves that thrust Arctic-cold waters aboard. "Salt water freezes at 26°," Sykes reported in his memories of that trip. "We [ended up with] a foot of ice on top of the trawler's pilot house. The captain was experienced in very cold weather travel, so instead of just letting the ice continue to form and remain on the ship, he sent us out with knives and hammers to chip away at it." The captain's order might have made the difference in the two boats caught in the storm. Bob's ship survived the ordeal; the other did not.

"My original ship," Bob reflected, "floundered and all were lost. Only one body and a hat were ever found." In his retirement years, Sykes explained to a newspaper reporter that the scheduled five-day journey would turn into "nine harrowing days and nights." The reporter capped his article of Bob's epic journey with carefully chosen words, pointing out that Sykes "joined the crew in a battle against his great love: cold, nasty weather."

Moved by his fortuitousness, Bob annually retold the story of his brush with death. Every Christmastime, when delivering his holiday forecast on WSGO, the radio station in his future hometown of Oswego, New York, Bob reflected about this most troubling episode of his time in Greenland. He not only wanted to share with listeners an important detail of his pre-Oswego career, he also wanted to give thanks for his life.

Not everyone serving in Greenland would be as lucky as Bob and his boat mates on that trip home. While in command of the Arctic weather stations, Sykes would bear the responsibility for dealing with several horrific deaths of fellow servicemen. The first, as could be expected, took place in one of the remote territories under Bob's responsibility. When glaciologist Max H. Demorest joined Sykes and his men on a mission to locate appropriate settings for additional weather stations, the experienced Greenland explorer set up a crude shelter in the difficult-to-navigate northern regions of the island. While at the site, Demorest witnessed the crash of a B-17 bringing in supplies for the station. He and an assistant set out by motor sled to assess the situation and found the pilot injured, but alive. During a rescue attempt, Max broke through a snow bridge, falling more than 100 feet into a deep crevice. No trace of his body was ever found.

The crashed B-17 was responsible for a second tragedy when a rescue plane made an attempt to bring the injured pilot to safety. When the plane crashed in a snow squall, all those aboard perished. Hazardous weather prevented further rescue attempts and the B-17 crewman endured severe Ice Cap conditions for nearly five more months. All who were aware of his precarious situation could do nothing more than wait. "It was a period of horror and nightmares," Sykes remembered, "until a rescue was finally achieved." As Bernt Balchen, who led the final and successful rescue attempt, so aptly described the horrendous challenges of Greenland: "It was not a war for territory, it was a war for weather."

Conditions at sea – even along Greenland's shoreline – were also life-threatening. Three of Bob's men perished traveling on water between observation stations during turbulent weather. Another serviceman drowned during a simple military exercise using a newly-crafted kayak the officer had just built with the help of a native Greenlander. When rough waters filled the vessel, it overturned and the soldier perished. Bob had the arduous task of writing the soldier's mother with the news, noting that because of the distant and remote location of the accident, he had few details of her son's death.

A kayak built by a Greenlander using processed seal skins drawn over a light wood frame. Since most Americans were not familiar with kayaks in the 1940s, the photo was included in Bob's Arctic training paperwork received prior to his Greenland assignment.

But perhaps the most harrowing death for Bob during his commanding duties in Greenland involved the circumstances that led to Corporal Donald William Eddy's demise. Though the men assigned to Bob's posts in Greenland were cognizant of the work and location challenges prior to their arrival and were selected for their proven ability to withstand physical and emotional hardship, military screening was not always foolproof. Otherwise healthy and stable servicemen, such as Eddy, could easily buckle under the stress.

The corporal had enjoyed a solid and successful career prior to Greenland and it appeared he had a happy life back home waiting for him. But while he was stationed as a weather observer at Greenland's Prince Christian's Sound, one of the most isolated sites that Sykes' officers manned, Eddy shot and killed himself. It would be months before the weather would clear enough for Bob to make it to the location and retrieve the soldier's remains.

Sykes was devastated, taking full responsibility for Eddy's death: "I should have reacted differently," he expressed. "If I could recall the times, I would take a different course of action than I did...I regard these as failures on my part."

Tragedies such as this were disheartening for Bob and his men, but they were part of the harsh reality of wartime. And though Bob and the troops he commanded would never see combat action, this is not to say that the horrors of the battlefield did not come frightening close to them. While Sykes and his men had done a fine job establishing a weather station presence in the southernmost part of Greenland, there was still a large part of the country – nearly 80% of it – that was uninhabited and unpatrolled. Allies were always concerned that Germany might attempt to use Greenland as a radio and airfield site in its northernmost regions, and at one point during Sykes' command on the island, they did.

In an effort to keep Hitler's forces at bay, early in the Allies' war efforts Denmark ordered the governor of Greenland, Eske Brun, to establish a troop of men whose job it would be to patrol the most wilderness areas of the island, six hundred miles beyond the Arctic Circle. Fifteen men – Danes, Norwegians and Eskimos – none of them combat-trained soldiers, were selected and led by Ib

Poulsen, a Dane who had helped Sykes establish his first weather station. Poulsen's men were assigned to work in pairs and they continuously traveled a 500-mile region on sleds, each powered by a team of eight or ten dogs, watching for any sign of an enemy. They were known as The Sledge Patrol.

This aerial view of Greenland's shoreline illustrates how uninviting the territory was, but Hitler's soldiers still managed to find their way ashore.

In the summer of 1942, a German boat left their home country with two radio operators, a team of meteorologists and a doctor – nineteen people in all – looking to secretly set up a weather and radio station presence in Greenland. Their captain, Lieutenant Ritter, had never been to Greenland and was unsure where he would find a location hospitable for the group's goal, but he knew he wanted to go as far north as possible to avoid Sykes and his established worksites. Just before the weather turned cold enough to jam up travel routes, Ritter's ship arrived at Shannon Island, 200 miles from the Sledge Patrol's home base. Radio transmits started to be sent to Germany, with plans to guide submarines and aircraft to the island, putting Sykes, his men and his weather-forecasting project at great risk.

The Germans' work went unnoticed until March 11, 1943, when one of the Sledge Patrolmen out on a regular watch happened upon a human footprint in the snow. Poulsen and his men were shocked; since the troop's inception, the area was thought too inhabitable to support life without special equipment and supplies. But upon searching the area, the men found an unoccupied cabin, still warm from a recently-used stove. There were half-empty coffee mugs on the table, and hanging on a hook by the door was a jacket of an unfamiliar greenish color. On the coat's breast was a swastika.

The Patrol quickly left to report the news, splitting into two teams, but not before having been spotted by the Germans who were returning to their cabin. Lt. Ritter's order was to follow the men, find out their whereabouts and bring them back, preferably alive. The race between the Patrol's request for military support, which had to be radioed to Sykes, and the Germans' pursuit to capture and interrogate the Sledge Patrol was on. The Germans took the upper hand, capturing two men, one being Poulsen, and killing a third during the encounter. The Eskimos, a peace-loving people, had abandoned their Sledge Patrol assignment, fearing any sort of violence.

The two Patrolmen were held captive until Poulsen, using a mixture of hand gestures and smooth double-talk, convinced Ritter to let him out of his sight. Escaping by foot, Ib braved a 200-mile trek without adequate clothing, shelter or food. Once at his command post, he radioed news that Germans were on the island and retaliation for this discovery was expected. Though the Patrol was hundreds of miles from military assistance, Poulsen held out hope of the Allies' eventual support. When none came, he surmised that with the Germans establishing radio presence in Greenland, they had most certainly retrieved his urgent message before it could reach the Allies. Deciding to hand-deliver his request for military intervention, Ib took off on sled for a six-day journey to the nearest command station.

While Poulsen struggled to establish contact with the much-needed help, the second of the two men captured by Lt. Ritter managed to overtake him and return to the commander headquarters by sledge, where the German leader surrendered. Ritter's counterparts, however, were still at large and unaware of their commander's surrender. While planning how to withstand a possible attack from Ritter's men, word finally arrived from the Allies. The Army Air Corps, deeply entrenched in the fighting taking place in Europe, had been delayed in sending support. Poulsen and his men could only wait.

When an American bomber finally dropped a container with four machine guns at Sledge Patrol headquarters, a team traveled with firearms to the German cabin. Though it was found empty, the men managed to destroy all radio-transmitting equipment, as well as lifeboats and other settlement necessitates. Shortly thereafter, on May 29, 1943, the Allies, led by their leading expert on raids, Colonel Bernt Balchen, bombed the Nazi's Arctic site. However, no Germans were killed during the mission; having feared their commander's demise, the rest of Ritter's troop had already boarded ship to return to their homeland.

In late 1943, Bob traveled north to look for suitable weather station locations for the Allies. Accompanying him was Ib Poulsen, whose knowledge of the area assisted him in his site assessments. During their work together, the two men established a friendship that continued well after the war had ended. Bob visited Ib in Copenhagen several times, and Poulsen returned the kind gesture with stops to see the Sykes family in America. Both Barbara and Bruce remember the visits by him, as well as other Danish friends that Bob had met during his war years in Greenland.

With dangers like German infiltration and his soldiers perishing in harsh weather conditions, Sykes had no choice but to look beyond the realities of war and maintain focus on his assigned tasks. Doing so would give him reason to realize a sense of accomplishment: By the end of 1941, just five months into their mission, Bob and his command (now grown to 22 servicemen) were already operating three stations in Greenland and had achieved an improvement in both the quality and regularity of the much-valued weather reports. Two years later, Bob's success expanded to 26 weather stations. (Some were the older, ineffective stations originally built by the Danish and brought to U.S. standards by Sykes' men.) That number would peak at 32 locations by the time his work was completed in late 1945.

Bob's superiors back on United States soil were following the impressive progress he carried out while stationed in Greenland. Accolades would accrue almost as rapidly as the number of his fully-operating stations. By February 1942, seven months after his arrival, Bob was promoted to first lieutenant. A short four months later, at the age of 25, his grade would rise to captain. In August 1943, with Greenland's reputation as a principal meteorological command center firmly established, Sykes was promoted to major. Those who served under and alongside him would long remember his efforts, honoring him with the nickname "Mr. Greenland."

Bob kept his military skills sharp while in Greenland.

Bob's success in the Arctic followed him well into his later life, with friends and colleagues who never knew him as a military man still acknowledging his work there. Bill Gregway, a weather observer for over 50 years in Oswego, New York, remembers discussing Bob's Greenland experiences with him. Gregway sees his fellow weatherman's accomplishments as a real contribution to U.S. and Allied military efforts, and explains why he feels Sykes helped shift the fate of the war:

"It was during World War II when weather observers first started learning about and working with the jet stream. With planes able to fly higher and higher, they began to understand how the airflows in the Earth's atmosphere affected weather. In 1942 or '43, Bob was able to take that information and study the jet stream that would come over Greenland and head to Europe."

Wouldn't Carl Gustaf Rossby, who had carried out groundbreaking studies on how those jet streams operated, have been impressed that the student he rejected from MIT's graduate program would one day apply his theories to help win a war?

When Bob taught meteorology at The State University College at Oswego, his students often heard about their professor's experiences in Greenland. One of those students, Dave Eichorn, who went on to become a respected Central New York meteorologist and a lifelong friend of Sykes, had this to say about Bob's time in that Arctic environment: "I had the impression that, of all of Bob's life, his time in Greenland might have been the most invigorating for him."

Another student and close friend of Sykes, Bill Wall, remembers hearing Bob describing his experience in Greenland: "He saw some spectacular weather phenomena – the Northern Lights in particular. At that latitude, there's nothing to keep it from being brilliant. Bob both loved the isolation and hated the isolation. It was such an unusual and unique experience to spend years – summer and winter – there. But, at the same time, it's horribly remote. It was kind of a love/hate situation."

Wall suggests that some people, like Sykes, can be drawn to a remote and stark life in the Arctic. In fact, the inclination toward cold-weather isolation has its own name: "the Arctic bug." Those "suffering" from it are generally believed to possess a strong sense of individualism, a trait Bob acknowledged possessing when, in 1942, he volunteered to participate in a training* for what he described as "isolated Arctic-type duty. I pursued this aggressively." Years later, Bob described himself as having a tendency toward introversion, which has strong correlations to this Arctic bug. Sykes also maintained a second attribute to those with the bug: People with this trait may often be referred to as "characters."

Whether viewed as an eccentric or not, honors for Bob Sykes' work during his time in Greenland served as a testimony to his success. In 1945, shortly before he left his first military assignment, Sykes was awarded the Legion of Merit for "his meritorious conduct in his performance of outstanding service as a weather officer in Greenland from July 27, 1941 to December 31, 1945." The award acknowledged the adverse conditions Sykes led his men through and the improvements they made in Greenland.

Bob's efforts were also heralded outside the military. The story that Sykes' troops had successfully created a radio and weather station network across the North Atlantic was good news for America. The military, which so often was required to remain tight-lipped about the harsh realities of war, found an opportunity for some "happier" publicity with Bob's Greenland achievements. This was positive press, with little controversy to taint it, and Bob's superiors took full advantage of publicizing these wartime success

---

*Sykes would eventually participate in just such training during one of his return trips from Greenland to the United States. The training for weather communications staff, cooks and medics working in remote areas was held in the mountains of Colorado.

stories. Still, to assure that the information America read would meet their approval, military commanders chose someone from among Bob's charges to tell the Greenland story.

After spending two years as Bob's administrative assistant at the District Weather Control Office, Andrew Brown became a military-approved "reporter" for *National Geographic* magazine. Brown covered the work being performed by its weather station personnel in his article, "Americans Stand Guard in Greenland." Published in October 1946, the first-person narrative about military life in Greenland would showcase the accomplishments of Bob and his men, as well as the harsh realities of the work conditions they had been enduring. *National Geographic,* known for its outstanding illustrations, supplemented Brown's narrative with photographs of Greenland's rustic terrain, including several pictures from Bob's personal collection.

There are few photos of Bob Sykes in Greenland; one would have normally found him behind the camera.

Brown had praise for all the men who served in Greenland, but made special note of Bob's ability to lead by concluding the article stating that Sykes' group "took pride in their job, sending out vital weather reports to make North Atlantic flying safer and to hasten the European victory."

It would be another six years after the *National Geographic* article before a non-military journalist would be allowed to enter the Arctic region and report on the work Sykes and others had performed. In the summer of 1952, *Collier's Magazine* released an investigative report on Greenland achievements in an article spread over two of the periodical's issues. Entitled "On Guard at the Pole" and written by *Collier's* reporter Bill Davidson, the article emphasized the extreme conditions officers worked under, noting that some of the weather stations Sykes commanded were actually closer to the North Pole than points in Alaska, and temperatures in that part of Greenland were known to plunge to 60° or 70° below zero. Davidson concluded that "not even Eskimos live in the northernmost parts of this rock-and-ice wilderness."

Sykes is featured in several of the photographs accompanying the article, including a chilling scene of he and fellow military officer Thomas Gray heading toward a rescue plane after being marooned for 11 days at a weather and airstrip site only 450 miles from the North Pole. This event was not documented in Bob's career retrospective, and since much of what he was commissioned to establish while in Greenland fell under the auspices of military intelligence, we will never know the complete story of all that he accomplished and endured. Bob was a private man, not prone to draw attention to his successes. To him, it was an endeavor he willingly accepted, and when his time in Greenland ended in December 1945, he would remember it simply as being "an excellent job and among the most meaningful in my life."

After surviving that late-1942 boat ride across the Atlantic during a winter storm, Bob spent some of his time in the States advising military personnel and providing presentations for service organizations. But the leave also gave him his first opportunity to spend time with Marie since their relationship had started to blossom beyond friendship. "Marie and I became reacquainted in

January of 1943," Bob reflected. "Soon after arriving in Yonkers, I contacted her and we re-met, so to speak, and began dating. Before I returned to Greenland, near the end of February, we became engaged on a bridge that crossed over the Sawmill River Parkway, which was in the valley between where Marie and I lived. To seal the engagement, we exchanged quarters." Recalling this memory near the end of his life, Bob confided that he still had possession of that special coin.

The now-formal relationship continued as best as it could once Sykes returned to Greenland; the couple again relying on letter writing to plan their wedding day, targeted for January 1945. On a second return to the United States in 1944, this one for follow-up meetings and strategizing for the still-expanding weather services in Greenland and other Arctic regions, Bob and Marie had the opportunity to finalize wedding plans. "We were married at Marie's home on the 20th of January, 1945," Bob recalled. "My mother and father, of course, were present, and some friends and relatives of Marie's. My father was Best Man. Richard Pease, a friend from Brown University and an Episcopal priest, was present."

But the joys of marriage were brief for the newlyweds. After spending their wedding night at the Waldorf Astoria, a favorite hotel for Bob, he and Marie enjoyed their honeymoon at Mohonk Mountain House, a Hudson Valley resort center. Then it was back to Washington for Sykes, where he spent time with his commanders, discussing the goals for his final months in Greenland and exploring options for his next assignment. A few days later, Bob headed back to the Arctic for an eleven month tour.

Finally able to begin an extended time together in late December 1945, Bob and Marie moved to Suitland, Maryland, a suburb near Washington. When Sykes met with his commanding officers to review his work in Greenland and make recommendations for officers who would replace him, he received orders to report to his newly-assigned military base, Fort Meade in Lanham, Maryland.

It was a volatile time for the United States Army, which saw its organizational structure undergo changes after the important role airborne military played in World War II. Many believed that because of this, the Army Air Corps should become its own entity. All who had served in the division, including special-assignment meteorologists like Bob, were faced with a decision: remain an officer of the United States Army or take a transfer to the newly-forming United States Air Force. The effect this would have on each officer differed depending on their previous military service. If the soldier had built up seniority in the Army, he could risk losing his military rank, which influenced salary and job assignments. Bob discussed the pros and cons with Marie and made his decision. In 1947, he applied for, passed the required tests, and was recommissioned into the United States Air Force.

Within days of accepting this new position, Bob received his new Air Force job title: Special Assistant of Arctic Operations to the Commanding General. Planning to utilize Sykes' Arctic weather competency to expand their control of those regions, their cold-climate enthusiast was heading back north, this time to Fort Pepperrell, Newfoundland. Though looking forward to the assignment, Sykes was forced to delay his start when a family tragedy struck. His father, who had suffered a debilitating accident early in 1946, died in November of that year. Wanting to stay close to home and provide support for his mother, Bob requested and was granted a delay in his date of departure.

Once in Newfoundland, Sykes learned that his new position, unlike his tenure in Greenland, would require extensive travel. His first trip, in fact, returned him to his original Arctic home to complete an analysis of his newly-built weather stations' effectiveness. Bob ended up making several "survey trips" to Greenland, with his work there including the transference of Greenland's weather station command from U.S. military to the Danes. Facilitating that shift required Bob to also travel to Denmark.

These trips were often prolonged, which frustrated Bob and Marie, now parents of their first child, Barbara. Desiring to begin life together as a family, arrangements were made for Marie, Barbara and their dog, Sandy, to also reside in Newfoundland. Traveling by boat in June of 1947, they reunited with Bob and settled into a home in the Field Officers' quarters in Fort Pepperrell. Their plans were promptly interrupted, though: within five days of his family's arrival, Bob was sent on duty for eight months, this time into the Canadian Arctic and then back to Greenland.

With those trips continuing, Bob later explained this time in his family's life with a measure of remorse: "Once back in Newfoundland, I was soon gone for three more months. And then soon after my return, it was off to Denmark. Marie knew the garbageman better then she knew me during that period." In an attempt to offer Marie and young Barbara company, Bob's recently-widowed mother visited, staying long enough to be on hand for the arrival of the Sykes' second child, Robert Bruce, born in 1948.

Chapter 7

Highest Honors and Troubling Setbacks

D uring one of the rare opportunities when Bob was not traveling, he was able to take possession of a letter sent to him at his Newfoundland headquarters:

August 30, 1947
From Hans Bertelsen, Counsellor of the
                              Danish Embassy
Washington, D.C.

"It affords me great pleasure to inform you that His Majesty the King of Denmark has been graciously pleased to confer upon you the Cross of Knight of the Order of Dannebrog (Dannebrog, Bob later noted, means Danish flag.) in recognition of your valuable services for Denmark's cause during the war. I forward herewith a letter to you from the Royal Chapter of the Order, containing the patent of appointment and the decoration."

While the meritorious service award had been bestowed months before Bob received his letter, matters such as these must first move through proper channels: from Denmark to the U.S. War Department, to the Air Force (still in its formative stages), and finally, to his commanding officer. An official ceremony was held in the Brigadier General's office, where Sykes was formally decorated with the Cross of Knight of the Order of Dannebrog. Along with the medal and its official documentation, a citation described Bob's proficient organization of weather data and use of intelligence to provide for the many North Atlantic operations that led to the war's successful conclusion.

Bob took pride in the award, remembering its important symbolism throughout his life. But he never considered it as a momentous affair. Instead, he saw the work this award acknowledged as part of his duty to serve his country and others in need; the medal itself was secondary. In notes summarizing his life, Bob mentions the honor, but does not expound on it.

The medal itself never found a prominent display spot in his home or office walls, and most who met Bob later in his life, including students and faculty at SUNY Oswego, were unaware he had received the award. In fact, Chrystal (Laird) Cardinali, a student of Bob's whom he hired to help with office work, remembered once having to find something he needed for a class in his desk. Feeling through the untidy desk drawers, she came upon the award's official-looking "regal" document deep in a corner. Bob had never mentioned it to Chrystal, and she never told him that she'd stumbled upon it.

Bob remembered his two and a half years in Newfoundland as an "excellent" assignment, though "in all but about eleven months of the time, I was traveling." He had some incredible stories of life in cold-weather climates to share with his family during those rare stays at home, including a situation that occurred when Bob was stationed for a period time at the North Pole. "It was there that he experienced snow blindness," daughter Barbara explains. "In the bright sunlight, without enough protection for the eyes, you could temporarily go blind. Dad described it to me as if you are hallucinating in a desert."

When the Sykes family was able to return to the States and settle in their new home at Washington, D.C.'s Air Weather Service, Bob's trips to cold-weather climates continued. His first took him to Alaska, where he worked to establish weather station radar operations for America's newest state. In 1950, while still working in Arctic regions, tragedy struck a fellow military man and again change the course of Sykes' career.

"Charles Hubbard, who was the American head of the Arctic project for the United States Weather Bureau, was killed along with some twelve Canadians in an air drop of supplies to one of the most remote United States-operated weather stations in the Arctic islands," Sykes explained. "I was asked if I wanted to replace Hubbard, and the person who first spoke with me about this was Admiral Richard E. Byrd.* Arrangements were to be that I was - temporarily reassigned from the Air Force to the Weather Bureau and act as the head of the Arctic project. The Air Force subsequently billed the Weather Bureau for my salary."

This increased responsibility, though it reflected the confidence Bob's commanding officers had in him, did not guarantee his being stationed at a single location. Nor would it mean that he would be spared life-threatening experiences such as Hubbard's. In early 1952, Bob led a team of weather professionals assigned to a return trip to the Arctic, this time to survey the north-

---

*Admiral Byrd was an American naval officer, well known for exploring Arctic regions.

ernmost wilderness of Greenland known as Pearyland. Sykes had long had his eye on the site as an ideal location for a weather station, but the region's remoteness and perilous weather conditions made the project seem improbable. Recent advancements in the military's understanding of the Arctic's harshest regions gave the team, including Sykes, reason to move forward with the idea.

When the officer originally selected to be in charge of the station's construction had an accident exiting his aircraft at the site, Sykes stepped up. Though lacking the officer's expertise, he and his men agreed to push on, with Sykes relying on his familiarity with Greenland and diligent study of area maps and photography. All was going as well as could be expected until, as Bob recalled, the day he noticed trouble in the sky:

"Clouds were thickening in the southwest. There was a period of six to ten hours of our return trip to base operations when we had virtually no visibility, traveling by erratic compass and subjected to severe weather conditions. We were under continuous threat that a breakdown in our Weasel, a Studebaker variety, would have left us in dire, if not worse, straits." The storm, Bob learned after their eventual safe return, was powerful enough to have caused significant changes in their recently-surveyed site's surface conditions.

Back in the States from the Pearyland expedition, Bob received an abrupt directive to leave his position with the Weather Bureau and return to active weather service duty in the Air Force. The news, a surprise to Sykes, stemmed from some negative interactions that had been taking place between the United States and Denmark over the proposed Pearyland site. Improper air shipments being received at the site caused friction between the two countries, and though Bob was in Washington when the mishandled airdrops happened, his role as leader of the Pearyland project meant he was to shoulder the blame. Despite his promotion in 1950 to Lt. Colonel as a result of his weather-related work supporting the military in hostile outbreaks with Korea, Bob was presumed unfit to continue in the Weather Bureau leadership role.

It was puzzling to say the least, but such abrupt changes happen in the politics of government and military service. The directive from his superiors came in the form of a choice: retire from the military and permanently join the Weather Bureau, or resign from the Bureau and return to atmospheric duties with the Air Force. Sykes considered his options. He knew he was looked upon as "a qualified weather type, quite aggressive, and very much liked by the chief of the United States Weather Bureau," but still he was unsure what the long-term consequences of joining the Bureau meant. He presumed it would result in continuing with the Arctic Project, but beyond that, his role was unclear. It also meant starting over with a new organization, losing seniority and pushing a reasonable retirement from the military ahead to 1980.

After talking with Marie, Bob decided to continue his military service, now in its eleventh year, though he later admitted that he never knew if he'd made the right decision.

A return to the Air Force did open up some new assignments for Bob, including one with the National Security Agency. In conjunction with the NSA, Bob's superiors negotiated his participation in some exploratory work to establish a substantial-sized airstrip in the Arctic that would satisfy "America's desire to be able to land B47s and perhaps B52s in flights across the Polar Ocean. You know where they were interested in going," Sykes said, referring to the United States' growing concern with the Soviet Union. Though common knowledge today, in the early 1950s this was top secret intelligence.

Aside from the Weather Bureau snafu, by this time in his

military career Sykes was being heralded as an expert in Arctic weather. He repeatedly denied this, noting that he'd had enough "humbling experiences to disagree with the term 'expert,'" and doing "whatever I could to get myself exempted from its use in my direction." At any rate, "it would not be too helpful to me in regards to the military."

Sykes was referring to his attempt at advancing his career with a promotion to Full Colonel, which in 1952 was denied. Tracing the reason back "to the trouble between my people in the Weather Bureau and the Danes," this declination was deeply felt by all who cared for Bob. Marie became so angry that she sent a letter to Bob's commanding officer. Barbara recalled this difficult time and the circumstances surrounding the decision: "To be promoted, you had to be evaluated by a group of officers and then recommended for promotion or not. Apparently there was an officer on the promotion board that didn't like Dad for some reason and voted no and that was the end of it."

While decisions made by others regarding his career were disappointing, home life offered a refreshing balance. In 1952, son Fred (named after a king of Denmark – Fredrick) was born in Washington. Two years later, Cindy, the last Sykes child, joined the family. In the years from 1950 through 1956, Bob and Marie lived with their young family in a small three-bedroom apartment in Suitland. But soon the family outgrew the apartment, so they built their first home in Seabrook Acres, near Lanham, Maryland and moved into the split-level house in October 1956.

With four young children at home, Marie continued with the full time care of her family. (It would be only after all were school-aged that she returned to her Home Economics career, starting with substitute teaching in the Maryland/Washington D.C. area.) Among the happy family memories in Washington, as

96

Barbara recalled, was "when the cherry blossoms were blooming on the Potomac. We would go as a family to see them."

The Sykes children. Left to right: Fred, Barbara, Cindy and Bruce.

Chapter 8

Europe!

Bob's final military assignment would be markedly different from his previous tours of duty. Though he was again stationed in a foreign country, Sykes was not using his weather expertise in a frigid Arctic setting, but in warmer European climates. As a plans officer in the Second Weather Wing, Bob was charged with helping to rebuild U.S. weather stations in war-torn countries. Though the work was far from the Sykes' home and would take months to accomplish, this time there were to be no long separations from his loved ones. In fact, the entire family was headed for Bob's first work assignment in Wiesbaden, Germany in the fall of 1958.

Everyone was excited, especially Marie, who had ties to the country of their destination. Her German-born parents had taught her to speak their native language and she was excited to use this skill and to visit locations she'd only ever heard her family talk about. But there was more to Marie's desire for her family to accompany Bob to Europe. Barbara shares this memory from the Sykes' last few months in Seabrook Acres, as her parents discussed the possibilities for Bob's next assignment:

"One night, I crawled into bed with Mom and Dad and heard them talking about moving. Dad's preference was Alaska, but Mom actively campaigned and won for the chance to go to Germany. She saw the long-term benefits for the family: historical, exposure to many other cultures, etc."

Once settled in Europe, the Sykes children were enrolled in the American Dependents Elementary School.* The family's thought that Bob would be able to spend more time at home did not look probable when his first travels took him to England, Africa, Greece and Turkey. Upon return from this extended trip, after living in Wiesbaden for less than a year, the Sykes were sent to Heidelberg, Germany, where Bob assumed the position of commander of the 7th Weather Squadron. Along with supporting the continued restoration work by the United States Army, Bob also oversaw weather stations in Italy, Germany, and France.

In the summer of 1959, the Sykes family again moved, this time to a complex known as The Patrick Henry Villages. The children settled into another American Dependents Elementary School, and one day while on the way there, Bruce learned something about his father that he never forgot.

"It was a hot sticky day in the late spring," Bruce relates, "and Dad was taking me to school. The kids there all had some long, black stick pens with "Property of the U.S. Army" stenciled in gold. I asked Dad to get me a few of them. His answer would be a beacon of light and a treasured inspiration for me through difficult times that lay ahead. 'Son, those pens belong to the U.S. Govern-

---

*One of a network of schools that were founded in 1946 to serve United States military personnel while on duty outside their home country, American Dependents Elementary School assured children who'd been uprooted from their communities of a good education and support system while overseas.

ment and it would be wrong to take them and give them to you,' Dad told me. It was a lesson on honesty, taught not by preaching, but by example and it guides my actions as a trial lawyer to this day." The rest of Sykes family and Bob's friends and colleagues learned of this poignant memory when Bruce shared it his father's funeral.

There were other ways that living in Europe influenced the Sykes children. Also living at The Patrick Henry Villages was a Protestant chaplain, Don Helm, who would prove instrumental in Barbara and Bruce's religious development. Helm presided over services at The Worms Cathedral* and arranged for the two oldest Sykes children's confirmation there. Though the Sykes normally attended services at the base's chapel, they visited the Cathedral on this and other special occasions.

Cindy and Fred's American Dependent School photos.

While Bob was away traveling, Marie made sure the children explored their surroundings. "When we lived in Germany," Barbara remembers, "my mother wanted to take us to Berlin. Dad couldn't go, because it meant he would have had to cross from West Ger-

---

*A church with historical significance, the Worms Cathedral, built in the 12th century and renowned for its Romanesque architecture, was where religious radical Martin Luther was called before the German imperial parliament in 1521. Threatened to either recant his spiritual beliefs or face torture and possible execution, Luther refused and proclaimed his inalienable right to believe what he wished.

many to East Germany. This was before the wall went up in August 1961, but he still wasn't allowed into East Germany because he was military intelligence. So my mother took the four of us alone."

In time, Bob would be able to join his family in exploring Europe. The end of the 1959-60 school year and start of summer vacation opened up the opportunity for the Sykes to embark on an extended driving tour, starting with the French and Italian Rivieras, and then through Monaco. Along the way, they tent-camped in places such as the foothills of Mont Blanc, offering the children a vista of one of the world's most beautiful mountain ranges.

Cindy on a Sykes family trip while in Europe.

Further along on their journey, the whole family was treated to a meteorology lesson that blew in while camping in St. Tropez. Referred to as a "mistral" and only experienced in southern France and the northern Mediterranean regions, this rare weather event features extremely strong and cold winds. The Sykes happened to be in the right place when one hit, which Bob enthusiastically described: "[During a mistral] the wind comes off the Alps and down the Rhone Valley into the Mediterranean. I and one or two of the kids were in a tent; the rest were in the Volkswagen camper bus. It had been wet, but the air dried very rapidly. The wind picked up and it looked like we were going to lose the tent, so we all got in the car and drove over into the protection of some trees. The wind must have gusted to 60 mph or higher.

"The next morning, we prepared to go for a swim. The evening before, the water was very comfortable, with temperatures around 72°. In the morning, I went down to the waters' edge, put the thermometer in the water and the temperature was not too far from 40°. What had happened, of course, was that the wind had blown the surface water more or less southward and water from underneath had upswelled."

Europe was rich in educational and cultural experiences for the children, but some weren't appreciated as much as others. The youngest Sykes child, just six years old, had to learn how to use a bathroom in locations without modern conveniences. "At one stop we instructed Cindy where the bathrooms were," Bob recalled, "and when she got there, she found in the floor a couple of raised sections where one puts their feet, with a hole underneath, more or less matching the natural exits from the body. Cindy couldn't take to this and came yelling back to Marie."

A second trip that summer, this one into Italy, gave Bob and Marie a rare chance to travel on their own. Beginning with a scenic drive through Munich, Berchtesgaden and the northern part of the Bavarian Alps, the couple then boarded a bus down into Italy for a ten-day trip through Venice, Florence, Rome, Naples, and the islands of Capri. In Rome, they saw St. Peter's and the Sistine Chapel, just prior to its restoration process. (Bob would return years later and remark on the Chapel's rejuvenated beauty and bright colors.)

Among the highlights for the detail-oriented Sykes were the spectacular marble structures of churches and cathedrals. Taken by their beauty, he and Marie made purchases to be shipped back to America, knowing that wherever life took them next, they wanted their home to reflect the memories this time in Europe had provided.

The Sykes' interest in how fine art had influenced European home construction was also heightened on the trip. Noting the styles and care given to houses along the roadways they traveled, Bob and Marie gathered design ideas and purchased sample blueprints of their favorites. Packed away in suitcases, these options for a new home gave the couple much to talk about on their relaxing vacation. Shortly before departing Heidelberg for their return to the States, the Sykes bought some paintings from a traveling salesman. They would be thoughtfully displayed at their next home, back in America and, in fact, remained with the Sykes for the rest of their lives.

As Bob's assignment in Europe was completed and his 20½ years of military service to his country ended, acknowledgement of his most recent work was added to his growing list of accomplishments. In June 1961, Bob received the Air Force Commendation Medal, its letter of recommendation stating:

"As Plans Officer, Headquarters, 2 Weather Wing, Military Air Transport Service, Lindsay Air Station, from 10 July 1958 to 7 July 1959 and The 7 Weather Squadron (MATS) Commander, from July 8, 1959 until July 19, 1961, Robert Sykes was responsible for coordinating, supervising and integrating wing programs and planning activities, including processing program changes, reorganization requests and emergency war plans. In order to accomplish the duties and obtain the maximum efficient results, it was necessary for Lt. Col. Sykes to develop a detailed knowledge of weather operations in Europe. [His] scientific aptitude and thorough understanding of the Air Force's overall mission enabled him to develop concepts and make concrete, realistic plans in phase with current trends.

"[Sykes was also] responsible for providing weather service to the United States Army in Europe...The leadership initiative exhibited by him during the embryonic stages of establishing and organizing the new unit are highly commendable...Lt. Col. Sykes manifested keen foresight and devotion to duty by establishing and maintaining a beneficial and propitious relationship with German Army Meteorologists...The results of his efforts reflect his ability to grasp the broad aspects of the problem and to relate them to their proper perspective to the end objective: the ultimate mission of the United States Air Force in Europe."

This award, bestowed upon Bob just a month before his July 19th retirement, was the only such honor given out to an Air Force serviceman during this chapter of United States military history.

Bob accepting one of several awards he received during his military service.

Awards such as this, along with his growing reputation as a skilled Arctic surveyor, made Bob a viable candidate for membership into The Explorer's Club. Originating in 1904, members of the club were travel enthusiasts with a particular interest in exploration. Those proclaiming membership to the Club included Sir Edmund Hillary, who was the first to climb Mt. Everest; Robert Peary, first person to the North Pole; Neil Armstrong, first man on the moon – men Sykes was honored to be counted among.

Membership required an invitation and Bob's was extended by Bernt Balchen, a fellow Greenland serviceman and Admiral Richard E. Byrd.* Bob remained a club member for life. As a bonus, attending the Club's annual conference in New York City gave Sykes a chance to visit his former commanding officer and mentor, Arthur Merewether, who was also a member.

As the Sykes closed the European chapter of their life, Bob and Marie contemplated what lay ahead for their family. Throughout their 16-year marriage, three quarters of it had been spent with Bob's work taking him far from home. The children ranged in age from seven to 15 and had lived in a half dozen locations throughout the world. It was time for the Sykes family to set down roots. But where?

Bob was surely wondering about what lay ahead in terms of his career. He had successfully completed a greatly-admired military tour of duty. That would have been enough for many who could look forward to a quiet retirement after fulfilling a contribution to

---

*Byrd, of course, was a U.S. naval officer noted for his exploration feats. His pioneering work as a polar explorer included successfully crossing sections of the yet-uncharted Arctic Ocean. While Bob was in the military, he and Byrd had frequent discussions regarding the weather's role in such risky travel.

their country. But Bob Sykes, at forty-four years of age, had acquired an assemblage of meteorological experiences few would ever realize. Settling into a life of complacency was the furthest thing from his mind. He was fervent about expanding his exploration of the weather – and he was eager to share it with others.

SUNY OSWEGO PROFESSOR (1961 – 1983)

"Not what we give, but what we share,
for the gift without the giver is bare..."

- James Russell Lowell,
    "The Vision of Sir Launfal."
    read at the celebration of Bob's
    life, February 3, 1999.

Chapter 9

Fate Pays a Visit

Arriving at New Jersey's McGuire Air Force Base as August 1961 came to a close, the travel-weary Sykes family headed off to Marie's parents in Mahopac, New York. The Lips had made arrangements for accommodations nearby, where the new arrivals could have a little respite before beginning to put the pieces of their future in place. Too tired to even unpack, Bob and Marie settled the children into bed and turned in for the night.

Sykes was the first one up the next morning, and it was he who answered the usually early phone call. It was Marie's mother. She had news of someone stopping at the Lips' home who very much wanted to visit with the Sykes. Keeping the person's identity a secret, Bob's mother-in-law encouraged him to wake the family and hurry over. As the Sykes pulled up to the Lips' home, they noted a Cadillac parked alongside the house. Curious to see who might own such a car *and* be looking for them, Marie and the children had Bob leave them at the sidewalk. While parking the car, Bob heard his wife let out a joyous scream.

It was Harold Richardson, Marie's high school chemistry teacher. Having been an excellent student, she had made an impression on Richardson, which led to a friendship between the two families. The couples stayed in touch even after the Richardsons moved to Stanford, Massachusetts for Harold's new teaching position, where he found a job for Marie when she graduated from Syracuse University. Whenever the Richardsons were in the area, they made a point to call on the Lips.

Since he'd last seen Marie, Harold had earned his Ph.D. and accepted a science professorship at a State University of New York college upstate, in the city of Oswego. When Richardson called on the Lips, he heard about the Sykes' recent travels and Bob's military career. Once informed of his accomplishments in meteorology, Harold had a second reason for wanting to visit with the Sykes: Oswego State was about to embark on an aggressive period of expansion and student recruitment, and recent staff meetings at the college's science department had been spent developing plans to diversify their Geology division. Included in the changes was the addition of a small concentrate in weather study.

The possibility of teaching on a college campus was not an entirely new idea for Bob. As he neared the end of his stay in Europe and was pondering his future, Sykes had considered just such a career path. He even explored the idea by contacting universities with weather study programs, including Ohio State. A letter to their Polar Studies director in early 1961 inquired about possible teaching positions. Bob filed the director's response, a cordial letter indicating that the college had no openings at the time, in his career portfolio. Had Bob been discouraged by this rejection? Had he already given up the concept of a career in academia? He needn't have been; Harold Richardson had an idea.

As a professor in Oswego State's science department, Harold kept in close contact with the Earth Science faculty and he was able to explain the concentrate's current course offerings to Bob, including a few classes in weather and astronomy. (Bob later remarked that, although he was excited to see one of his lifelong hobbies included in Oswego's science curriculum, he thought the inclusion of astronomy was "a little bit strange, because it is hardly an Earth Science.") Sykes listened as Harold explained the details of a professorship at Oswego and then responded with an honest portrayal of his academic training. While forthcoming about his limited work in geology, he made sure to express his great interest in snowstorm phenomenon. Harold liked what he heard and encouraged Bob to think about the possibilities of a teaching position at Oswego. Less than 24 hours on U.S. soil, Bob's job prospects seemed surprisingly hopeful.

Three or four days passed after that chance meeting. The late-summer weather in downstate New York was brutally hot and the Sykes spent most of those days at a friend's swimming hole, relaxing into their new life. But, in the middle of one of those peaceful days, another phone call came for the Sykes. It was Harold Richardson, calling with a question: Would Marie and Bob be interested in taking a trip to Oswego? Unable to let the idea of Bob joining Oswego State's faculty lie idle, Richardson explained his serendipitous meeting with Sykes to the science department chair and college president as soon as he'd returned home. Faculty and administrators alike were interested in meeting this man with such a diverse weather career and suggested Sykes make the trip north.

After some discussion, Marie and Bob decided that he should accept the request while she stayed behind with the children, and the following day, Bob was on his way to the city of Oswego. Barely settled in for his stay with the Richardsons, he and Harold headed for the foothills of the Adirondacks, to the summer residence of Foster Brown, president of the State University College at Oswego. A friendly conversation covered Bob's career and study interests, and then the talk turned to job positions at Oswego. When all indicated their positive reaction to the discussion, Foster suggested that Bob visit campus the next day for a tour and interviews.

Early the following morning, Sykes was sitting with Dr. Charles Turner, a long-time administrator of teacher education at

Oswego; Sherwood Dunham, Vice President for Academic Affairs; and Science Department Chair Harold "Hop" Powers.* While on tour of the campus, Bob got his first look at the Great Lake Ontario, just a short distance from the walking path through the college.

By afternoon, Sykes returned to the Brown's Adirondack cottage for further conversation. Before he retired for the night, he called Marie to update her on what had transpired over the few days. He'd be home soon, he told her, and they could mull over all that he'd learned while in Oswego. But once he was back with his family, there would hardly be time for that conversation. Two days later – barely a week after returning from Europe – the phone rang once again. It was Hop Powers, offering Bob Sykes a position at Oswego State University.

---

* Turner and Dunham later both had tenures as SUNY Oswego's college president.

Chapter 10

SUNY Oswego's Newest Professor

W ith only a few days to prepare for his career change, Bob made a rushed return to Oswego. Welcoming him to his new hometown would be some of Upstate New York's typical late summer weather: a last shot of the season's humidity, a passing cold front carrying its first autumn-like chill and a few scattered showers. When the skies again brightened, Lake Ontario's waters glistened. As Bob hurried across campus toward his first responsibility as a professor – helping at student registration – the lake's beauty again caught his eye. There hadn't been a lot of time to consider the weather, but the change in atmospheric conditions during his first few days in Oswego wasn't lost on Sykes. This Great Lake, he noted, seemed capable of great weather.

1961 would prove to be a monumental year, not only for Oswego's newest professor, but also for the college on that great lake. The school was celebrating 100 years since its founder, Edward Sheldon, first opened it as a training college for primary grade teachers. Starting in a humble setting within the city limits of Oswego, the college moved two years later to its lakeside location. Growth was slow in its earliest years, and by the time Bob arrived on campus, the college still consisted only of its original structure, Sheldon Hall (a statue of its founder presiding over the grounds), an Industrial Arts building, gymnasium, library, and three dormitories – one near Sheldon and two more along the lake.

But college administrators had aggressive plans as the school began its second century. The '60s and beyond looked to be years of rapid growth for Oswego State in several curriculum areas, including the sciences. A national shift had been taking place in how colleges approached that course of study, and in an attempt to rise to those standards, Oswego's science department in 1961 had grown to include chemistry, physics, mathematics, philosophy, and the earth sciences: geology, astronomy and weather. To accommodate this and other curriculum area expansions, within Bob's first decade at Oswego, 29 buildings were erected; one of them a science building.

Piez Hall* was one of the perks Bob was promised during his interview for the college position. He heard about the new building's spacious offices and classrooms equipped with state-of-the-art science study tools. Eventually Bob's earth science department *would* end up in Piez Hall when it opened a year after his arrival. But to start preparing for his first semester at Oswego, Bob was brought to the site where he would begin working and teaching: an old Army barracks.

With enrollment already expanding – the student body would quadruple from 1960 to 1975 – temporary buildings were required during the construction phase. New programs like weather study were relegated to those structures, which Bob soon learned were carryovers from World War II; prisoners-of-war were held in the buildings on land adjacent to the campus. When the property

---

*The SUNY Oswego science building was named in honor of Dr. Richard Piez, Industrial Arts and Psychology teacher.

was later acquired by the college, the well-worn stockades were included. Ray Schneider, a geology teacher hired the same year as Sykes, remembered those makeshift classrooms: "They were the same style that you saw all over the country, post-WWII type barracks. These were not brick buildings, they were all wood. And they were crowded."

Some would have decided to hold off accepting additional students and starting new programs before adequate space was available. But the man at the helm of all this development, Oswego State President Foster Brown, had a vision he was anxious to see fulfilled. Bob liked what he had heard about Brown's plans for the college, and in short time, a friendship was formed beyond teacher and administrator responsibilities. Though some of the faculty didn't care for Brown's overbearing presence and stoic interpersonal manner, Bob liked what he saw. It may have been because Brown operated like many of Sykes' military supervisors: men with assertive, strongly-opinionated personalities. Brown may not have been a perfect match for those accustomed to academia, but Sykes felt right at home.

There had been no complaints from Bob when Foster directed Earth Science Department Chair Hop Powers to offer Sykes a job at the lowest of the three levels of professorship: Assistant. (The other two levels were Associate and Full Professor.) There were also paygrades for each level and Bob, as a first-year professor, was also assigned its lowest grade, his annual salary starting at $5,800. With only his military pension to serve as the family's source of income, Bob and Marie decided the college's offer would have to be adequate.

But Foster Brown had some brighter financial news for Bob when he stopped to see the new professor on his first day of work. Brown, who made a habit of circulating the registration room on the first day of each semester, checked in to see how Sykes was managing. Bob was, in fact, struggling with the registration process, finding it a world of difference from his two decades in the military.

Asking to speak with him privately, Foster led Bob out of the whirlwind of activity to explain that he had reconsidered his salary, raising it to $6,200. There was more good news: Brown was adjusting his job title from Assistant to Associate Professor. Reasons weren't given and Bob didn't ask.

Once registration of the students was complete, Bob quickly shifted his focus to the details of his new job. He would be teaching between 18 and 21 semester hours, a typical first-year professor's workload. As SUNY Oswego's first professional meteorologist, Sykes was expected to develop a new course covering equal parts of geology, astronomy and weather study. In addition to teaching three classes of that course, Sykes would also offer one introductory class focusing fully on weather. Developing study plans from scratch and examining existing equipment for science experiments, Sykes took a look around his stark, echoing classroom, preparing to greet his first group of students.

With all the activity involved in those first weeks at the college, Bob found little opportunity to think about his family. There had been no time to look for adequate housing in Oswego, and knowing it could be weeks or longer before they would be able to do so, Marie and Bob decided to register their children for the school year in the Ossining School District, where her brother lived. As soon as life was somewhat settled, Marie traveled north to tour her family's new hometown and start house hunting with Bob. They began their search near the campus, in the predominantly rural Southwest Oswego area. When nothing surfaced there, they looked within the city limits, along the Oswego River which cuts through the city and even up river to the next community, the village of Minetto. It was well into the fall before the Sykes found and purchased a home in Oswego, at West Sixth and Seneca Street.

Conditions there were not ideal. Shortly after moving in,

Bob and his family learned that some road construction was being redirected from Oswego's main thoroughfare to Seneca Street, making their neighborhood noisy and commuting difficult. The new Sykes home also had its challenges: With four children and two pets,* living space was crowded. Oldest son Bruce found himself in close quarters on the third floor. For safety, Bob rigged up a knotted rope as a means for emergency departure from Bruce's window. The house was also a problem on the outside; the lots within Oswego's city limits were notoriously small. All of the Sykes wanted more space, but especially Bob, who was anxious to spend time outside in what he kept hearing was going to be some amazing winter weather. The search for an appropriate home continued.

The Sykes Family. Back row: Fred, Bruce and Barbara. Front row: Marie, Cindy, Bob.

---

*Bob and Marie made good on their promise to Cindy and Fred for the adoption of a cat and a dog. Once arrived in Oswego, Moe the cat and Sam the dog joined the family.

At the suggestion of Astronomy Professor George Pitluga, the Sykes revisited the area southwest of the city. There they found land owned by William Brown, who had recently put lots up for sale not far from Route 104, on a little dead-end road he'd named Brown Drive. The Sykes liked what they saw until they calculated the purchase price for the land and new home construction. With Bob's small military pension and still proving his worth at a new job, making Brown an offer seemed like too much too fast.

It wasn't just the cost of a new home that caused Bob and Marie to think conservatively about their finances. Any extra money the family might manage to save was earmarked for a career plan Bob had been contemplating. After teaching his first classes as a college professor, Sykes began considering the possibility of continuing his education toward a Ph.D. Doing so would certainly strengthen his standing at the college, where most of the new staff hired had already achieved this highest of academic standings. And then there were the Sykes children. Daughter Barbara, who by 1962 was 16, was looking beyond high school. The prospects of paying for two college educations at once, and with three more children following close behind, Bob decided that family finances "looked pretty gruesome indeed." Building and moving to a new home would have to wait; furthering his own education would never be realized.

With money concerns always a consideration, at the end of his first year at SUNY Oswego Bob decided to discuss his future as a professor with Foster Brown. Reactions from both students and faculty had seemed generally positive, and after checking with Bob's immediate supervisor, Dr. Powers, Foster agreed to the discussion. All reports on his work were good and Sykes was welcomed to continue teaching at Oswego. But that wasn't all. To prove his faith in him, Brown had decided to grant Bob his tenure.

Tenure without a Ph.D. and after teaching a single year? What could Brown have been thinking?

There are a variety of opinions about the college president's generosity to Sykes. "Foster Brown was very fond of my father in regards to the whole concept of starting a weather program," says Barbara. Faculty at Oswego also speculated that Foster's remarkably-early tenure gift might have had something to do with Sykes' prior achievements and military ranking. He had, after all, already successfully completed a notable career, unlike most of the other new hires, fresh from their Ph.D. programs.

But the reasons for granting tenure went beyond Bob's previous accomplishments and Foster Brown's admiration of his work at Oswego State. Brown certainly was trying to help the State University's plan for radical changes on their campuses. With the study of weather making huge technological strides in the 1960s, colleges – including Oswego, with its limited weather curriculum – were anxious to stay in line with the progress.

Prior to Bob's first meteorology classes, the college offered only one introductory course in weather and that was taught by a chemistry teacher. For students desiring a career in elementary education, this basic course sufficed. But for future science teachers at the high school level or for those looking for a full-fledged career in weather, the college offered little to help fulfill their meteorology requirements. Bob Sykes was seen as an important piece of the university's plan to rectify that and they didn't want to lose him. With his job security looking favorable, the Sykes purchased the land on Brown Drive in 1963.

Once Bob's classes were in place, Oswego hoped that the offer of a new weather-study program would help SUNY's goal of building enrollment. The college began accepting meteorology students, and those who were expecting a comprehensive curriculum in that subject area would have thought they'd found what they needed when they arrived on campus for the 1962-63 school year. Freshman met their teachers in the newly-opened Piez Hall. Besides no longer needing to study in Army barracks, Piez was equipped with up-to-date weather-observation equipment, including some of the campus's first computers.

But students looking for a degree in meteorology in Bob's earliest years at Oswego were disappointed with the program's limitations. One student, Bill Wall, recalls the contrast between his initial excitement about attending Oswego and his frustration once he began classes: "I had always been interested in the infinite variety of weather, and in summer 1962, my family met Bob Sykes when we were vacationing at Whiteface Mountain. My father started up a conversation with Bob, who mentioned the weather degree program at Oswego State College. After graduating from high school, I applied to Oswego, and in August 1964, I began my studies there.

"After I'd been at the school for a while, I realized that there was no real meteorology department, per se, and no degree in it. If I had stayed there, I would've had to have gotten an education degree with, perhaps, an earth science major. I liked going to school in Oswego; it certainly had the kind of weather you had to see to be believed. But I wanted a meteorology degree and Bob understood. I transferred to NYU at the end of my first year.*"

SUNY Oswego heard the concerns from students such as Wall and initiated efforts to provide a certifiable meteorology course of study. A second instructor was hired in 1965. However, the professor was barely on staff – he was so new, in fact, that he hadn't

---

*A few years later, Bill Wall returned to SUNY Oswego and continued his education there. He and Bob remained friends, as well as Wall becoming part of the Sykes family when he married Barbara. After their marriage ended, Bill and Bob maintained a friendship throughout Sykes' life.

yet moved his family to Oswego – when The Blizzard of '66 inundated the area. Soon after, the new hire left the faculty, not even completing his first year. Perhaps, Bob surmised, there was just a little too much weather for the out-of-place meteorologist.

The college tried again to attract a willing professor for the 1967-68 school year, and this time they hit a double jackpot. In quick succession, a second meteorologist, Dr. Eugene Chermack, and then a third, Dr. Peter Caplan, joined Oswego's fledging program. Both professors found their way to Oswego when New York University decided to close its meteorology program. Once they learned that their department was being eliminated, both men began to search for colleges looking for professors in their field. Chermack and Caplan learned about the growing weather study program at Oswego, and along with Bob, they would become the core of its meteorology program.

As had been expected of Sykes, the two new hires were instructed to develop appropriate courses for Oswego's new science curriculum. With all three professors offering innovative weather-related courses, students who had declared a major in meteorology now had a full range of applicable classes to prepare them for their career field. Moving from Sykes to Caplan to Chermack as their educations at Oswego unfolded, the meteorologists-in-the-making were offered distinctive differences in how each of their professors approached the study of weather.

It wouldn't have been hard to notice. Chermack and Caplan, their training as meteorologists strongly influenced by time spent in academic settings, were teaching primarily in a textbook, lecture-based classroom environment. Just down the hallway, Bob Sykes relied on his years studying the weather in a variety of climates, employing observation and hands-on experience to introduce theory to his students. The uniqueness between teaching styles quickly drew attention, with students having opinions on the pros and cons of each professor, along with their personal preferences. In the years that followed, Dr. Al Stamm and Dr. Robert Ballantine joined the department, further expanding the permanency of meteorology on the SUNY campus.

Much of the buzz among college faculty concerning Oswego's dynamic meteorology curriculum focused on the first professor hired to teach it, the one who'd learned the science while serving his country in the Arctic and was now using unconventional methods to convey his knowledge. Within Bob's own department, Geology Professor Ray Schneider noted that Sykes "was always a very enthusiastic guy as far as meteorology. He was effective for the material he was teaching... the biggest thing he did was arranging for all the observations."

Dr. Luciano (Lou) Iorizzo also began teaching at SUNY Oswego in the early sixties, and he remembers those years when the entire Oswego faculty was small enough for everyone to know each other. Though Dr. Iorizzo taught History, he and Bob became acquainted and he remembers the impression Sykes had on the faculty: "There was a cafeteria near Moreland Hall and faculty from various departments would go there to eat. Bob was a very sociable guy, but I think some looked at him as an alarmist. He would always be alerting people to what was going on weather-wise. Most of the time, though, he was right on target."

Bob Maxon, the weekday morning meteorologist on *NBC Connecticut News Today* grew up in Oswego and attended Oswego College's Campus School. Sykes was an early role model for Maxon and he has a thought about why Bob might have developed this reputation among his peers: "I think because he was a bit introverted, the people in Oswego thought he was a little like Einstein. He avoided attention and I can almost picture him walking in the hall when I was at the Campus School. It was an image like he was a kid walking down the hallway along the lockers with his head down."

As more and more people learned of his zealous interest in the weather and unorthodox approach to studying it, Bob Sykes began to draw attention through the Oswego campus. Those meeting him were often inclined to either be fascinated by his way of looking at the world or consider him odd and perhaps a bit standoffish. His college president and friend, Foster Brown, was one who remained in full support of Bob, which made the news Sykes learned about the man that brought him to Oswego even harder to take.

Just a few years after instating Bob's tenure, Brown left Oswego State, assuming the same position at St. Lawrence University. In a letter sent to Foster concerning this decision, Bob expressed his admiration and appreciation. He wanted the first administrative supervisor of his teaching career to know that he was "especially indebted for making my transition from military life to college so easy and happy. But more than this, you have provided an inspiration for my meeting the testing tasks of one of the really vital career fields."

Foster Brown had offered Bob Sykes a new and exciting road on which to journey, but no one could have foreseen how extraordinarily this weatherman would navigate it.

Chapter 11

The Classroom Comes Alive

"It didn't take me long to get interested in Bob Sykes as a teacher; he was a unique individual." So says Tom Moore, a SUNY Oswego student from 1970 through '74, and he expresses the realization that many of Bob's students had soon after meeting their new professor. Right from day one, students heard the important and somewhat nontraditional goals Bob had for them and for himself, and those goals were as lofty as the clouds the students would soon be introduced to. Evidence of his desire to truly inspire his classroom of future weather observers can be found in his course curriculum notes, including this tangible definition of meteorology:

"Let us work out a practical definition, a bit different than that given by Aristotle, which was namely 'the study of things above the earth.' Yes, as a practical view, meteorology is the study of the physics of the gases surrounding the earth...but my definition differs from the usual, as does my differentiation of meteorology and weather. I view weather as those portions of meteorology which pertains to the part of the atmosphere where we do our primary living. All in all, weather is not an exact science, although 'hard science' (physics and math) are vital in the supporting equations into the description of motions and interactions."

Notice how Sykes paid homage to the struggles he endured to finally comprehend mathematics in his college years. But listen to how he made sure his students knew that they will be studying weather beyond those hard sciences: "Nevertheless, advances based on modern applications have yet to cause outstanding developments in the effective forecasting of the weather which you and I earnestly desire."

How did students respond to Bob's definition of meteorology? Was it just words, carefully chosen and eloquently stated? Would this middle-aged man, who tended to ramble on with his explanations, hold their interest? In time, students figured this out for themselves, and to be sure, Sykes was not everyone's cup of tea. But when it came down to *how* he taught his definition of meteorology – the understanding of it at the level where we do our living – his former students had much to say. Tom Moore explains why he found his new teacher so unique:

"I had two classes with him and one was Current Weather Patterns, which he developed himself. I was in that class the first time he offered it and it was perfect for Sykes to teach because he could ad-lib the class. He could just talk about weather situations and expound upon that – and he loved it!"

Francis Quirk, a biology student at Oswego in the late '60s, took Bob's meteorology course as an elective and found himself in the presence of a teacher who did not distinguish learning from living. "He was just phenomenal as a teacher," Quirk states. "I took the course from him in summer school, when classes were two or two and a half hours a day, but the time just flew by.

"He told a lot of stories about his previous meteorology work while in the service, and he told us about things like wind-chill. At that time, none of us had ever heard of 'the wind-chill factor' before; it wouldn't have been part of a typical weather forecast, but he explained it to us. He'd get real excited talking about snow, and this would be in July. I remember I did really well in the class, and since I was taking a summer school course, you could probably figure out that I wasn't the greatest student. But I got almost a 100 average with him because he was just so interesting."

Les Austin, who attended SUNY Oswego in the late '70s and applied his meteorology studies to a 37-year career in aviation, remembers how good Bob was at communicating what he was thinking and when describing how weather events happened. "Most of his classes were taught in the real world," Austin points out, "and he was always talking from his experience. A lot of the other meteorology classes that we took were math-based, theoretical kind of things, which were kind of dry. But you never fell asleep in one of his classes."

It wasn't just those assigned to one of Bob's courses who learned from his unique methods of instructing. Some students, on their way to their own classes, would walk by his room and just have to stop and hear what all the fuss was about. "One of my classes was in 305 Park Hall," Industrial Arts major Tom Frawley remembers. "Bob Sykes used to give a lecture in the same room, ending just prior to my class. That particular classroom had windows that allowed you to look out over the lake and see the weather changing. This mesmerized me in my own class. So I would get my cup of coffee, go up and sit on the interior steps outside the classroom and listen to him give his lectures. I saw how he was drawing those students out. And after his class was done, he would always stay. Many of the professors were in a rush, but Mr. Sykes was one to stay and talk with the students. People would be lined up to ask him questions, quiz him on concepts and for clarification from his lectures."

One of the students in that lineup waiting to talk to Bob was Dave Eichorn, who today is one of Central New York's most well-known and respected meteorologists. "As the class cleared out, I would always end up staying to ask questions," Dave recalls. "I used to joke that I was the luckiest person in the world that I had [Bob as] a walking meteorological encyclopedia. Everything I saw, everything in the natural world that I could witness and watch living so close to Lake Ontario gave me so many questions. And sometimes there aren't always answers to these things, but then you can have conjectures. Bob might say something like, 'Well, I don't know exactly what it is that we are seeing, but in all probability, here's what's going on conceptually.' This three-dimensional conceptual view of what was going on around us was something that could be taught to anyone who was interested, but I don't think that it was readily being taught. So as a college student, I was very fortunate to be exposed to that right from the get-go."

Edward Sheldon most certainly had no idea when he moved his new college to its lakeside location that Oswego State would one day become a mecca for weather lovers. But by the time the college entered its rapid period of growth in the 1960s and '70s, faculty were well aware of Lake Ontario's ability to produce powerful storms, and from them, equally powerful educational opportunities. Though the city of Oswego seemed rather typical itself, many had a reaction like Greg Stumpf did when he first arrived on the campus by the lake in 1982:

"I thought *Wow, this is beautiful!* My first impression, weather-wise, was that it was really nice. Autumn is very beautiful in Oswego and I was aware that it also had its reputation for lake-effect snow and that didn't bother me; in fact, it was something I wanted to see."

Indeed, the SUNY College's reputation for impressive snowfall totals and hard-to-imagine lake-effect snowstorms made Oswego an intriguing starting point for those seeking a career in weather. Adding in Bob Sykes' fervor for observing and evaluating storm systems only enhanced the key components of a memorable college experience. Tom Niziol, who spent many years as a forecaster for the National Weather Service in Buffalo and then went on to become a winter weather expert on *The Weather Channel*, got his meteorology training at SUNY Oswego in the mid-1970s. Neither of Tom's parents had gone to college and he was the first of his siblings to do so. He looked at some of the big schools, such as Penn State, but then found out about a school not far from his hometown of Buffalo that offered a meteorology program. Tom clearly remembers that first drive to Oswego, seeing the campus and meeting Bob Sykes:

"My dad and I drove there and we got just this wonderful feeling when we talked to Bob. Oswego was a small program where the faculty cared and it was on this great location by the lake. [To this day] I consider the Great Lakes one of the most wonderful, natural laboratories to study weather in the world." Like many of Bob's former students, Tom can easily recall how his teacher used the lake and its famous weather as an instructional tool: "Everyone knew that from inside a building you could use your sight to observe what was going on. But from the outside – where you could hear the wind, feel the wind and the snow – that's how Bob taught us to study the weather."

In fact, many of Bob's classes didn't take place in a classroom. Instead, they were conducted on top of that new science building, Piez Hall, where the wind proved to be one of Sykes' most powerful teaching tools.

Bob leading a class on top of Piez Hall. (Photo courtesy of Thomas Moore)

Wind played a major part of a lesson Bob was teaching on Piez Hall's roof that Tom Niziol found especially memorable. It started with a cloudless day and very light winds, and Tom recalls that "we guys in class were busier looking down at the coeds than the weather. Bob, of course, noted this and commented on it, as he would. Then he looked at us and said, 'Here's your quiz for the day: Tell me what direction the wind is coming from.' Well, typically, you're going to look to see if there were any flags waving. There weren't. You couldn't look at Niagara Mohawk's smokestacks next door to see if there was any smoke heading in a particular direction, because there wasn't. There were no visual cues to tell us what the wind direction was.

"So everybody's kind of looking around and scratching their head, and Bob's got that wily smile on his face. He looked at all of us and said, 'Alright, smell the air.' And we all thought, *Smell the air?* 'Take a deep breath,' he said, 'and smell.' And, as we began to do so, we could smell a sweetness in it. It was chocolate from the Nestlé plant in Fulton! The wind was moving from the south, heading north toward Oswego."

Students probably wished that all of Bob's impromptu classes on Piez's roof could have been as sweet as that. But inclement weather never stopped Sykes if there was a good lesson to be learned; in fact, it only inspired him *and* his dedicated students. One of those students, Chrystal (Laird) Cardinali, who had been hired by Sykes to work in his office, remembers the day she got a phone call from him when he was off campus, alerting her of a storm heading toward Oswego:

"He was excited and said, 'Go up on the roof and check.' Paul [Cardinali, another student of Sykes and Chrystal's future husband] was with me and we went up together. On the roof there was the section encased by a large amount of metal that held all the weather instruments. We stood up there and watched the thunder and lightning – it was wonderful!"

Then the couple heard a buzzing sound and noticed a glow. "It was St. Elmo's fire," Chrystal was certain, "which is an electrical discharge before lightning strikes that causes a buzzing and sometimes an illumination on a surface. Paul yelled to me, 'Get down the stairs!' and pushed me toward the staircase. We pulled the door shut and then we heard Kaboom!"

Another of Bob's students, Jack Kaplan, also had a St. Elmo's fire sighting, but his wasn't on top of Piez Hall. Kaplan was on the ground, several miles from campus, working on a weather study project for Bob at Niagara Mohawk's nuclear power plant, located on the east side of Oswego. "I was in the trailer at the plant," Jack explains. "It was 4° below zero and snowing heavily off the lake, but you could see the stars above. And everything was glowing! I called Bob to explain what I was observing. 'I think the nuclear reactor is going down!' I said. 'Really?' Bob replied. 'That's St. Elmo's fire! I'm on my way there to see it!' "

After the event, Jack made sure to research the phenomenon he had witnessed, learning that St. Elmo's fire is static electricity that results when snow is unusually dry.* "You know how you rub a balloon and then it sticks to a wall?" Kaplan asks, as part of his explanation. "Well, when lake-effect snow is light and dry, it will stick to things and that's static electricity. Because it is electricity, it will glow and you'll see it around the trees and bushes. Everything will light up, and it's quite beautiful."

Many who took a course from Bob Sykes would acknowledge that Piez Hall's roof was their favorite learning environment – and not just during the daylight hours. In wanting his students to fully understand the complexity of studying weather

---

*St. Elmo's fire can also be attributed to weather conditions such as lightning storms, which is what the Cardinalis experienced. In fact, most reported sightings of St. Elmo's fire are during rainy conditions. Reports of it during winter storms are rare.

systems, Bob challenged them to immerse themselves in it, no matter what the conditions or the season or the time of day. He developed observation schedules to mimic those carried out at National Weather Service stations, and since this work was done around the clock, Bob set up shifts, with students working in pairs. Les Austin will tell you that these co-workers were important when going up to the top of Piez Hall on a windy winter evening:

"You never went up by yourself, because somebody would have to hold onto the person taking measurements with their handheld anemometer. If you didn't have that person anchoring you, you could end up being blown off the roof." Other students agree. When Clark Warner-Long studied under Sykes while earning his teaching degree at SUNY Oswego, he referred to those extra-fierce windy days on top of Piez as "high toupee-alert days. You needed to hold onto your pants because a 40 mph wind on the shoreline would transfer to 75 mph on Piez Hall's roof."

But Warner-Long remembers that learning from his surroundings was well worth the risk involved. Besides determining wind direction by following smells and observing meteorological phenomenon as rare as St. Elmo's fire, Sykes also showed students how they could interpret weather by birdwatching. "Bob taught us to watch the direction that the seagulls were flying," Clarke shares. " 'If the gulls are flying inland,' he would say, 'a storm is coming. They can sense the change in barometric pressure and that will send them to other environs rather than hunting on the shore.' How would my teacher have known that? No book that I can think of would have contained information about the habits of seagulls in the city of Oswego."

Besides Lake Ontario, there were other great teaching tools Bob utilized in the neighborhood of Piez Hall. Niagara Mohawk Steam Station's smokestacks, a fixture for both community and campus since they were built in the 1940s and '50s, were ideal weather study "instruments." Their location on the lakeshore, less than a mile from campus and rising 350 feet from the ground, proved a bonus on windy days when those stacks were billowing. Paul Cardinali found a way to use the stacks not only to learn, but also to impress his friends. Walking with some classmates into the college's Hewitt Union on a beautiful spring morning, with the smoke from the stacks blowing out over the lake, Paul noticed that a small flag near the base of the plant was showing the wind blowing inland, away from the lake.

"I knew that on warm spring days as the land heated, cooler air from the lake would move inland to replace the warmer rising air," Paul explains. "I knew that the dark plume from the stacks was a landmark for showing wind direction, so I said to my friends: 'It's about time to change the wind direction!' and voila, like magic, the plume from the stacks rose and reversed its direction. They thought it was an amazing magic trick!"

Niagara Mohawk Steam Station smokestacks: great teaching tools for Bob. (Photos courtesy of Paul Cardinali)

Niagara Mohawk's famous structures even became a classroom of sorts for some of Bob's braver students. Jack Kaplan climbed to the top of the smokestacks a few times. "We had some meteorology equipment up there," Jack remembers. "There would be the stairs and then some elevators inside the stacks that you would go up to get to the top."

Bob's use of weather observation tools like seagulls and smokestacks seem primitive compared to meteorology's modern-day instrumentation. And though some of Bob's methods seem almost childlike in comparison, his former students who use today's technology see a correlation. For example, this learning experience told by Tom Niziol, which involved a common children's toy: "Bob had us send a thermometer up on a balloon that we had tied to a rope, marked off at each hundred feet. As we sent the balloon up, the thermometer would mark a certain temperature and stay at that mark. We'd bring the balloon back down and could actually take a sounding of the lower atmosphere, of what the temperature was up there. From it, we could learn how the air in higher altitudes on a calm, clear night cooled more quickly than it did just above the ground. Today, we can use radar and all kinds of other sophisticated equipment to do that, but, back then, we used a balloon and a rope with a little thermometer on it."

Just because students were learning experientially didn't mean that a class with Sykes was easy, as Chrystal Cardinali can attest. Chrystal both studied under and worked with Bob, so she well knows his hands-on approach. The informal setting of his classes and activities encouraged student interactions, which is how she met fellow science student and future husband, Paul Cardinali. But there wasn't a lot of time for either to think about romance when they were taking Bob's classes. Chrystal points to the high standards Sykes held for his students as an example of the "pure hell" some of his classes were for her:

"He was a very, very intelligent man, and many times when he was teaching, he would skip over the obvious angle right to the glory part of it. So as a student, you are 'down here' and he was 'up there' and there was no connective 'tunnel' between you. His tests were bad, too – he'd make up a question, and if you knew all the parameters, then you could guess at it."

Others echoed Chrystal's experience with Bob's combination of dynamic teaching and grueling testing methods. This included some who knew Bob better than most, such as his daughter, Barbara, who took a class from him as an adult. "I had moved back to Oswego, and took a few courses at the college," Barbara explains, "one being Dad's Introduction to Weather. It was fascinating. He was fair, but demanding, and could not tolerate lazy students. The class I took from him was a beginning meteorology course, and because a lot of students had to take science, they took his. When they took the test, some of them wouldn't even know how to spell the word meteorology correctly and he would be furious."

Barbara studied harder than she had for any other class, suspecting that her father wasn't going to be generous just because she was related. She even took it under her married name, "so I wasn't a Sykes in the class," she notes. "Hopefully, no one knew I was his daughter. But he gave no preference whatsoever."

Barbara wasn't the only Sykes family member to experience Bob as an instructor. Marie tried her hand at it, as well. Once again, there was no forgiveness because of familial ties. "Mom was livid," Barbara recalls, "because he wouldn't even answer her questions. She would have to ask other students because he didn't want to show any partiality."

Those who managed to keep up with Bob and follow the tangents of his course lectures eventually understood why they enjoyed the experience despite their struggles. Paul Cardinali, who graduated from Oswego with a degree in Earth Science in 1965 and taught the subject for 33 years, realizes why Bob's classes worked for him: "He would ramble sometimes. He would capture the memory of when he was in Greenland or when he worked with this or that, and he would go on about describing the phenomenon, which was fantastic. And his exams were rambling, too. But I liked it, because my mind also rambled with weather. I had read all the books and I knew what he was talking about. So if you had a devious mind, like I did, you could follow him."

Along with exciting real-life stories and practical applications to meteorology theories, students could also enjoy that Bob managed to inject humor into his weather study. Tom Moore liked hearing how Bob wove the school rivalry between Oswego and its neighboring city, Fulton, into what was happening in the weather. "Bob liked it when the wind was out of the west and his hometown of Oswego got all of the lake-effect snow," Moore remembers. "But if the wind was slightly north, Fulton got it and he didn't like that. One day, he was in class and drew an outline of Lake Ontario to show the weather patterns from a recent storm. He started writing his own made up two-letter identifiers for location names. He said, 'For example, we'll call Oswego OS, Mexico MX, and of course, Fulton I would designate as FU.' "

There's a perfectly good reason why some of Bob Sykes' students were drawn to him while others were not. It's something that most of his impassioned students wouldn't have been able to identify until much later in life, but it turns out that there's a common trait found in the SUNY Oswego weather enthusiasts who Bob befriended: when they aren't observing the weather, they're talking about it. And though some attribute this characteristic to their deep-seated interest in meteorology, others, like SUNY Oswego alumni Jim LaDue, use a much more colorful expression: "I was a weather weenie. Weenies are people who are really interested in talking about current weather. Bob was one, too."

So it was not only natural for Bob's students to understand his insistence that they immerse themselves in weather, but they also found it inspiring. Here was a teacher who willingly chased after unusual weather situations and then wanted to dissect and examine it through discussion. Sykes was a role model for emerging weather watchers, but not in an aloof manner. He was approachable, almost friendly, and when word of this unusually welcoming meteorology teacher began to spread, some selected Oswego State as their institute of higher education because of him. That's how Dave Eichorn found his way to Bob Sykes.

"I grew up and went to school in Webster, New York," Eichorn explains. "My biology teacher lived in Sodus, and he would always open up his class with a brief discussion of weather and the jet stream, which to me was just awesome. Because my teacher lived in Sodus, he was keenly aware of lake-effect and he was the one that originally suggested that I go to Oswego and contact this guy named Bob Sykes, who was already gaining quite a reputation for working with lake-effect snow."

Arriving on Oswego's campus in 1974, Dave made sure to take his biology teacher's advice and registered for Bob's Introduction to Meteorology class. He was impressed with his teacher, remembering him as being "educated and highly cultured, with an unbelievable command of the English language. After the first class, I went up and introduced myself to him. His first impression of me was probably that I was brown-nosing, but he listened to me.

"One of the things he told me was that there's a difference between a weatherman and meteorologist. A meteorologist is someone dedicated to the science and understanding of meteorology. But he was trying to impress on me and the other students that a weatherman is somebody who, when they first walk out the door, the first thing they do - they could be in the middle of the most intense conversation - but they always look up. They took a visual measure of what was going on in the atmosphere.

"When he said that during our first class, I knew that was me as far back as I could remember. So I had found somebody who was as engrossed in the subject as I was – particularly in what I call the romantic side of meteorology. That's the part that, whether you're a scientist or not, it's the part that holds you in awe. Whether it's a dark sky or storm you remember as a kid, or something that makes you go, 'Wow!' – it just gets to some people. And Bob touched that nerve in me."

The impact that Sykes had on his students reached beyond the classroom and was demonstrated in ways other than his unique teaching style and course curriculums. For a young college student, memories can be made with the smallest of gestures. "He was also a father figure for me," Tom Niziol says. "I was away from home for the first time and Bob knew how to bring along his students who were experiencing that on their own.

"At a graduation party that we both attended, he was telling stories and he looked over at me and said, 'I remember your dad.' I said, 'You remember my dad?' 'Yeah,' he said. 'You may not have known it, but when you and your dad came here to visit, he pulled me aside and said, 'You know, he's never been away from home. I just ask you that if you have the opportunity, keep an eye on him.' Bob never told me anything about that while I was at college, but he did that for all of us."

Greg Stumpf stayed in touch with Bob after he graduated from Oswego and he would get calls on all the holidays from his former teacher. "We'd chat," Stumpf explains, "and I'd give him an update on how things were going for me in grad school, the kinds of storms I'd seen, and he would talk about the weather. It was almost like your grandpa calling to check and see how things were going."

Even those outside academia can spot an exceptional teacher when they see one. Mark Kramer, who was hired by Niagara

Mohawk in the 1970s as a meteorological consultant when the company began building its nuclear power plants in Oswego, spent time with Bob reviewing his thorough weather data. Kramer observed him developing several projects that required student input and witnessed Sykes' dedication to teaching. "The way he talked about his students made it quite obvious how he felt about them," Mark says. "I once did a small stint as a teacher, and I know it takes a special person to get young people to do something extra. He had quite a crew for years that did additional data collection and research fieldwork for him."

That crew, it turns out, benefitted greatly from participating in the work Bob's weather study projects required. Getting onto one of Bob's project teams often resulted when he observed something about the student that seemed to go above and beyond class time. Earth Science major Tom Galletta took all the electives he could in meteorology, including one Bob taught called Weather and Man. Galletta and Sykes found they enjoyed working with each other, and in his senior year, Bob offered him an independent study. "I needed another three credits to graduate," Tom points out, "and Bob was working on this program that involved some analysis of lake-effect storms."

Along with projects that earned them college credit, Bob's students were also able to benefit financially when a project was supported by grant money and included stipends for assistantships and work study. Some of those students would eventually turn their special assignments into full-time positions and fulfilling professions.

A review of the diverse weather-related careers that Bob's students are carrying out today illustrates his far-reaching influence. Those he taught show up on television, radio and the internet, both in front of and behind the scene. Others work in fields such as aviation and climate-dependent commercialism, and they regularly defer to their weather training. A few have chosen careers that seem to have no connection to meteorology, but these former students of Sykes still find thoughtful ways to weave his insight into their work.

What began as admiration for their professor, now are lifelong testimonies to Bob Sykes' inspiring gifts as a teacher.

Chapter 12

Career Retrospective

Over his tenure at SUNY Oswego, Bob Sykes taught 43 semesters of weather-related classes. In addition, he was an instructor for special workshops such as Elderhostel, an educational program for senior citizens. Over the course of his life, as his meticulously-kept records indicate, Sykes would instruct 4,200 students. His notes would elaborate on those numbers, pointing out details such as his largest class (90), smallest (3), the number of field trips he took with students (75), and this staggering number of weather observations either with students or done by students under his direction (over 400,000).

Those numbers are impressive, to be sure, but Bob was mindful of including in his notes what he determined were the shortcomings in his attempt to be the best teacher possible. Something had to give in his 24 hours per day, and though he was intent on accomplishing all he could, his late-in-life reflections pointed out where he felt he had lacked:

"Being too aggressive in lake-weather snow studies to the extent of exclusion of some other matters, including my family, was a big mistake I made. Such extended emphasis really began in 1964

143

and continued until the time of my retirement in the early 1980s."
Not only did Bob feel he had slighted his family, but also his
students. He regretted "not being more active in student advisement.
I could have done more and perhaps been more helpful in this
arena of academic activity."

There were other regrets. He would have liked to have paid
closer attention to procuring recording and observation equipment
for the college as science and technology advanced. He confessed
his lack of spirit for college department policies and admitted to
what some professors had already noted: a lack of attention to
theoretical knowledge. But in the end, Bob remained aware of what
he felt his best teaching work included, and he noted it as he
watched his students moving into their own work. "Nevertheless,"
he concluded, "I did help a number of various weather-oriented
students develop in their career interests, so that I probably should
not be considered as totally failing in respect to my responsibilities."

Despite the high regard his students had for him and the
numerous careers in meteorology that he helped launch, Bob never
rose to that esteemed level of Full Professor. The position of
Associate Professor bestowed on him by Foster Brown in 1961
would remain his title throughout 23 years at SUNY Oswego.

There were reasons that his rank of professor remained the
same. This was academia, of course, an institution that expects its
faculty to work at developing theories and subjecting them to peer
review and publication, and these were not areas where Sykes put
his boundless energy. As time passed and administrators came and
left, the enthusiasm for weather study that Foster Brown admired in
Sykes would not be as coveted. And so he did not advance.*

---

*Upon Bob's retirement in 1983, he was acknowledged at the college's
graduation ceremonies by SUNY Oswego President Dr. Virginia Radley,
who bestowed on him the honorary title of Professor Emeritus.

But like the policies and misperceptions that kept him from obtaining the grade of Full Colonel in his military career, the outcome of his college advancement would not merit much concern from Sykes. He knew what was important regarding the education of his students and he never gave up advocating for what he felt they truly needed to develop themselves as effective weather observers.

In 1983, the year he retired from teaching, he was still advocating for the betterment of education. He wrote to New York State Governor Mario Cuomo with a long list of what needed to be done to improve the State University's meteorology program and course curriculum. (He took special delight in mailing the letter on President Lincoln's birthday.) Such action on behalf of his students, undertaken time and again during his teaching career, expresses how, in many important ways, Bob Sykes *was* a full professor.

OSWEGO'S FORECASTER (1961 – 1989)

"I'd like to be remembered as an avid observer – not a meteorologist, but a weather guy..."

- from Bob's videotaped interview with son Bruce, September 12, 1998.

Chapter 13

A Weatherman in Demand

As if twenty years in the military weren't enough, nor the twenty-two devoted to inspiring young people, during his lifetime Bob Sykes would amazingly realize a third successful career. Running almost concurrently with his professorship at SUNY Oswego, his role as a winter weather specialist and radio forecaster was not something Sykes actively pursued; instead, the opportunity came to him. And while this expansion of his weather prowess first presented itself on Oswego's campus, the launching of this third career did not take place in the classroom, nor would it initially involve his dedicated students. It was his fellow faculty members who set the wheels in motion.

Foster Brown was among the first to tap into Bob's collective weather knowledge. As the end of Sykes' first year of teaching came to a close, Brown was facing one of his annual challenges as a college president. Charged with determining if Oswego State's mid-May graduation ceremonies could take place outside or would need to be forced into a more crowded indoor location, the decision was always dicey for Foster. Inclement weather – including a last-hurrah snowstorm – is a real possibility in Oswego. Having someone to help him in this weather-prediction conundrum would be a load off Foster's mind, and Bob Sykes, he decided, was the perfect candidate.

Evidence of Brown's pleasure with Bob's forecasting skills shows up in a May 1962 letter, after what sounds like some "nail-biting" weather conditions for that year's graduation day. In it, Brown pointed out that Sykes' information "gave us the courage to delay making a decision. The extra hour made the difference and we are grateful to you for your assistance." Once established as the man in the know regarding campus weather, Bob's expertise in this often-volatile process would carry on throughout his SUNY career and after his retirement from the college.

Soon, other schools in the Oswego area got wind of his forecasting talent and superintendents and principals were trusting Bob with their special events. Sykes and the Oswego School District, for one, had an annual agreement for his advisement. One letter approving this work read: "Whereas the meteorology information provided by Mr. Robert B. Sykes, Jr. was helpful in determining whether to close schools during inclement weather, etc. during the 1979-80 school year, therefore be it resolved that on the recommendation of the superintendent of schools, Mr. Robert B. Sykes be and he hereby is authorized to serve as a meteorology consultant for the school district of the city of Oswego, NY for the 1980 - 81 school year, at the cost not to exceed $550." A similar agreement was also in place for the city of Oswego's Department of Public Works. These daily duties required an early start time: 4:30 a.m., with weather updates continuing as needed until after the supper hour. Both agreements would continue throughout Bob's career at SUNY Oswego.

As early as his first year of teaching, Bob's eagerness with which he approached his Oswego State professorship brought him opportunities that expanded beyond his classroom role. In late 1961, he was offered an opportunity to chaperone and mentor meteorology students on a trip to Flagstaff, Arizona. As the adult responsible for eight youth from various eastern U.S. colleges, he also had the opportunity to participate in their special weather-study challenges once they'd arrived in the Southwest.

Sykes counted the trip as one of his most satisfying as a teacher/advisor for college students, as he would another trip, this one to Colorado State University that resulted from an invitation from an old military buddy. Herbert Rhiel, who was one of the 11 students in Bob's NYU military cadet training, had established himself as an authority on tropical weather, and post-military, he became chairman of the weather department at CSU. Remembering Bob's interest in unusual weather, Rhiel extended him an invitation to the special teacher training.

Awareness of these opportunities came from Sykes' involvement with the Atmospheric Sciences Research Center. The ASRC, developed by the State University of New York's Board of Trustees, was in its infancy in the early 1960s. Founded as a university system-wide center for promoting and encouraging programs in the sciences, the group dedicated itself to those issues that dealt with atmospheric conditions. When the ASRC began their search to find college faculty interested in research programs, Sykes, who was also just beginning his tenure at Oswego State, was seen as a worthy candidate.

After Bob's enthusiastic participation in the Arizona and Colorado trips, more doors opened. He was seen as an ideal faculty member to represent SUNY Oswego at the Eastern Snow Conference, scheduled for spring 1962. Founded in the 1940s, the ESC was a joint Canadian/United States organization that sponsored annual meetings to cover topics on the rapidly-changing theories of weather observing and forecasting. Winter storms had been a dynamic conference topic for decades, and since many of the ESC's meteorologists were stationed in areas strongly influenced by lake-effect snowstorms, conference organizers made a pledge to investigate these largely unknown weather systems.

Compared to our knowledge of lake-effect snow today, the study of these powerful weather systems prior to the early '60s was inadequate, to say the least. Meteorologists were only certain that Northeastern United States weather often originated in Canada, and that it was carried by swiftly-moving winds over 200+ miles of the Great Lakes. It didn't take a meteorologist to know that the weather those winds brought could be extreme and debilitating for certain areas along the lake, but no one knew exactly why this happened. Whatever observational data had been collected was fragmented, narrowly focused and scattered throughout the region's hardest hit areas. The ESC planning committee's ambitious goal was to develop a comprehensive project to look at this lake-effect phenomenon.

The plan called for the development of a system of weather data-collecting stations situated along the lee side* of Lake Ontario which often incurred the brunt of lake-effect storms. Ontario was selected because it is the Great Lake that experienced the least amount of freeze over, keeping it an active storm producer throughout the winter months. Sketching out the details of the plan was the first step toward launching the project and these were carefully considered. Next, they turned their attention to the one point that all agreed was pivotal to the project's success: Finding just the right person to head up this endeavor.

Committee members needed only to review his work in Greenland and other Arctic settings to convince them that Bob Sykes was their man. After hearing of his demonstrated ability to not only observe and record severe winter weather data, but also to successfully lead and complete complex projects, administrators were sure they had the right person. But they also knew he was just

---

*The "lee side" is the side or direction away from the wind, or downwind.

one person. How would Sykes be able to manage and direct a detailed project that covered such a widespread geographic area while continuing his SUNY Oswego teaching duties?

A thorough examination of their potential project leader's tenure in Greenland would have set ESC committee members' minds at ease. Sykes recognized the similarity of the distances between weather stations dotting Greenland's vast wilderness and the committee's plan for observing snow activity throughout Upstate New York and Canada. After all, he'd worked and traveled in blizzard territories many times before. Ultimately, in the autumn of 1962, Bob was selected to be the project's first director. (Though his agreement with ESC was to only see the project successfully launched, Sykes continued to oversee its progress until 1971.)

But there were some aspects of the project that even Sykes was leery of being able to overcome in order to assure its success. With money for the project limited, the weather observing stations, unlike those in Greenland, would have to be manned by unskilled volunteers. Before the data collection could begin, Bob needed to recruit and train the right people for the project. Not only did they have to be the sort of person who could handle adverse weather, but they also needed to live in specific locations. And Sykes needed dozens of these willing amateur weather observers.

Finances for the project were given a shot in the arm soon after it established itself with a proper name: The Lake Ontario Environmental Laboratory (LOTEL). When word about LOTEL's ambitious goals were passed through the learning institutions associated with the Eastern Snow Conference, many signed on. Along with the two initial colleges, the State University at Albany and Oswego, many others in the SUNY system eventually committed what resources they could make available.

Despite the committee's solid support, Bob struggled at the onset of the program. Since LOTEL's goal was to *understand* storms and their influences from the lake, thus allowing weathermen to better forecast lake-effect snow, he attempted to familiarize himself with the data he would be analyzing. Unfortunately, he found no textbook studies or research papers* that had examined comparable winter-weather conditions. Sykes, it turned out, would be one of the first people to comprehensively study the lake-effect snow phenomenon.

LOTEL's administrators needn't have worried about the immensity of their ambitious plans. There was one trait in Bob's weather study protocol that the project needed if it was to succeed: the mile-to-mile variables along a lake-effect storm's course would need to be painstakingly tracked, and Sykes had long devoted himself to observing weather at such a micro-level.

In order to collect the necessary data he needed to analyze lake-effect storm systems, Bob focused on two important decisions: determining what equipment could best capture the data and selecting the ideal locations for his series of weather checkpoints. He began by first collecting what he knew each volunteer observer would need to carry out the work he was requesting of them: a thermograph to record temperature fluctuation, a barograph to document air pressure changes, and some wind equipment.

Next, he focused on where to place these "mini-weather stations" along the area east of Lake Ontario, deciding that they should reach from Canada, head south through Lowville, Boonville and Rome, and then arc toward Rochester. Once the stations were in place, data collection would begin, and theoretically, Sykes could track a typical - if there was such a thing - lake-effect snowstorm.

---

*Bill Wall, a former student and colleague of Sykes, recalls that there were "ocean-effect snows in Japan that came close to this project's work," but little had been written about them. In the United States, no such investigative work had been conducted.

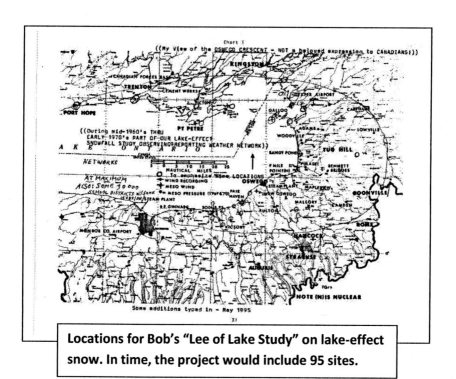

Locations for Bob's "Lee of Lake Study" on lake-effect snow. In time, the project would include 95 sites.

Along with observing the areas directly on the lee side of Lake Ontario, Sykes also thought it important to include locations inland from the lake's shoreline. For years, meteorologists had heard about the phenomenal snowfall that piled up in an area known as The Tug Hill Plateau, a 150,000-acre expanse due east of Lake Ontario. Its gradual rise to 2,000 feet above sea level makes The Plateau a perfect spot for moisture-dense clouds coming off Ontario to deposit several feet of snow in one storm. The conditions were run-of-the-mill for Tug Hill locals, but largely a mystery to weather scientists, and Sykes was itching to unlock its secrets.

But those lake-effect storms didn't always head for the higher elevations of Tug Hill. Sometimes the powerful winter weather systems would head southeast toward Syracuse, 40 miles from the Lake Ontario shores. As a major U.S. city that could be crippled by lake-effect snow accumulations, Sykes was given the challenge to not only learn how those storms developed, but also to determine what influenced their often unpredictable pathways. Bob expanded his observation sites to include Tug Hill, Syracuse and other important areas for the study.

Volunteers to become Bob's eyes and ears for this groundbreaking project needed only one common denominator: a sincere interest in the weather, thus increasing the likelihood of committing to the required daily testing. The rest - the science of it all - could be taught. Thermometers and wind instruments were basic enough for most anyone, but the barographs - machines with a rotating drum covered with graph paper and a free-floating pen to record changes in atmospheric pressure - required some special instruction.

Patiently, Bob explained to each weather recruit that the needle would rise and fall as the atmospheric pressure did the same. Should the needle sink down, Sykes enthusiastically advised, that would indicate a storm approaching. The only requirement was to make a daily observation, preferably at 7:30 a.m. If there was an outbreak of lake snow, Bob asked recorders to report three times that day: the early-morning regular check, and then at noon and five p.m.

Bob had no trouble finding willing volunteers in most of his targeted locations; farmers, small-business owners, school teachers and stay-at-home moms agreed to participate in his project. But there were a few important sites where the right person did not come forward, and in order to have all locations covered, Sykes needed to do some gentle persuasion. Bernadette Crisafulli, who grew up on County Route 1, in East Scriba, remembers a knock on her door back in the early '60s.

"This gentleman introduced himself as Bob Sykes," Crisafulli remembers. "He explained that he was doing a research project and he had this machine with him - the barograph - and I remember my mom really worried about being responsible for such equipment. She was afraid she was going to break it, but he kept assuring her that it was fairly easy to operate. He explained how it worked and that the only thing we needed to do was change the paper every day, dating each page."

Bernadette's mother tried to talk Bob into going to a relative's house down the road, assuring him they would love doing such a project. But Bob was adamant. "He said, 'It's got to be at this house,'" Bernadette explains. "'Even 1/10 of a mile down would be inaccurate.' So my mother reluctantly agreed to do it. We had it in our basement on a stool and my mother used to refer to its daily care as 'Change the Baby.' She'd say, 'Okay, I've got to go change the baby.'"

Though Bob eventually developed a dependable system of checkpoint observers, they still needed his support, and even making an occasional visit to all sites meant a lot of traveling. To compensate for this, ASRC loaned Bob a Land Rover and it became a fixture around the Sykes home and on campus.

"It was a really clunky, military-looking industrial car," Bruce Sykes recalls, "but very functional: four-wheel-drive, big heavy snow tires, and it had a winch on the front so that if he got stuck somewhere along the way, he could get himself pulled out. He used to give me a ride to school in it and it was like riding in a tank."

Bob Sykes' Land Rover.

Sykes ended up spending a lot of time in that Rover during his years orchestrating LOTEL. "He would go to visit his network of observers from time to time. Our family called them 'weather trips',"" Fred Sykes recalls. "He usually wanted one of the family to go with him and the task usually fell to me or my younger sister, Cindy." Along with the long hours in the Rover as they traveled to each weather observer, there was also a little bit of fun along the way. "My father always stopped and bought Archway cookies to take with us," Fred goes on to say. "Those trips were done in good weather and they were usually day trips. But there were a few overnights up to Canada."

Over LOTEL's first few years, Bob built an observing network of 49 stations around the eastern end of Lake Ontario. Eventually, that number grew to a total of 95 sites. By the late '60s, the program involved nearly 400 high school students from 40 school districts who were selected because of their interest in meteorology and earth science. Chrystal Cardinali played a major part of the collection and collation of all the data these locations produced, and she believes the project was one of the first computer studies ever done at SUNY Oswego.

"We worked with something called 'Mark Sense,'" Cardinali explains, "which were used with Fortran computers. These were those cards with little ovals lined up across in columns. The first two columns would identify the school and location, the next two would be the students' names and then the rest were for weather variables." After the schools filled the cards out, they were sent to Chrystal, who ran them through a computer, effectively producing an image of the pattern of weather on a given day.

"Bob would analyze this data for meteorological assessments about wind direction, etc.," Chrystal continues. "I didn't do any of the analysis, but it was my job to write the data on the strips and then prepare them for permanent storage. In order to do that, I had to decipher what Bob wrote, and he had terrible penmanship!"

But Chrystal's struggles with Sykes' shoddy handwriting were worth it. What Bob was able to infer from the miles of statistics was what he and LOTEL had hoped for. After analyzing months of the barographs' records, Bob was able to see patterns of he called "Vs"

– little ups and downs that the needle sketched over time. These small and intense activities, Sykes theorized, were meso-low pressure systems and indicators of strong storms moving through. Dave Eichorn, who discussed these observations with Bob many times, points out that "with Doppler radar today, we can confirm this." But in the 1960s, Sykes work with the LOTEL project was unprecedented, as SUNY Oswego meteorology student Bill Wall notes:

"At that level of what Bob was doing to try to understand the dynamics of lake-effect snow and be able to forecast what was going on, I had never heard of anything like that before. What he was doing was micrometeorology.*"

LOTEL's planning committee wholeheartedly agreed with Wall's explanation, noting that the work accomplished would have been impossible for U.S. and Canadian Weather Bureaus to achieve on their own. Bob, though, was more pleased than anyone else. The LOTEL project was included on a list of "The Greatest Positives of My Life" that he compiled at the end of his SUNY Oswego career, and in it he thanked "the selfless aid by many hundreds of cooperatives in the widespread weather networks and data-gathering programs making up our Lake-Effect Snow Studies."

Included in his thoughts about LOTEL was his satisfaction in "providing for more than a score of students who worked in my weather projects in such ways that substantially aided in directing their professional careers." Indeed, beginning with LOTEL, Bob was able to offer many of his students the opportunity to explore career options in truly unique learning environments, not only opening doors for them, but also creating powerful memories that is still influencing their work today.

_____

* Micrometeorology is the study of weather conditions on a small scale or within a small geographic area.

An unidentified SUNY Oswego student, one of many young people who enthusiastically helped Bob in his studies.

Bob's trips to LOTEL's check stations weren't always in the company of his family; there were occasions when one or more of his college students came along to help with the data collection and routine maintenance on the instrumentation. Often, those trips took place in the middle of one of the lake-effect snowstorms LOTEL was investigating, and Tom Galletta remembers driving through more than a few of them with his teacher. If the Land Rover was out of commission, Sykes used the family's Chrysler Imperial, which Galletta noted "had Michelin tires that he bought special for it."

Other times, Tom and his fellow students followed Bob, driving their own vehicle during intense snowstorms. In order to communicate what they were witnessing, Bob had purchased a then largely-unknown piece of equipment for each vehicle: mobile phones. "These phones had this big power pack that you had to mount in the trunk," Tom explains. "They had just come on the market and Bob bought a couple of them – he often paid for things out of his own money."

The phones would come in handy, for sure, with some of the weather Bob asked his students to drive into. But he never had to worry about finding willing participants to travel with him through less-than-ideal travel situations. Bill Wall says he can list "a coterie of students – fanatics – crazy enough to go out and drive through the snow. There were some hair-raising events associated with this work. Paul Cardinali had an old Chevy, and there were times we drove it when visibility was literally zero.

"I saw snow bands where I thought that it couldn't possibly be snowing that hard. It was almost like it was materializing before your eyes, like being in the thickest of fogs. You couldn't see past the hood of the car and you had no idea where the road was. You tried to feel if you were going off the edge of the pavement. Once or twice, we'd run off, and once you're off the road, you'd be there until the snowplow came."

Cardinali remembers those excursions with Wall and Sykes, and also several with his future wife, Chrystal, when the two of them drove into storms to track the endless weather studies Bob was working on. Chrystal describes a typical Sykes "assignment" like this: "Bob might say, 'It's storming and there's a band of snow west of here. I want to know how wide the band is.' So we would get in the car, drive to the site, and mark our odometer when we entered the storm and then check it when we drove out of it. From that, we'd be able to figure out how wide a band it was."

"Another thing he had us doing," Chrystal continues, "was 'snow cores.' When we'd get snow, if it was that light, fluffy stuff, it was probably lake-effect, which doesn't have a lot of water content. But just to be sure, you could take a core sample. We'd have these three-foot-long metal tubes that were pushed down through the snow. We'd pull them up and place them into a bag, mark the location of where we got it and proceed on until we had maybe half a dozen to a dozen samples. We brought them back home to our living room, where we had these pans waiting. Once the snow melted, we measured how much liquid was in each snow core. From there, you could figure out whether it was lake-effect snow or not."

"Sometimes, we would be out chasing storms to take photographs of snowflakes," Paul says. "Up in the north country, we were off on the side of the road and I had my headlights shining on a piece of black cloth, taking pictures of snowflakes. All of a sudden I looked up and I saw lights flashing. A police officer had pulled up behind us."

Chrystal picks up the story: "The trooper sat there for a few minutes, probably running our license plate number, until he finally got out. 'What are you doing? Are you in some kind of trouble?' he asked. Well, just like Bob, Paul is very intent in what he is doing and doesn't want to be disturbed when he's working, so he didn't answer. The officer repeated, 'What are you doing!' Paul never looked up and answered, 'I'm photographing snowflakes!' Well, the officer didn't know if Paul was serious or whether he was on something, but he said, 'Well, I think you better finish your work and get back to where you belong.' "

Sometimes, participating in Bob's pursuit of the weather could turn into a lucrative deal for the perennially poor college students. Aside from recruiting native New Yorkers and Canadians to man LOTEL's check stations, Bob also found another pool of candidates in his classroom. Certain that this data collection experience would be an ideal real life experience for future meteorologists, he arranged work study programs so that his more advanced students could be involved. For many who had nearly completed their undergraduate degree, developing an independent study and a topic for a research paper could also serve as a catalyst for this work.

"I found out you could apply to work with Bob," Francis Quirk says he learned after his class took a "field trip" to Sykes' house. Quirk noticed the cellar's shelves filled with weather instruments, and when he asked about them, he was told he could be set up as one LOTEL's weather stations. Bill Wall explains more about work possibilities with Sykes: "This equipment was always in need of changing the graph paper and records and things like that.

162

We would try to service that stuff, particularly the wind-recording machinery set up close to Lake Ontario, which was particularly susceptible to being iced because of the spray coming off the lake. Bob used to spend the summer taking apart and repairing 100 barographs, 50 thermographs and 20 or 30 pieces of wind equipment."

Once the stations were set up and proved to be operating successfully, LOTEL received additional grant money, allowing for the expansion of testing beyond its original scope. Some of the grant money would cover SUNY Oswego students' service hours. (When that money ran out, Bob provided them their promised compensation from his own pocket.) A portion of the grant also went to the establishment of a more sophisticated weather station. Located in Granby, a few miles south of the Oswego campus, the station featured some complex weather instruments that needed round-the-clock monitoring. Assigning two workers per shift, Bob gave many students their first hands-on experience in professional weather forecasting.

Doug Stewart was one of the lucky students involved in that aspect of the project and describes the setup for his participation: "There was a graduate student who met us at the Granby station. He was like the supervisor to check in with when we got there. He'd make sure we were sober, etc. He'd leave, and then every hour we would do a reading. It was five or ten minutes of work: temperature, wind, humidity, visibility. We also photographed snowflakes at that site."

"I also worked the night shift," Pat Brennan recalls. "You could split the time with the other person; one would stay awake to check the instruments and do their homework, while the other slept. We would write down a few things, and depending on how the wind was blowing, we might indicate that there was a 'chocolate' wind: a wind coming from the Fulton/Nestlé direction. It was the cushiest student job you could ever have: two eight-hour shifts a week, and if you were lucky, you'd be paired up with one of the smart kids and they'd help you with homework."

With his success as a college professor, his expanding role as a dependable weather predictor and his accomplishments with the ASRC and ESC, Bob came to the attention of The Niagara Mohawk Power Company. Founded in the late 1920s when 59 local utility companies merged, Niagara Mohawk had become the biggest power supplier in northern New York by the 1960s. In '63, in an effort to continue meeting its customers' utility needs, the power company chose a lakeshore location in Scriba, a small town on the east side of Oswego, to construct a nuclear power plant.

Early in the plant's planning stages, Bob and a fellow weather observer from Oswego, Elmer Loveridge, were invited to meetings with Niagara Mohawk's administration. The company was looking to tap into Bob and Elmer's meteorological knowhow, including their weathermen's perspective regarding the power plant's viability and safety.*

Niagara Mohawk had good reason to want to understand how weather would affect normal plant operations, especially weather coming off Lake Ontario. They also were anxious to determine what could happen should there be an accident at the plant: In what ways would the region's weather contribute to the fallout and its aftereffects? Would adverse weather conditions hamper Niagara Mohawk's ability to provide protection for the surrounding area's population in such an emergency?

Mark Kramer witnessed the process of establishing Bob Sykes as Niagara Mohawk's go-to man. Kramer, who was employed

---

*In exchange for his weather expertise, Sykes was offered the power plant's location as an additional site for LOTEL's "Lee of the Lake" study.

by Smith-Singer Meteorologists Inc. (later known as Meteorological Evaluation Services, Inc.), had been assigned to serve as a meteorological consultant for the power company. Mark made many trips to Oswego, having been instructed to provide an overview of the weather conditions that could be expected, including worst case scenarios. Mark remembers that one of the key questions the plant wanted to know was in regards to "lake breeze penetration": how far breezes would travel inland, with what frequency, etc. This pertinent information was closely tied to Bob's LOTEL Project and Kramer had been advised to contract him as a consultant.

"We had no problem finding Bob Sykes," Mark recalls. "Everyone knew him in Oswego. From my very first discussion with him, we met at the Oswego Raceway. Bob liked meeting at the Raceway's restaurant because it had a great view of Lake Ontario and he always wanted to be aware of any weather coming in off the lake. Bob willingly shared his data, but it was not digitalized; everything was in paper copies. Still, we ended up digitalizing a lot of it so that it could be compared with the onsite data. We also found Bob's weather tower at his home in Southwest Oswego to be one of the better ones in the area regarding lake breezes farther from the Niagara Mohawk site."

Over time, a number of Smith-Singer's staff were former students of Sykes. One of them, Pat Brennan, got his first job as a meteorologist at Mark's company and Pat believes that because of the company's longstanding working relationship with Bob, it might have had something to do with him getting the job. Like Brennan, Tom Galletta also benefitted from work with his college professor on the Niagara Mohawk project. Under Bob's supervision, Tom collected data for the power plant and converted them into digital form. This project would work in Tom's favor after his graduation from Oswego. Another power company, Rochester Gas & Electric, had constructed a weather tower in Sterling, New York, about 35 miles from the Oswego power plants. RG & E was monitoring that area, which they were considering as a location for a nuclear plant, and when the company contacted Bob in need of some research, he gave them Tom's name, who they hired as a technician to collect weather data.

"It was a two-year program," Tom remembers, "and that experience led me to a job as meteorologist at Oswego's Nine Mile Point. It started my weather career in nuclear meteorology, which is the field I've worked in for 23 years.* Galletta had a chance to return the favor when he hired Sykes to help him in his work at Nine Mile: "I had to write an article applicable to the nuclear plant and hired Bob to critique it. I also contracted with him to confirm the accuracy of our weather data – we needed someone else in the Oswego area who collected regular data. Bob would give me a report each day to show that my information at Nine Mile Point was accurate. He was like my sanity check!"

Bob's association with Niagara Mohawk began in the mid-'60s and continued on through the '70s. (After Nine Mile One, a second plant owned by the New York Power Authority was built adjacent to it at their Scriba location. When it began operation in 1975, it also benefitted from Bob's weather data.) He monitored the site on a regular basis, including one visit prior to the plant's start up that occurred in the middle of an intense lake-effect storm.

Though he had no idea at the time, Sykes was driving through the first stormy stage of The Blizzard of '66. He remembers being one of the last cars that was able to maneuver over Oswego roads before the storm fully erupted, "barely making it to my Brown Drive home before the roads were closed. A car following me was stopped at the bottom of Perry Hill [just a short distance from my house]. I was that close."

---

*Today, Tom works for the Nuclear Regulatory Commission in Rockville, Maryland.

Working from his house for several days following that harrowing car ride, the blizzard delivered more than an intense storm for Bob to diligently monitor. It also brought him his greatest challenge as a weatherman to date. Unbeknownst to him while he was thoroughly engaged in his nearly continuous observation of the four-and-a-half-day storm, the dedicated weatherman would realize his greatest meteorological achievement, earning praise for his role in helping Central New York survive the blizzard and its aftermath.

However, by the time The Blizzard of '66 found its way into local history lore, Bob Sykes would also find himself in the middle of a controversy that put his meteorological knowhow in question.

Chapter 14

Tracking The Blizzard of '66

Sykes had been waiting for a storm like The Blizzard of '66 since he first accepted a teaching position at Oswego State. Harold Richardson, in his attempt to sweeten the job description of a meteorology professor at the college, surely would have mentioned the infamous winter weather waiting for Bob on the shores of Lake Ontario. After hearing about Sykes' enthusiastic prowess in Greenland's blizzard conditions, it was a safe bet for Richardson to think that tales of Oswego's substantial winters would factor into Bob's decision-making – and he would have been right. Once Sykes learned about the cold-climate weather associated with his new hometown, he was anxious to set down roots and wait for the big snows to arrive. But he would have to be patient.

The first few years of living in Oswego were rather disappointing weather-wise for its new resident. From 1961 until '66, though there were occasional opportunities to witness unique storm cloud formations rolling in on the lake, they offered little significant snow accumulation. December of 1963 brought a snowfall memorable enough to show up on Bob's 30+ years of Oswego observation data sheets, and there were a few other storms that caused minor disruption in the Port City's day-to-day routine. These made Bob aware of how ill-equipped the area was for inclement winter weather and he started warning his colleagues, students and neighbors that if a big storm were to hit, Oswego and its surrounding towns and rural expanses could be in trouble.

People listened. Many were lifelong Oswegonians with firsthand knowledge of the dangers Sykes was talking about, including memories of earlier Central New York storms, such as those in 1947 and '58. They knew that not only had those storms been inconvenient, but also potentially life-threatening. With this awareness and gratitude for his offer, Sykes began helping school districts and municipalities create plans for winter storm situations.

True to the effectiveness of a small town's "grapevine," word spread about the work Bob was doing for the safety of children and families. Soon, more and more people wanted access to his weather information, and the local radio station seemed the best vehicle for this. By the time The Blizzard of '66 rolled in, Bob Sykes' forecasts were being transmitted by Oswego's WSGO station.

Actually, WSGO's loyal listeners had been benefiting from Bob's weather-observing abilities before they ever heard his voice over the airwaves. Starting in 1963, Sykes was helping the voice that people *did* hear, that of Ray Falconer. A SUNY Albany professor and founding member of the Atmospheric Sciences Research Center, Falconer was broadcasting regular weather reports for various radio stations around the state, including Oswego's WSGO. Through their work together on ASRC projects, Falconer had come to respect Bob's thorough and consistent weather data and asked if he might use it to supplement his long-distance forecasts.

The information share from Sykes to Falconer continued into early January 1966, when Ray was asked to travel to Yellowstone National Park for a cold-weather study project. In his absence, he asked Bob to stand in for him and provide the daily weather broadcasts around the state. In those first few weeks of January, WSGO took a liking to what Bob was offering its listeners and they offered their hometown weather watcher a steady forecasting job exclusively with their station. And just days after the ink had dried on their agreement, The Blizzard of '66 made its grand – some would remember it as monstrous – appearance in Central New York.

Neither Sykes nor WSGO could have anticipated the fortunate timing of their new business association. The winter of 1965-66 had started off rather uneventful, much like the last few winters had. Temperatures in December and early January were seasonal and even a bit above normal. Finally, in the third week of the new year – a week before the blizzard began – there was a coastal lake-effect storm that dropped 10 to 12 inches of snow on most of Oswego County. At least, people were saying, it started to look like winter. Then, in the last full week of the month, the coldest weather of the season (including a record-setting low of -26° in nearby Syracuse), set a chilly stage for what was to follow.

The massive storm, as Bob suggested in his December 1966 essay, *The Blizzard of '66 in Central New York State – Legend in its Time*, should actually be remembered as consisting of three separate phases*: "1) The first wind or 'small' blizzard; 2) The quiet period [with] locally heavy snows with little or no wind; 3) The climatic blizzard or second wind," this last phase effecting much of the Northeastern United States.+

---

*Never one to consider a subject closed until he had looked at it from every angle, Sykes would in his later years determine that the storm actually happened in *four* phases.

+Years later, when people started comparing the significance of the '66 Blizzard to more recent storms – 1993's nor'easter, for example – Bob would remind them that the '66 storm covered a much wider area than the others, estimating its influence spreading over nearly 20,000 square miles.

"The first phase," Sykes reported, "[took place] Thursday, January 27 and Friday, the 28th. A deep coastal low, originating in the Gulf of Mexico on the 25th, moved northeastward to south of Newfoundland by the 28th." This pressure system, while producing some snow, was not out of the ordinary for Central New Yorkers, but still carried enough of a punch to put a damper on their comings and goings. Paul Cardinali was a first year teacher at Central Square High School living in Oswego in 1966, and was, like his college professor, an avid daily weather observer. Paul's Friday, January 28 journal entry reported: "Horrible driving to Central Square in a.m., only to find out school closed. Got back as far as Fulton. Stayed there until 1700* when I was able to head back to Oswego."

Many drivers found themselves with similar poor road conditions. Once snow clouds started gathering over Lake Ontario, and with winds gusting between 20 and 40 mph, the falling snow at times gave the area, in Sykes' unique phrasing, a "zero-zero visibility." By noon on Friday, he noted that the "dramatic 25 degree veering of the wind included a speed decrease from about 26 mph to about 17 mph." During phase one of the blizzard, Bob recorded 20 inches of new snow, and once the winds picked up again, it began swirling it and the new snow that began falling into an "effect that was likened to 'snowfog,' " he stated. (He would later rename it 'snowdust.')

This storm, primarily lake-effect, was "characterized by wide variations in flake size and fall intensity and," Sykes theorized, "by a single snow band." Curious to test out his theory and see what was happening beyond his Southwest Oswego home, Sykes embarked on a precarious trip heading toward Fulton. Sure enough, he drove out of that narrow band of snow "approximately six miles southeast

---

*Cardinali, like most serious weather observers, records time using the military "24-hour clock," with 1300 indicating one p.m., etc.

of Oswego." His theory was further supported when he headed back home and got a glimpse of the clouds clearing over Lake Ontario. Phase one of the blizzard, certainly nothing that would have ended up in record books on its own, had ended.

The second phase, which Sykes suggested took place primarily on Saturday, January 29, brought with it steadily diminishing winds and a sense of calm to Central New York. Snow was falling, but gently. Though some areas had gotten a substantial accumulation in phase one, once the clouds broke, the only thing that seemed necessary was a shovel and strong back to return life to normal. The steady, but diminished snow activity during the next 24 hours gave Bob a break from his continual observations outside his Brown Drive residence, allowing him a chance to find out what was happening in the surrounding areas. What he found was surprising.

It turned out that phase two was particularly fickle as it moved from town to town and country road to country road in Oswego County. Bob recorded another 10 inches of snow at his Brown Drive weather station, but found only two inches on the SUNY Oswego campus, four miles to his east. At Oswego Center, three miles south of the college, there were 14 inches. Cardinali concurred with Bob's findings, noting "5 to 12 inches of new snow varied greatly in amounts over a very few square miles." Snowfall totals in regions beyond Oswego County were hit and miss. Wherever the snow fell, it floated gracefully to the ground, offering a sense of peace over the region. People settled in, ready to enjoy a quiet winter weekend.

But as Central New Yorkers sat back, congratulating themselves for having made it through another lake-induced storm, phase three had already begun organizing. Sykes described the phase "in the form of a developing cyclone over the southeastern states," drawing moist ocean air into its growing mass. Things weren't boding much better to the north of Central New York: Up in Sykes' old stomping ground, Greenland, a blocking high pressure system was affecting the weather of an enormous area from northeastern Canada to southwestern United States. The system was spreading extremely cold air over two thirds of North America. By Friday the 28th, this Arctic blast penetrated deep into central and west Texas; by Saturday the 29th, it was into the Gulf of Mexico. It turns out that the record low of -26° recorded for Syracuse on January 26 was a result of this much larger system, carrying the potential for major weather problems across America.

But no one had more reason to be worried than Upstate New York, for on its way south, this frigid frontal system moved in over the Great Lakes, and as if those rock bottom temperatures clogged up its gears, the system slowed to a near standstill.

The blizzard's most critical phase hit the Northeast on the 29th, when that stalled Arctic air met the rapidly-moving low pressure system from the south. The low traveled from southern New Jersey to Burlington, Vermont in 12 hours, Central New York right in its pathway. Then this low pressure, like its cold-weather kin heading down from the north, decided to slow to a mere 10 mph. When the two weather systems hit over the Great Lakes, something momentous – and something Bob Sykes had been waiting for – was unleashed. But not just weather enthusiasts like Sykes would notice the weather taking its ominous turn.

Around Central New York and along the lee side of Lake Ontario, faithful residents who had been monitoring Bob's barographs for his LOTEL project took note of their machines' sudden and erratic behavior. On January 29, Bernadette Crisafulli, whose family in Scriba had been fulfilling their barograph duties day in and day out, noticed that the needle gauging the pressure systems' highs and lows had sunk to its very bottom. "Nobody had *The Weather Channel* back then," Bernadette points out, "and we had no idea what was happening. My mother was so upset, because she thought we had somehow broken the machine."

No, the barograph wasn't broken; it was merely doing its job. Had more people owned such equipment and understood the needle's variable storyline, perhaps they would have been prepared for what came next, when the two merging systems created, as Bob described it, "a 34-hour blizzard condition." A smothering winter blanket covered the Northeast, fueled by moisture from the Atlantic. Central New Yorkers, however, would have the added "benefit" of Lake Ontario to keep that snow machine churning when a subtle but meaningful shift in the winds took place.

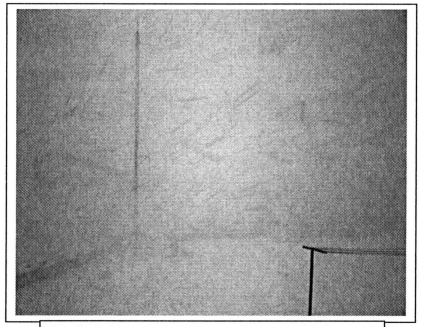

The view outside Bob Sykes' back window on January 30, 1966, during the height of The Blizzard of '66.

Diligent weather observers would have noticed the wind shift. On Sunday the 30th, snow crystal formations changed from cyclonic snow (such as that closely associated with a typical nor'easter) to lake-effect snow. Looking back on the storm in a 1991 newspaper article appearing in Syracuse's *Post-Standard*, Bob would describe phase three of the blizzard as "culminating in an absolutely chaotic situation. By [Monday] Jan. 31, the flakes were averaging one-half to three-quarters of an inch in size.* It was like taking a pillow," Sykes noted, "and dumping it over the area for hours on end." (Years later, in an attempt to illustrate for an audience what it was like to experience just such a lake-effect blizzard, Sykes emptied a pillowcaseful of down feathers onto the conference room.)

But it wasn't just the heavy snow. The importance of the wind to the 1966 storm, as many who witnessed it insist, should not be overlooked. Along with causing a sustained near-zero visibility, the blizzard winds were wreaking havoc with the snow that had fallen. Their incredible force had resulted in a "nearly clean scouring of many areas," Sykes explained. "Conversely, there were also the hard-packed drifts...commonly found in polar regions." He would have seen these sights in Greenland, and once he realized what was happening, Bob launched into the observation practices he had perfected in his former Arctic home.

Fred Sykes, still living at his parents' home in 1966, remembers his father being awake for the blizzard "the whole time; at least it seemed like that. He wanted to observe all of it, because he knew this was something exceptional. Being up all night wouldn't have bothered my dad; he was excited in what was happening." Indeed, Bob would log more than 40 *continuous* hours of his Arctic-trained observation skills; that number would be part of the 125 hours he logged during the entire seven days that included the storm. And once it was all over, Sykes had recorded 102 inches of new snow during the storm's three phases.

Not everyone was as excited as Sykes to watch those inches

---

*While there is no "standard" size of a snowflake, they are generally seen as between ¼" and ½" in size.

add up. Many people were wondering if the storm would ever end. To appease their worry, most Oswego County radios were turned to local stations for updates, since TV weathermen from Syracuse and Rochester weren't much good to those trapped in rural areas. Those larger cities were being battered with snow, too, but what they were reporting just wasn't matching what places like Oswego and Fulton were enduring. People needed information about what was going on in their neighborhoods and they needed reassurance that things were going to be OK. Bob Sykes answered that need; his analysis of the blizzard heard on WSGO over 100 times as the storm unfolded. For some, it seemed he was on continuously.

But everyone listening to Sykes wasn't automatically impressed with his forecasts and weather recaps. Some people began questioning his 102-inch snowfall total: How had Sykes come up with those numbers? Why didn't it look like there was 102 inches of snow outside their homes? For the first time since Bob had started sharing his winter weather observations, his methods were in question. Just how did Bob Sykes measure snow?

The Blizzard of '66 storm was monitored and measured where Sykes had been keeping weather stats since his family's move to Southwest Oswego: at his weather station on Brown Drive. His measuring tools – the same ones commonly used by weather observers during that era – included a ruler, a snowboard* and his visual observations. Intent on keeping an accurate account of what he quickly realized was going to be an unforgettable storm, during its most intense phases Sykes was almost continuously measuring and recording his findings. Other dedicated weathermen were measuring, too, but they were coming up with much smaller totals, and once those numbers were compared to Bob's, people wanted to

---

*Normally a 24" x 24" square, a snowboard is usually made of plywood, painted white and set on the ground where falling snow can collect.

know why there was such a difference.

One reason for the disparity between Sykes' and other measurers' numbers is quite obvious to most longtime Central New Yorkers. During many storms, and especially when it is of the lake-effect variety, snow activity varies greatly from location to location. People in Oswego are used to talking with friends and relatives in neighboring towns and hearing about substantial variations in snow accumulation.

Years later, Bob would theorize that, in all probability, the worst of the storm actually *had* played out in the general vicinity of his home. Other areas, he concluded – some only a few miles from him – did indeed see significantly lesser amounts of snow. But when considering snowfall totals, the variability in those amounts could also come from the *frequency* of their measurements and here is where Bob Sykes differed from his weather-observing peers.

Sykes had developed an observation standard that involved taking measurements much more frequently than what would be considered typical. The National Weather Service, considered the United States' most trusted weather data-collecting organization, requires that a snow observer take measurements minimally one time, *but no more than four times,* a day (or every 6 hours). However, in a storm as exciting at The Blizzard of '66, waiting hours to take measurements just wouldn't work for Bob. He wanted to size up what was happening as it happened – morning, noon *and* night. In trying to record the significance of the blizzard seemingly snowflake by snowflake, Sykes was working around the clock.

Time between snow measurements matters for one key reason: compression. Everyone who has watched lake-effect snow gently pile up as it falls, and then see that pile hours later shrunk and densely-packed, innately understands the science of compression. 11 inches of snowfall recorded in six hours might look more like seven or eight inches at the 12-hour mark.

Variations in measurement frequency also have to factor in a weather condition that is unique to blizzard storms. Along with the changes that happen to the snowflake's composition over time, the blowing and drifting that results from a blizzard's high winds will be factored in differently from observer to observer. When snow has fallen and then is quickly swept away, infrequent measurements miss out on those numbers.

There was one more variable that The Blizzard of '66 added to a weather observer's challenges. Not only was the blizzard moving snow before it could be properly measured, but its strong winds began hammering the snowflakes until they lost all semblance of their original form. This resulted in the snow becoming so densely-

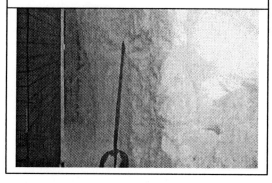

Concrete-like snowdrifts were common during The Blizzard of '66. (Photo courtesy of Paul Cardinali.)

packed that people used the phrase "concrete-like" to explain what they were seeing. It was an accurate description. When many ventured out after the storm to start their cleanup, they weren't shoveling snow, they were chiseling it.

Sykes had an explanation of why this phenomenon happened during the storm: "[After the heavy winds,] a powerful magnifying glass revealed very small segments of crystals with approximate diameters ranging from 1/50th to 1/100th of an inch. It appeared that the original crystals in the ½" to ¾" size had been broken down into perhaps hundreds of small fragments of ice by multiple collisions. No wonder, therefore, that these small flat pieces formed into drifts that could readily be walked upon with few remaining traces."

When snowfall measurements are as tenuous as they were during The Blizzard of '66, another weather observation tool beyond rulers and snowboards is needed, and once again, Bob

Sykes was in possession of just such a tool. His years spent in Arctic's long winter season had made visual analysis – the *observation* part of being a weather observer – one of his strongest weather-measurement practices. Sykes shared this skill with his students, many who still recall how Bob visually computed measurement totals. Bill Wall can still rattle off the formula that Bob explained to him back in the early 1960s:

"If his visibility was ¼ of a mile, figuring in the flake type, the snow rate was about two inches an hour. If it was snowing extremely heavy and his visibility was near zero, then it would be at more like five to six inches per hour."

Landmarks like telephone poles were another tool Sykes used to aid his measurement strategies, especially when driving through heavy lake-effect snow on the back roads of Oswego County. Actually, any large, dark-colored object would work, "such as a tree," Chrystal Cardinali remembers Bob teaching her. "You measure the distance from where you are to that point, and then, during the storm, if you can or can't see that far, you could guess what the visibility is with fairly good accuracy."

With the '66 winds raging for hours, and the fallen snow swirling into new-falling snow, even experienced blizzard-weather observers like Sykes had their work cut out for them when it came to measuring. "You can only *estimate* the amount of snow that would have fallen during a blizzard like '66," says Bob's former student, Jack Kaplan. As Bob would have taught him, Jack notes that "you can measure the height of the drifts and figure the wind speed and direction and come up with a good estimate of the amount of snowfall."

This is what Bob Sykes did, hour after hour, day after day, using his vast weather knowledge to arrive at his best estimate of what that unprecedented storm had delivered to Central New York.

While Bob was deeply engaged with what was going on in the world smaller than a pulverized snowflake, some in the larger world were questioning his numbers, his measurement methods and his current position as the National Weather Service's designated Cooperative Station Observer* for Oswego. In January 1966, there were three Cooperative Observers closely monitoring the blizzard's rage on Oswego. Besides Bob Sykes, who had been designated the official NWS Observer as a result of his position in SUNY Oswego's expanding meteorology program, Elmer Loveridge and Max Morgan also had their keen eyes on the storm.

Loveridge had a long military career as a meteorologist and came to Oswego to oversee the Army's First Order weather station in 1939. After the seasoned observer retired, Elmer continued keeping Oswego records, taking measurements at his West Third and Ellen Street home. Like Sykes, Loveridge used the traditional measuring stick and snowboard.

The third weather observer was SUNY Oswego Earth Science Professor Max Morgan, a colleague of Sykes. Morgan took his measurements on the Oswego Campus, just a few miles from Bob's home weather station, but garnered his snowfall totals differently. Preferring to use a complex method known as snow-to-water conversion, Morgan collected fallen snow from a designated area, melted it into liquid form and then weighed it.

Though the three men were less than five miles from each other, their totals were markedly different: Loveridge would report

---

*Cooperative Observers are volunteer weather monitors for the National Weather Service. Anyone – a meteorologist or not – is eligible to become an Observer, but they are required to use official measurement equipment and follow observation standards. There is often more than one Cooperative Observer in a given area; currently there are nearly 900 active locations in the Northeastern United States alone.

the city of Oswego accumulating 71.5 inches, Morgan concluded that 68 inches had fallen on the college campus, and of course, Sykes' 102 inches recorded at his Southwest Oswego home. With Bob's designation as Oswego's premier Cooperative Observer, his would become the official total, and word of his remarkable number quickly became big news – at least for a while.

After the blizzard had passed, a closer look at the three men's totals was taken, and some people, including the officials at the National Weather Service, concluded that Sykes' 30+ additional inches of snow in his total added up to some kind of mistake. Many of Bob's former students understand the controversy regarding the divergent Oswego totals. Jim LaDue knows that "there is no single measurement of snowfall that means anything without the context that it is in. When the media quotes a certain amount of snow," Jim points out, "it can be anywhere from a six-hour to a 24-hour measurement rate. Without knowing the source, you can't really put a lot of trust into *anyone's* measuring and reporting."

All of Bob's students would have been advised by him about the problems associated with accurate measurements, and many acknowledged the stringent observing and recordkeeping he kept. But his students were not the standard setters, and ultimately, Bob Sykes' record of the blizzard's 102-inch snowfall was rejected by the National Weather Service. His measurement methods had not followed the NWS guidelines and his total would be deemed too disparate from the other observers around him. It was replaced by Elmer Loveridge's 71.5 inches.*

Privately, Bob maintained the belief that his numbers accurately reflected the conditions Oswego and the surrounding

---

*Despite the storm total debate, Bob and Loveridge remained lifelong friends, continuing to trade their results after measuring major Oswego snowstorms.

areas experienced during the blizzard. He claimed his accuracy by citing his nearly 1,000 observations during the storm, the analysis of conditions during the 14-day period covering the week preceding and after the blizzard, and the scores of telephone calls he made to other observers in the area to discuss their results.

But, most of all, Bob was certain that "conventional snowfall measurement procedures, particularly those done [only] once or twice a day, could hardly reflect what actually happened [in that storm]. Oswego, with its high incidence of wind during cyclonic and lake-effect snow situations, would mean a once-per-day depth measurement would have questionable meaning. The vast quantities of blowing and drifting [should always] raise serious doubts to what has been measured."

Sykes held on to his beliefs even as modern technology helped advance meteorological proficiency. In a 1983 newspaper article, Bob acknowledged a "predictable improvement in the past five years for forecasting weather. However," he pointed out, "this is related to general forecasting, not for specific places like Oswego, [where] the weather can vary within a 10-mile radius." Others would support Sykes' claim. Even with today's most sophisticated weather-measurement instruments, there is still one variable that cannot be trusted with technology, and longtime weathermen like Bill Gregway well understand it.

"A machine can do temperature, rainfall, cloud cover and sun exposure," says Bill Gregway, who's been using measurement tools to keep weather numbers in Oswego for over half a century. "It can do everything except snowfall. Snow still has to be measured by a person." Gregway adds an interesting reflection that links Bob's work in Greenland to his aptitude in observing and measuring snowfall during harsh winter storms like The Blizzard of '66: "Because Bob was very familiar with Arctic conditions, he probably could measure snowfall horizontally!"

Perhaps Bob Maxon offers an appropriate closure for the question regarding Bob Sykes' controversial 102-inch snow total. As a New England meteorologist since August 1995, Maxon is not only well-versed in National Weather Service observation procedures, but also cognizant of the other methods weather-watchers have developed for garnering snow totals over the years. As an Oswego native, Maxon knows that Sykes' frequent measurements of lake-effect snow are going to look inaccurate by comparison with others. "But what is real measurement?" Maxon asks. "That will be debated for centuries."

Though we will never know exactly how much snow fell during that extraordinary blizzard, we *are* able to measure Bob Sykes' legacy that resulted from it. When people got tired of referring to the event as The Blizzard of '66, they started calling it "The Sykes Storm." Far beyond Central New York, people heard about the storm and about Bob's 102-inch total for Oswego, which started showing up on state and national newsfeeds.*

Barbara Wall, who was away at St. Lawrence University in 1966, called home when she learned how hard the storm had hit Oswego. "We only had about two feet of snow at St. Lawrence," Barbara says, "but I heard about Oswego on TV and radio, so I called my family. My mother said that Dad was on WSGO almost round-the-clock. After the storm was over, she always said that he could have been elected mayor of Oswego."

Bob himself remembered the public's reaction to his near-continuous reporting a little differently. "It's kind of like CNN now with reports from overseas," he suggested in a 1991 news article.

---

*Sykes' 102-inch assessment continues to be used as a benchmark for the '66 storm. Syracuse's *Post-Standard* used it in a "local history" column as recently as 2014. Talk to old-timers from Oswego about 1966 and they'll still use that number to prove the impact of the blizzard.

"People were sick of hearing about it, but they couldn't not listen."

But listen, they did. As a result of Bob's thorough coverage of the storm, local businesses and municipalities learned that they could depend on him when winter days proved especially challenging. People like Clyde Upcraft, town of Scriba Highway Superintendent, relied heavily on Sykes to keep his snow removal crews informed. Upcraft was moved to express his gratitude in a January 1978 letter, stating "I listen to you every day on the radio and plan the day by your predictions."

Even the staff at WSGO joined in on the letter-writing. In a February 5, 1966 correspondence from Cliff Harris, WSGO's owner and manager, to Dr. James Perdue, then president of SUNY Oswego, Harris wrote: "You should be very proud of the State University's Robert Sykes. Bob provided us with authoritative weather information under difficult circumstances and conditions of personal discomfort. He broadcast hourly reports and gave complete information, which kept the public fully aware of what was happening and enabled them to take suitable precautions. His broadcasts may well have been responsible for the fact that Oswego suffered no loss of life due to the storm. While many persons have spoken well of the radio station during this emergency, many of them have singled out Bob Sykes for particular praise."

And those WSGO broadcasts during the storm inspired a few future meteorologists as well. Native-born Oswegoian Les Austin, 11 years old in 1966, remembers hearing his future teacher on the radio: "One of the reasons I went to SUNY Oswego and studied meteorology was because of Bob Sykes. I was always interested in science and math, and as a kid, I remember hearing him and his weather forecasts – especially during The Blizzard of '66, when he was on almost continuously. I listened to his commentary and was fascinated."

Just five years after his arrival in Oswego, his faithful WSGO listeners were embracing Bob Sykes as one of their own. He felt likewise, and his children well remember their father's interest in doing what was best for their new hometown and its people. Bruce could tell from conversations with his dad and from observing him at his work that he was committed to figuring out Oswego's unique weather. "He was trying to understand it," Bruce notes, "and then trying to forecast it. He wanted to help people that could be hurt by the weather, to warn people when bad things were coming."

Barbara recognized the genuine love her father had for Oswego: "He took the city, the college and the weather seriously. I think Oswego was probably better off for having had him there, because when he did his reports on the radio, he didn't dumb it down, the way weathermen would do when they were talking on the street or to 'non-weather' people. I remember saying to him once, 'Dad, you need to say it differently.' And he said, 'No – that's weather.' He wanted to give real weather, not pabulum like you did a baby. He wanted people to understand it."

In another entry from one of Bob's many compilations of memorable events – this one found on his "Happiest Moments" list – was "the forecasting and public service performed during the 4.5 days of The Blizzard of '66."

Though he referred to this experience as "happy," many saw it as something much more meaningful. Happiness couldn't cover all the emotions people felt as they listened to Bob's voice during the blizzard's darkest moments. It was the '60s, after all; a time before nonstop dependable news reports. Those literally buried in snow and without any sign of the storm's ending had reason to fear for their lives. Bob's explanations for what was happening, and that an end to the tempestuous weather *would* come, helped ease those fears. Many Central New Yorkers were thankful that WSGO had the good sense to hire a man who knew his way around winter weather.

Chapter 15

The Voice of Oswego Weather

C liff Harris was well aware of what he was looking for in a radio weatherman. By the time he became owner of the WSGO radio station in Oswego, Harris had already spent years in the medium. Beginning in Philadelphia, where he worked for a station owned by Gimbel Brothers Department Store, Cliff had learned the effective - and not so effective - techniques of radio broadcasting. As he identified the qualities of good radio, Harris dreamed of one day owning his own station, and an important part of that dream included working with his son, Cliff, Jr., also known as "Fritz." In 1961, Fritz had just received his honorable discharge from the military and was eager to join his dad in a broadcasting venture. But there was one major sticking point: the father and son team wasn't sure where to make their dream a reality.

The Harrises zeroed in on the Upstate New York city of Oswego only after surveying areas across the country. Once they'd determined that the small, but vibrant city without its own radio presence was an ideal location, WSGO AM1440 was born. It wasn't too long after the Harris' arrival in Oswego that they met Bob Sykes. "Our association with Bob started because my dad really tried to make connections with people at the college," Fritz recalls. "Dad felt that Oswego State was a worthwhile endeavor, so as he was building up those relationships with professors, he met Bob Sykes."

Though Bob had already been working with the station through Ray Falconer's statewide weather reports, it took The Blizzard of '66 to put WSGO and Sykes' unique version of radio forecasting on the city's radar. As a result of the storm, most of Oswego and the surrounding area began regularly tuning in for Bob's daily reports, offered Monday through Saturday. Starting as a single broadcast per day, demand for his weather predictions expanded his forecasts to a morning, midday and late afternoon format, plus specials whenever the weather dictated it, including Sundays and holidays.

During his first seven and a half years of weather forecasts on WSGO, Bob's broadcasts were a public service. "He felt there was a need for more local forecasting," Fritz explains. "At the time, we were getting our weather news from The National Weather Service and sometimes those weren't very specific to our area. Bob wanted our listeners to know what was happening locally so that schools could make plans whether to open for the day and businesses could let their staff know about reporting in for work.

"Bob would call in from home and we'd record his conversation. Then, when it was time for the weather report, we played it. People always thought he was broadcasting live, but it was usually on tape. However, if he saw something changing the weather – if something didn't look right – he'd make a special call-in to keep people posted about bad weather coming in and such.

"People used to listen to Bob Sykes like they listened to their preacher. If he told you that it was going to do something on a certain day, it was going to do it. The only criticism Bob would get, from time to time, was that he talked too much. But it wasn't just idle chatter. I think in many cases when he was talking about the weather, he felt like he was in front of a classroom of students. And maybe some of the general public wasn't able to accept that. But you learned a lot from Bob about what was going on with the weather here, so when he was on our radio station, we let him talk."

Some of Bob's meteorology students agree with Harris' assessment of Bob's style of broadcasting. Tom Moore likes to point out that there is a big difference between how most of us look at the weather and how Bob did: "I might look at a snowstorm and say, 'Wow, it's really coming down!' But Bob would look at the same storm and say, 'It's coming down at a certain rate, an inch an hour or two inches an hour.' He would probably have also described the snowflakes that were falling: 'It's clinging flakes, dry flakes...' Then, when he gave a radio weather report, he would say something like, 'The lake-effect snow will begin at 6:30, and at 7:00, the winds will shift from the northwest to the west and then, by 10:00, to the west-northwest.' He would give you an hour by hour wind-shift forecast and nobody does that! His reports were as meticulous as his recordkeeping."

When Jim LaDue looks back on Bob's radio show, he's amazed at what his former teacher created in those lengthy reports without the aid of any internet or computer weather-data models. "He would watch the morning weather on PBS and study it. There was enough detail from those programs so that he could determine what the large-scale pattern was. He used his knowledge of the lake and local environments to come up with what he thought Lake Ontario would do to those large-scale patterns. And he did all this from his experience. He was basically equating what he saw in the forecast and 'pattern-matching' it to his previous experience and understanding of the science at the time."

LaDue noted that Bob also had to be aware of conditions throughout the county and state, what the visibility was like, and how they were treating the roads. "He talked a lot about the subtleties of snowfall," LaDue adds. "Things like the effects of settling with lake-effect snow and special-density snow. He knew all those details and he was familiar with the atypical hazards; things like falling icicles and such. Those were issues that you wouldn't find in a typical forecast, but he felt they would be important for his listeners."

Once Sykes befriended LaDue, Jim benefitted from his teacher's radio work in more ways than just by listening. Bob recruited him to report the daily forecasts on WSGO when he had to be out of the area. "I watched and learned how he put those shows together and modeled my reports after them," Jim explains. "Bob's show lasted seven minutes, which is unheard of in weather forecasting on TV or radio today. I'm not sure how many people actually listened to his whole forecast; they were very detailed and seven minutes is a long time for someone with a busy life."

Tom Galletta is pretty certain that there's never been anyone else like Bob Sykes on the radio. "He had the gift of gab, if anybody had it, and would sometimes talk in circles, but he would be talking about all the applications of weather. He might say, 'You could put your laundry out today, but you'll have to take it in by noon because it's going to rain later.'" Oswego historian Charles Young remembers those references to laundry: "He was always interested in the practical aspects. He would often give the report by saying if it was a 'one sheet, two sheet or three sheet' day. This had to do with things like the wind and the humidity – how quickly clothes would dry on the line."

Sykes worked hard at making his forecasts apply to people's lives, something Jim LaDue refers to as the "walking-biking-jogging" level: "This is the level of the atmosphere that directly affects a person and that was where Bob directed his weather forecasts. What were the conditions that people would experience? Perhaps instruments could capture some of that, but they could not address the entirety of the human experience."

Paul Cardinali also appreciated that Bob's forecasts were thorough, but he had to admit that sometimes they would carry on too long. "They could take ten or twenty minutes," Paul points out.

"When he'd get done, you'd think to yourself, *What did he just say? Is it going to snow or not?* So there were a lot of people who said, 'This guy is kind of a fruitcake.' "

Indeed, there were some who were sure Bob Sykes didn't know what he was talking about. Old-timers in the surrounding small towns oftentimes discounted Bob's predictions. SUNY Oswego student Tom Daniels, who lived in the rural Hannibal/Martville area, thinks this is because Bob was using terms and phrases that nobody had ever heard before. And though the word spreading about Oswego's weatherman wasn't always kind, Daniels points out that "people still talk about him. And those that know about him realize that he put his heart into forecasting. He made our part of the state and country unique."

One of Bob's students, Clarke Warner-Long, found a way to incorporate his teacher's radio work into his own career. After graduating from Oswego State and while teaching sixth grade science in Mexico, New York, Warner-Long rediscovered Bob by happening upon his WSGO radio show. Hearing his favorite teacher's voice, Clarke got the idea to somehow bring Sykes to his students:

"I brought my radio into my classroom. I needed to move my science class time from morning to afternoon because that was when Bob's broadcast was on, but he taught my class. Today they would call it distance learning, but that's what he did. The kids were rapt in their attention and it turned out that my class wanted to find out the same things that I did about the weather. I knew that my plan was getting to them because some of the more able kids said, 'I think that I want to go to Oswego and take Mr. Sykes' course.' As a teacher, it doesn't get any better than that."

Despite many people's enjoyment of his forecasts, complaints were getting back to WSGO about Bob's rambling and often-technical reports. After listening to these comments for several years, the radio station's schedulers took matters into their hands. Rick Gessner, whose father, Bob, purchased the station from the Harrisses, explains why and how Sykes' radio forecasts changed over time:

"Since Bob was a college professor and was used to teaching an audience of students, it was hard for him to adhere to the strict time requirements that went along with radio station programming. [Segments] were timed to the second, and WSGO's news programming started as soon as the sweep-second hand arrived at the top of each hour. Our staff asked Bob if he could end his weather forecast promptly before the top of the hour, but Bob quite often had trouble wrapping up to coincide with the start of the news segments. So a staff member came up with the 'Bob Sykes bye-bye tape.'

"This was an eight-second tape that was taken from a previously recorded segment that Bob had done, at the end of which he would say, 'This is Bob Sykes, chief meteorologist for the State University of New York at Oswego, reporting for WSGO.' When it appeared that Bob would run overtime into the news segment, the on-duty engineer at the radio station would slap in his 'bye-bye tape,' at exactly eight seconds before the top of the hour, and the news segment started exactly on time!"

Long or short, a Sykes forecast was often a listener's only warning of an impending storm, but there were times that Bob himself did not heed them. The entire city of Oswego could have just heard his prediction of a lake-effect snowstorm that was guaranteed to produce horrendous driving conditions and Bob's neighbors would observe him disregarding his own warnings. "I'd look out my picture window," Brown Drive neighbor Ken Peterson tells, "and there was Bob at the end of our road, with his car stuck.

Shortly after that, I'd hear a knock on my door and my wife would say, 'That'll be Bob. You gotta help him out.' Then, I'd have to put on my snowmobile suit and grab my shovel and I'd help dig him out so he could go about his business."

Despite his ramblings and eccentric ways, for the most part, Bob was highly regarded for his WSGO work. People faithfully tuned in right up until his last report of April 1989, when he retired from broadcasting. Native Oswegonian and columnist for the city's *Palladium-Times* newspaper, Mike McCrobie, sums up how many felt about Sykes: "He was *our* meteorologist. Back when I was a kid, in the '60s, Oswego was the kind of place that, if you didn't know a person's last name, you knew them by their first name and their occupation. So we had Dan the mailman, we had Pete the bookie...and it was Bob the weatherman. His voice was always there, coming out of that radio on the kitchen counter. It was like he was right in our kitchen."

Another Oswegonian, meteorologist Bob Maxon, also grew up listening to Sykes' radio reports. Along with his parents and siblings, Maxon relied on Bob's weather analysis as they coordinated their busy lives, and he reflects on how hearing those forecasts made an inspiring impression on him:

"It took quite a long time for me to comprehend the impact Bob Sykes had on me personally, but his radio program showed me the importance that meteorologists had in a place like Oswego. In the mid-'70s, when I was about 10 years old, I so clearly remember that we would stop whatever we were doing at 7:08 in the morning, or whenever it was that he came on the radio. A family of seven would come to a screeching halt for those few minutes."

Chapter 16

Living, Breathing and Being the Weather

W hat was it about Bob Sykes that made his weather forecasts so special? Why was he compelled to stay awake through the night in order to capture every nuance of a lake-effect storm? How did he manage to inspire so many others? And if Bob insisted that he was not a meteorologist, but a weatherman, what were the particulars of his personality that caused him to prefer that title? Understanding the complexities of Bob Sykes the weatherman actually begins quite simply, by remembering a concept we first learned in grade school: how to trust our five senses.

"With Bob, you had to feel it, taste it, smell it," says Jack Kaplan. "There were times I would be observing the weather from Bob's window at his home and he'd say, 'Let's go out into it.' Once, Bob and I were chasing a lake-effect storm that had a distinct beginning and ending. You usually don't see that. You might see it in a rainstorm, but not often when it's snowing. As we were going through the storm, in some places you couldn't see anything; in other places it was clear as day. So we stopped the car and started walking in and out of the storm. Walk in, walk out, like walking through a curtain of snow. I remember saying to Bob, 'Nobody's gonna believe this!' And he said, 'I don't care.' "

It's true. He didn't care what others thought. But he was always hopeful that someone might want to share what he was excited and learning about, which certainly informed his teaching style. His fascination with the weather also compelled Bob to share his knowledge of it with gusto, starting with his college newspaper's weather column and continuing through his string of radio broadcasts during one-of-a-kind snowstorms. He willingly exposed his excitement, convinced that others out there reading and listening to him felt the same. Add a third aspect of his personality – his attention to detail – and that completed his winning combination: the passion, fellowship and precision of Bob Sykes' version of a weatherman.

Sykes' daughter, Barbara, explains the basis for how her father managed to mold these traits into his own brand of meteorology: "Dad learned about the weather just like the early pilots learned to fly: by the seat of his pants. The skills those pilots acquired were achieved without depending on instruments. And Dad was that kind of weatherman. While instruments were part of his profession and he certainly used them, he wasn't dependent on them."

Barbara notes that weather tools like modern radar will often miss important local information which can't be seen on such a grand scale. In contrast, she can still hear her dad saying things like: "Wait a minute; those clouds are moving not the way that this radar tells me that they're moving." Because her father did this, Barbara concludes, "I think it made him more accurate locally."

He thoroughly enjoyed determining local weather idiosyncrasies that resulted from Central New York's stormy winters, and there's evidence of this fact in the opening paragraph of Sykes' 1971 essay, *The Climate and Snow Climatology of Oswego, N.Y* (co-written by fellow Oswego weather enthusiast, Elmer Loveridge and the National Weather Services' A. Boyd Pack). In his quest to understand weather at its micro level and then share it with others, Bob chose to introduce the article with a single photograph. The picture is of a city winter scene, and for the average Central New Yorker, it would simply show a snowstorm in action, just like those seen countless times. But here's how Bob Sykes described what *he* saw:

> "Photo was taken toward the west at about 0815 December 20, 1963, in the north central part of Oswego city during the snowburst. Car is about 55 feet, and house beyond, about 90 feet from camera. Snowfall started about 0455. By before about 1800, 24 to 26 inches of new snow were measurable (perhaps as many as 28 to 30 inches, if three or six hourly measurements had been made) on top of the previous snow cover (about six inches) at the site of the photo, West Sixth and Seneca Streets. Some compaction must have occurred by 1915 when the 24 – 26 inches were measured. Little new snow fell after 1700 to 1800 at Sixth and Seneca Streets. Accumulation depth here was greater than 1½ miles to the south (about 21 inches during the same period) or about three miles to the east (about 15 inches during the same period). Snowfall rates appear to have prevailed in the two to four inches-per-hour range from about 0800 to 1630. Temperatures during the snowfall ranged in the middle to upper teens. Wind in the heavy snowfall area of the city was "light"; only slight drifting was noticed. City schools were closed around noon; vehicular traffic into the city was stopped for several hours during the afternoon by the Mayor."

It was as if Sykes took the blank page of "just another snowstorm" and on it wrote a nuanced account in order for the world to truly understand it. Though most people have neither the scientific background nor the inclination to analyze such a scenario, this was how Bob approached his work; it was the only way he knew how to interpret his surroundings. But while those who studied the weather alongside him quickly learned to accept the idiosyncrasies of his personality, they also showed up in other aspects of his life. Fred Sykes describes how his father continued to use his ability for recalling detail well into his later years:

"Dad would come to visit, say after he'd seen an eclipse, and he would explain this to us, starting with him leaving Oswego and the airport and going through every detail of the trip. Then, if you asked him, he could do the same for a trip he'd taken five years earlier."

Though such thoroughness didn't always serve him well (as his overly-long radio broadcasts illustrated), it was what Bob Sykes knew how to do. He'd known it on some level when he first noticed a winter storm at age eight, when he poured over weather history data in the basement of Brown University and as he expounded on it in Greenland, chest-deep in treacherous weather. And those lucky enough to accompany him on his equally treacherous weather-observing excursions in Oswego County got to witness Bob at his meteorological best.

Tom Galletta speaks for many of Sykes' students when he describes this scene: "We used to drive up and down the eastern shore of Lake Ontario through lake-effect snow bands. Sometimes we couldn't see 50 feet in front of us and I loved driving in them. We would have tape recorders and talk our way through these bands, [figuring out] what the weather was like when visibility got really low."

This draw to study weather at its worst both excited and inspired Bob, of course, but oftentimes it was stressful for Marie.

"He would go out in the storms and forget to check how much gas there was in the vehicle," Barbara remembers her mother telling her. "He'd run out of fuel and this would really worry my mother. Once Dad got into the weather or into a storm he had no concept of time or anything else. It's like when you sit down and read a book, and the next thing you know, it's been eight hours. That's what it was like with Dad and the weather."

Bob Sykes on the trail of a lake-effect storm.

Over time, Marie learned to accept the reality of being married to a weather enthusiast. It was her husband's chosen career and she determined that he was carrying it out in the way he thought best. Others who closely worked with Bob also deferred to his unique relationship with the weather. While working in his SUNY Oswego office, Chrystal Cardinali observed him day after day, season after season, anticipating the weather.

"He was a person that, when the door came open, he would come bounding in if it was snowing," Chrystal remembers. "Everything was grand, he had a big smile and he was gregarious. But if it wasn't snowing, he'd come in and you'd see a big dark cloud over the top of his head and he'd turn into somewhat of a grump. Then it was just plain business – there was no fun and games."

Bill Wall uses the natural world to describe Bob's approach

to weather-watching: "Some animals are nocturnal and some are diurnal. Bob was winter. He came alive when it started getting colder and the snow arrived. He would be in full swing because he lived for the active snow periods, mostly the lake-effect storms. He liked to have me drive so that he could observe. He'd have his camera on the dashboard, his little recording device and his paper and pen. He'd be going constantly if we were going through an active snow band or weather situation.

"Watching Bob observing snow was like watching a prairie dog: he would always be in movement, looking at everything...the visibility sideways, forward, up. He'd sometimes make six observations a minute during heavy snow events. These would all be written down manually. After that task, while we were on our way to somewhere else, he'd fall asleep. But he was most active when he needed to be, to pursue the observation and that was his end all."

Chrystal also saw Bob's unusual active/rest/active pattern: "On the average, he'd sleep about four hours a night. Then, during the day, if he got tired, he'd take a mini-nap and keep on going. I think this was something he learned from his training in the service. He almost had some kind of biological "battery" that was just like jumping a car. If he was tired, he'd nod off for a few minutes and then – bang! – he'd be ready to go again.

"Once, he and I were coming back from a meeting he had in Buffalo, and when we got to the other side of Rochester, he said to me, 'I'm awfully tired; you don't have a driver's license do you?' I told him that I didn't and he said, 'Would you be offended or object if I pulled off at the next rest stop, so I can take a 20-minute nap?' And that's what we did – he sat in his seat and I sat in my seat and he took his nap. 20 minutes was all he needed, and he was refreshed and ready to go."

Students who emulated Bob's abilities as a forecaster, learned to adopt similar erratic sleep patterns. Dave Eichorn, who lived about a mile southeast of the city of Oswego for part of his college years, sometimes stayed up all night to compare notes with his teacher, who was doing the same thing on Brown Drive.

"Bob had an old piece of a meteorological tower that he passed on to me," Dave recalls. "I bought weather equipment and put it up on this 30-foot tower where I lived. If I could tell you the number of hours spent late at night on the phone taking observations every five minutes until one, two, three, four, five o'clock in the morning...There was no satellite, no radar back then, so we were making conjecture based on observations. Now, years later, with Doppler radar, I find out that, indeed, our conjectures were for real!"

Anybody who knew him well soon accepted that this passion for the weather and dedication to capturing its detail was his life. But even those just getting to know Bob Sykes quickly saw that this was what every day was like for him – even after an Oswego winter had dragged on far too long. Frank Castelli, who took meteorology classes from Bob in spring 1976, remembers being amazed at his professor's recap of a lake-effect snowstorm in March, late in the snow season. "You would think that it would be such a minor event after months of heavy snow," Castelli relates, "but Professor Sykes told us that he was up and awake at 3 a.m. to observe the storm!"

Once the Sykes family moved to Brown Drive, others who lived on the road grew accustomed to seeing their neighbor in odd situations: lying face up on their road for a better view of a changeable sky, or on his rooftop, extending his view of a weather system taking form over the lake. Karen Krause, a co-teacher of Marie's from Oswego High School, remembers dinners that the two couples would enjoy at each other's home. Once, during a snowstorm, Karen recalls Bob excusing himself from the table: "He'd be getting up every fifteen to twenty minutes to take his yardstick and go outside to measure how much more snow had fallen."

Weather was his job, and when a person works on something that changes every day – sometimes several times a day – it can become overwhelming. But Bob never thought of his work as a chore. Along with immersing himself in the technical science of studying the weather, he was also drawn to its beauty. Much like his weather-observing idol, Wilson Bentley, who spent a lifetime in amazement of the snowflake, every snowstorm held a mysterious beauty for Bob. But, then again, so did an interesting cloud formation or the cherry trees blossoming in Washington, D.C. Today, the Sykes children's homes display framed photographs of dramatic weather, such as lightning storms, captured by their father's keen eye.

One of Bob's grandchildren, Bruce's daughter Kathleen Sykes, can relate to how her grandfather merged the art of observing weather with the art of photography: "I used to study art in college and the thing that is interesting to me is that, when you look at a photograph someone takes, you can tell what that person was focusing on. If I take a picture, I might try to find the best light, the best composition, and Grandpa's photographs do have elements of good design. But you can also tell that he was taking photographs because he liked what was going on in the sky or the water. That's what was happening for him."

Kathleen and other Sykes grandchildren got to spend time with Bob as he observed the weather whenever their families visited Oswego. In the summer, they would often drive to "The Loop" on Lake Ontario for supper, always staying to watch the weather. Kathleen's sister, Sarah Sorensen, recalls one night when she realized her grandfather's attention to beauty: "There was a huge rainstorm and the waves seemed to be ten feet tall. I watched Grandpa watching them come in and he was just looking at those waves, in awe of them."

Sarah and Kathleen's cousin, Beth Sykes Collins, agrees that her grandpa "had a great appreciation for beautiful things. I would always take special care to wrap his Christmas presents, because presentation was important to him. In fact, I remember his house was full of beautiful objects that would fascinate and terrify me as a kid. There was a polar bear rug from Greenland, I think, and various Egyptian artifacts. And he had thousands and thousands of slides of 'just blue sky.' But he saw something in them that I could not see."

There were other triumphs for Sykes when encountering beauty. He claimed to be one of the few people who ever saw what he referred to as a "moonbow." In fact, he would see it twice: first, in 1944, while stationed in Greenland, and again in 1978, at his home in Oswego. "It's the nighttime equivalent of a rainbow," Bob explained. "The moon has to be low in the sky and it has to be raining, but opposite of where the moon is."

Rainbows are equally beautiful, but also rather common – unless you are a tireless observer like Bob. In 1962, while with his family on Whiteface Mountain, he simultaneously observed four separate rainbows, and in his notes of that auspicious event, he made sure to mention that five was the world record.

Many who listened to Bob's forecast on the radio got to hear his attention to detail and beauty. Rick Gessner offers this memory from one of the WSGO weatherman's broadcasts: "Bob was talking about being awake in the early morning hours to observe and take photographs of a rather dramatic display of the Aurora Borealis. His passion was evident in his meticulous description of the veils and curtains of colored lighting dancing in the sky." Jack Kaplan described Bob's reaction to these celestial and meteorological events as orgasmic. "Anybody who has a passion for the weather and observes it will understand what I mean by that," says Kaplan. "It's an orgasmic experience: that power in being able to live and see such an experience."

Bob also found that the beauty in details – the measurements, the endless variations of snow crystal formations, the subtle, but meaningful wind shifts – were as awe-inspiring as the photo-perfect scenes themselves. He never tired of noting observations. Even once he'd left the military career that demanded diligent detail and accuracy, he continued doing so in his teaching and broadcasting.

"Essentially, he was trying to measure every single change in visibility and snowflake character," Jim LaDue proposes. "At that time, very few people would have considered it important, but science has finally caught up with him. We now know the importance of understanding how details [as small as] a snow crystal can impact our lives."

Because he maintained friendships with students like LaDue who took up careers in meteorology (Jim works at the National Weather Service's Warning Decision Training Branch, teaching students how to forecast severe weather events), Bob was kept informed of how technology confirmed his theories. When Dave Eichorn started forecasting weather on Syracuse newscasts, he and Bob continued their frequent conversations.

"And that's when things started to reverse, when the flow of information shifted," Dave says. "I had access to Doppler radar and computer models, and with them, I was able to put into perspective some of the things that Bob and I had discussed all those years. He accepted this new scientific information with curiosity, but, at times, he would say, 'Forget it. This technology is awful!' And especially in the early years, he would've been right. There were a lot of wrong predictions, and he and I shared our frustrations with that. But we also accepted it, because that was part of the learning curve."

Tom Niziol remembers Bob calling him at the National Weather Service station to talk about the latest lake-effect storm and telling him about how snow crystals were changing from a quarter inch to an eighth inch, and as they were speaking, noticing them change again to a sixteenth of an inch. "People in my office would listen in and think that this guy was just crazy, or, to use a more respectable term, eccentric. Yet, if you went back and looked at his logbooks, during those storms he literally was taking observations three or four times a minute! He was trying to understand the atmosphere, trying to understand how snow – especially lake-effect snow – developed."

Greg Stumpf considers himself fortunate to have learned the attention to detail Bob insisted upon because it shows up day after day in his current job. Stumpf develops severe weather warning decision applications and technology to be used in events such as thunderstorms and tornados for the National Weather Service. "Especially during storms, there are a lot of rapid changes," Stumpf notes. "For instance, in the work that I'm doing today, we're doing our best to understand what symbols we see in radar data that can lead to tornado genesis and storms. And sometimes these signals occur very quickly."

Bob Maxon witnessed Sykes' detailed observations go head-to-head with computer technology when, in 1990, he saw his childhood hero give a talk to a room full of young meteorologists. It was at a conference sponsored by Lyndon State College in Vermont and Sykes was presenting a program that featured his finely detailed hands-on observations. "The keynote speaker that night was Jim Cantouri from *The Weather Channel*," Maxon remembers. "Jim is a friend of mine and he came to me after Bob's speech to express his amazement. 'You've got to be kidding me,' Jim said. 'The information and observation, the decades of weather analysis and forecasting in detail, the minute by minute observations...They are unheard of in this day and age and will never ever be repeated.'

"We Oswegoians took Bob Sykes for granted," Maxon concludes, "and we'd be sure to point out if he made a mistake. We might say, 'Oh, Bob Sykes was wrong again!' But he was probably right eight out of ten times."

Admitting he was wrong also showed up in the details of his work. Bob took time to correct his errors, even if he didn't learn of them until years later, like this minor fact about a 1972 snowstorm, which Sykes learned about when he and Tom Moore were reflecting on it years later: "I mentioned that a friend and I had gone out for a walk during the storm," Moore explains. "I told Bob that I had seen a flash of lightning on the walk. Bob hadn't realized there was any lightning with that particular storm. 'Well,' he said, 'I'll have to write that down in my journal.' And that's exactly what he would do."

Moore points out that, while conversations about weather most often centered on winter storms, there were times when Bob would talk about observations he'd made while experiencing conditions at the opposite end of the thermometer: "One time he told me: 'Last year, I was at the Taj Mahal, waiting in line for a tour. I was never so uncomfortably hot in all my life.' Bob was observant about *anything* that had to do with the weather, so noting the most uncomfortable heat he ever felt would have been important to him." Moore was sure that this detail, too, would have found its way into Sykes' journal.

Though the details in Bob's scrupulous records were primarily kept for his teaching or weather study-related work, they could also be a valuable tool for other purposes. There were instances during Bob's forecasting career when legal proceedings about accidents involving inclement weather needed accurate information on road or visibility conditions. Letters from attorneys found in Bob's career papers inquired about such details: At 10 o'clock in the morning on January 13, what was the temperature in Oswego? How much snow would have fallen in the Scriba area? How would the temperature and snowfall have affected road surfaces on County Route 1?

Having asked, one wonders if the lawyers seeking this pertinent information were prepared for the volume of data Bob provided. One such letter was dutifully answered by Sykes, and included in his response were not only measurements, temperatures and snowflake consistency, but also comparisons and contractions with the weather for that date a year ago, and then five years ago.

His collection of details was especially helpful when Bob was preparing a paper or planning to speak at a conference. Here, his preciseness could really shine, like in the article he presented at the 50th Eastern Snow Conference entitled "Seasonal Snowfall Totals from 1884-1885 to 1992-1993 for Oswego, NY." Prominently featured were the *monthly* snowfall totals covering a century of winter seasons. As a bonus, in many of those years Bob included measurements made from no less than nine different locations in the Oswego area.

Those journals and data reports were a fixture in the Sykes' home, and Fred has vivid memories of the volumes his father accumulated over the years: "They had pages that were 11 X 17, which had fine lines with 14 columns, one for each day. He had a whole series of things he would put down there: temperature, pressure, humidity, direction of the wind, etc. I can't say I under-

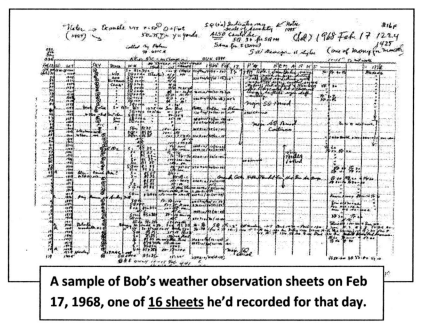

A sample of Bob's weather observation sheets on Feb 17, 1968, one of <u>16 sheets</u> he'd recorded for that day.

stood how he organized all that, and I'm not sure anyone else would, except him. But he knew where things were and he knew how to read them. He could find anything he was looking for, often in a stack of weather observations which was several inches thick."

Some of Bob's journals remain in the Sykes family and a review of them clearly illustrates the extraordinarily amazing effort he took to continually update them. In thin margins or on attached notes, Sykes would type or handwrite addendums to what he had previously written or, in the case of articles written about him, he would correct errors, often writing "No! They've got it wrong!" He wanted his life to read correctly. He wanted to be understood.

Understood, yes, but never idolized. As any weather forecaster quickly learns, on a daily basis, he or she puts their reputation on the line, and Bob, with his high profile after The Blizzard of '66, was particularly vulnerable. But he never let that bother him. In addition to his forecasts for Oswego radio audiences (where, he readily admitted, he ran the gamut of accuracy), Bob also made an annual prediction of the total snowfall for a given year in the Oswego area. He only shared these with a few close friends, "so they'll know I'm no humbug if I come close to the mark. Of the 14 times I have done this," Bob was quoted in a 1988 newspaper article, "I was a winner 10 times, two were so-so, and twice I was way off the mark."

One of those "way off the mark" predictions still gets talked about from time to time in Oswego. By the late 1970s, after years of successfully predicting Central New York snowstorms, Bob was being referred to as an oracle by many. Then, in 1978, his streak of accurate forecasts took a turn for the worse when he began tracking an extreme low pressure system (some would later say it was the lowest pressure recorded up to that time) creating some bad weather in the Central Plains. Around the Missouri area, the storm took a northeastern turn, barreling into New York State, first hitting Buffalo and then Rochester. Bob quickly called WSGO to announce the imminent danger of this mammoth weather system, warning businesses, schools and families to prepare for a storm with Blizzard of 1966 proportions. Everyone heeded his warning, quickly retreated to their homes and waited...and waited.

Today it's known as the Phantom Storm. Bob called it one of his career's great mistaken forecasts, but with this caveat: "Given the same information, I would have forecast it much the same."

It wasn't just errors like his 1978 miscalculation that prevented Bob from ever using the term "expert" to describe himself. Though others would refer to him as such, he wanted no part of that conversation. But he also went as far as saying that he never thought of himself as having mastered the *understanding* of weather, as his career papers reveal. He never explained his reasons for believing this deficiency to be true, but it's hard to imagine anyone putting more effort into research than Bob Sykes, especially when considering the insurmountable number of his weather observations.

True to his recordkeeping standards, he made sure to keep track of this aspect of his various weather careers. Just while teaching at SUNY Oswego from 1961 to 1983, Bob performed over 100,000 observations, breaking down those numbers with his usual flair:

5 years at an average of 8,500 observations or more:	42,500+
7 years at an average of 6,000 or more:	42,000+
4 years at an average of 3,500 or more:	14,000+
misc.:	3,000+

Add to this, his 21 years in the military and 16 years of post-teaching observations and surely this total would approach the quarter-million mark. There were more details.

Most observations at home (excluding field trips):

In a day: 230+
In a week: 680+
In a month: 1200+

In a year: 11,000+

Longest continuous workday: 40+ hours (carried out in 1966,'72,'77 and '78)

Longest workweek: 125+ hours (accomplished in 1961,'66,'68,'69,'70 and '72)

Most miles driven to observe or work in weather:

In a day: 685 miles

In a week: 1,800 miles

In a month: 4500 miles

In a year: 35,000+ miles

Numbers such as these suggests a measure of importance, and Sykes' certainly are impressive. But the significance of his forecasting career adds up to much more than an accumulation of observations. Rather than losing the essence of who he was in those numbers, in order to truly understand Bob Sykes' many contributions to the science of weather, one must imagine him achieving his success one observation at a time. And there was no place he enjoyed studying the skies more than at his Brown Drive home.

Chapter 17

A Weather Station in Southwest Oswego

W hile Bob certainly brought his avid interest and notable skills for weather study to the Oswego campus every workday, his opportunity for extended observations was always better at home. The volume of data he accumulated over the 37 years he lived in Oswego would not have been possible without a location as perfect for weather study as the Sykes' Brown Drive home. Selecting the site occurred only after Sykes diligently researched the Port City area for the best venue to examine atmospheric conditions. Once he'd selected his ideal setting, it wasn't what the weather was doing in Oswego, but, as the opening line for his WSGO radio show proclaimed: "This is Bob Sykes, reporting from Southwest Oswego," it was what he was observing from his home station that mattered.

Envisioning this forecasting location began back in the winter of 1962, as soon as the Sykes purchased two adjacent lots on the corner of Brown Drive and West Lake Road. Located in a predominately rural setting less than a mile from Lake Ontario's shoreline, there were only a handful of other homes on the road when they acquired the land. Bob immediately began drawing up blueprints, since it was imperative for him to oversee the architectural development of their home. There were important matters to consider: the house's orientation to the lake, the design and placement of its windows, and the possible sites for weather station equipment.

Though planning progressed favorably, Bob's newly-established college career demanded his time and the home's construction phase was delayed for two and a half years. While Bob was busy with projects like LOTEL and chaperoning cross-country trips for college students, the details of completing their house's construction and preparing for yet another move for the Sykes family fell on Marie.

When the time came to finally occupy the Brown Drive home – it would be summer of 1964 before the family was able to move in – last minute details delayed the actual moving day. With Bob out of town, Marie scrambled to find a place for the family to stay. She turned to her husband's college contacts to help secure temporary living space, and someone suggested a vacant sorority house in Oswego. But even this provisional solution fell through when the sorority sisters returned for their fall semester. Finally, in late August 1964, the Sykes were able to move; interior work on their new residence, however, took another year to complete.

The Sykes' new home on Brown Drive in Southwest Oswego.

At first glance, the newest home on Brown Drive wouldn't appear to the neighborhood as one that would play host to unusual weather observation activities. Fred remembers his family's house starting out like any other, including "a room on the side of the house that faced northwest," Fred describes. "This was my father's study, where he could develop his weather interests." But those interests wouldn't stay contained inside for long. Soon, they ventured outdoors.

"Gradually," Fred continues, "my father began to acquire weather-study equipment and his station evolved over time. He'd eventually have a thermograph for monitoring temperature, a hygrometer for measuring relative humidity, an anemometer to monitor wind speed and direction, and a barometer and barographs to measure and record the rise and fall of air pressure. He also built a tower attached to our house that had wind speed and direction instruments. A detached tower, higher and further away from the house, was added later."

The equipment was procured by Bob from his years in the Army Air Corps, purchased as surplus or outdated equipment from the United States Weather Bureau, or on loan from Oswego State. Bob's students, who today have access to state-of-the-art meteorology equipment, remember how primitive the Brown Drive tower and equipment were. Jim LaDue: "I'm not sure if it would have passed the FAA for an airport site, but he could get minimum and maximum mercury temperatures on an old-fashioned machine. Once you'd taken the temp, you would have to yank it to get the indicator back down. He supplemented that with a digital anemometer and a wind vane. He used the old digital red numbers with a big broad display that looked like an old Texas Instrument calculator."

"The tower measured about 75 feet," says Doug Stewart, one of Bob's students brave enough to scale it for repair work. "I climbed it maybe 10 or so times over the years, because Bob had a schedule for when he wanted to do the calibrations. It was anchored on a concrete pad with three triangular cross supports and guide wires coming off each side. A hinged part of the tower was about 25 feet up and there would be a boom coming off it maybe three or four feet long, with the anemometer wind vane on it and electrical wire going out to it.

"In winter, I'd be climbing halfway up, with my hands freezing, trying to calibrate his instruments. The tower had a boat trailer hitch on its lower part, and its upper part had an arm on a pivot so he could lower it. In high winds, that would be tricky to do. I might have had some sort of rope around me, not a harness really, but something for 'safety,' and I'd lean out to the instrumentation. I'd be communicating with Bob, who was in his office, by walkie-talkie. As I held the vane a certain way, he'd calibrate the instrument."

Bob's weather tower: quite a sight in his Southwest Oswego neighborhood.

College students weren't the only ones leaving solid ground to make adjustments to the weather station's equipment. Brown Drive residents like Ken Peterson watched and wondered what was going on at the new house in the neighborhood when he saw not only a complex antenna system on the Sykes' roof, but also Bob himself standing atop his house, fine-tuning the antenna. George and Cheryl Knopp, also Brown Drive residents, were privy to Bob's high altitude antics. "We used to look out our picture window and see something moving up on the roof of his house," George recalls.

"It would be him, looking out over the lake." As odd as that may have seemed, George also admitted the advantages of having such a keen weather observer next door: "Before I'd leave to go hunting up north, I'd always ask him what his weather forecast was going to be."

Not everyone in the neighborhood was willing to accept Bob's weather exploits as just part of his perplexing personality. An April 14, 1971 letter to Bob from Oswego lawyer Leyden E. Brown spelled out the displeasure growing among some Brown Drive homeowners:

"Some of the residents in the area of your property are quite upset. They point out that you have erected structures on the property where you now reside and upon the adjoining lot...We point out that in your deed there were a few restricted covenants that are for the benefit of you, as well as the other residents. We particularly call to your attention the covenant that the premises shall be used for residential purposes only...We write you in an effort to avoid future trouble and possible litigation compelling you to remove the structures. From the talk I am getting, I am quite certain that if you do not remove this structure, and continue to place other structures on your land, the other residents will do something legal about it."

The Sykes children recall hearing some the details of this neighborhood dissent. "The problem with the neighbors was that Dad was trying to put a radar weather tower on the vacant lot next to our house," Fred recalls, "and the concern was that such a tower might be dangerous and affect TV reception. As I remember my father's plans, he wanted to put the tower somewhere else, but my mother wanted it on the lot next door so my father would have easy access to the information and not have to drive off somewhere to get it. I don't know whether or not my parents talked to any of the neighbors about their plans. They should have."

"I think the idea was that people didn't want the neighborhood used for business purposes," Bruce inferred. "I can understand why they might be concerned. He had these big towers and guide wires everywhere, and this was not a typical look for the neighborhood. But what should have happened was that someone should have come over and told him their concerns. Instead, these people who were his friends sent this letter out of the blue."

Barbara remembers her mother being upset: "What bothered Mom most was that all these people came and swam in our pool. Dad did *not* make any changes."

Even if the outside of the Sykes' house hadn't taken on the look of a makeshift weather station, a peek inside would have offered numerous telltale signs of an impassioned and somewhat quirky weatherman. All of Bob's children have vivid memories of what their family home often looked like with their father's work-related accouterments. Barbara says that it started out pretty tame, with "Dad keeping all his materials in his home office. Well, at least that was the idea. Soon, though, his paperwork ended up on the dining room table."

"A good way to describe my father," Fred adds, "would be with the word 'sprawl.' He had the study and his observation area, but he also had the dining room table, good parts of the living room and major portions of the cellar. He had things pretty much wherever he wanted, which always irritated my mother and us. If we had company, he'd have to clean it all up."

"He saved them all," Bruce says, referring to his father's meteorological journals. "When he passed away, I went back to the house probably 15 or 20 times over the next two years to clean it out and save what I wanted to save. I probably threw away 25 or 30 years of weather magazines. Along with those, I also found tons of weather instruments." Fred: "He had a shop in part of the basement

216

where he could repair [those] instruments. Some of the students from the college worked with him on that."

"He had an interface to a computer where he could digitally store his weather data. But it always seemed to break down," Jim LaDue recalls. "Bob wasn't really a computer guy, so he would need help. Then there would be his ledgers and his raw observations; there were notebooks full of them and they would pile up day after day." The first time Greg Stumpf walked into Bob's house, he recalled having to "wade through" those piles of magazines and data reports in the living room.

Chrystal Cardinali was another person outside the Sykes family who had first-hand experience with Bob's weather paraphernalia's dominance over their home. When a snowstorm prevented her father from picking Chrystal up at the college, Bob extended an offer to stay overnight at his home, a short and more manageable drive from campus.

"We got in Bob's clunky old Land Rover and I was frozen by the time I got to his home," Chrystal remembers. "When you rode with him in the Rover, you never put on the heat. That would melt the flakes and he wouldn't be able to get a good observation. I was so cold by the time we got to his home, and he said, 'I've got just what you need. I don't give this to very many people.'

"He took out a bottle of scotch and poured out about three fingers worth. 'Drink this,' he said. Well, I took one sip of it and said, 'That's awful!' Marie never said a word; she just came over, picked up the glass, and dumped it down the drain.

"They made up a bed for me in his study, which had a number of recording instruments called Rustraks. These were on a mechanical roll that collected information about wind direction and speed. Those Rustraks made a noise because a stylus marked the paper roll and the pen sounded like a ticking clock in rapid motion. There were about half a dozen of these in the room, and with all of them running, I got no sleep."

An innovative weather station ably tracking Ontario's lake-effect snowstorms? A thorough, but unorganized library of meteorological theories and dissertations? A disruption to the quiet ambiance of a rural neighborhood? Which was it?

A description of what would be seen when arriving at the Sykes home varied from person to person, but the amazing Oswego weather that Bob Sykes was experimenting with and analyzing year after year eventually garnered attention from a group of like-minded people from around the country and beyond. Though most of those weather enthusiasts never had an occasion to visit Bob and see him in action on his home turf, they had admired his work long enough to accept an invitation to visit his snowy city in the Northeast – and in the winter, no less! And while many of these learned men and women had witnessed some amazing weather events in their life, their trip to Oswego turned out to be an experience none of them would ever forget.

Chapter 18

100 Meteorologists Snowed In!

L ike his home, which could often appear to be bursting at the seams, Bob's busy lifestyle also seemed to be overscheduled. When considering the entirety of his accomplishments: teaching and mentoring students, overseeing innovative research projects, daily radio forecasts and parenting four children with Marie, it's hard to imagine him fitting one more experience into his day. But because Bob could never resist communing with others who were as passionate about the weather as he was, opportunities to do so were always on his radar.

For instance, there was the Eastern Snow Conference, an annual event Sykes always happily anticipated, knowing that researchers would be sharing current theories on all sorts of topics related to cold-weather climates. By 1971, after several years attending the conference, Bob presented its planning committee with an idea that would add yet another nuance to his winter-storm notoriety.

Since the location of the conference alternated yearly between the United States and Canada, Bob began thinking that

Oswego, with its history of noteworthy winter storms, would make an ideal destination for snow enthusiasts. After persistently petitioning ESC coordinators to select his city as a conference site, they finally agreed, and plans were approved for the February 1972 Conference to gather in Bob's hometown. Excitement for the event built when ESC Secretary Gordon Ayer added a note to the registration packet for the event: "This will be a good conference on the banks of Lake Ontario, where they really have snow!"

Indeed, the '72 conference *would* become a memorable one for many of the long-time ESC members, but not because of the on-the-mark topics presented or even the plush accommodations at the city's newest hotel and conference center, The Holiday Inn. Instead, it was Oswego's weather, looking to stir up a little more history, which would take center stage in the memories of those that attended. On Wednesday, February 2 and Thursday the 3rd, attendees began arriving at the Holiday Inn from all over the northeastern United States and Canada; others came from countries as far away as the Soviet Union. Whether they traveled by car or airplane, the relatively mild winter weather made the journey into Oswego as welcoming as could be.

The registration table at the 1972 Eastern Snow Conference. Proud host Bob Sykes is on the right.

There was a happy chatter throughout the hotel as people settled into their rooms. Situated in the heart of Oswego, the guests' accommodations had a breathtaking view of the Oswego River meandering through the city and emptying into the Great Lake. Out-of-towners didn't think much about the clouds forming over the lake, or even the first snowflakes adding a sparkle to their vista. But by Friday afternoon, just before the conference's main event, heavy snow began falling. The few jokes about the blustery weather quickly turned sour as the snow intensified into the evening. Soon, conditions became blizzard-like, and those who'd only ever heard Bob talk about what it was like to be in the middle of a lake-effect storm, suddenly found themselves knee-deep in one.

Whenever weather-related programs took place on or near SUNY Oswego, Bob invited his meteorology students to attend. Several took advantage in 1972, feeling fortunate to be invited to a program as prestigious as the Eastern Snow Conference. Tom Moore still has vivid memories about the severity of the storm he had to walk through to get to campus after attending part of the conference:

"Some of the snowdrifts were over your head. It was a couple of miles to walk and the visibility was less than 20 feet. As my friends and I were walking, the people up ahead would just disappear."

A few hours break in the snow and a hint of the sun later Friday prompted several of the wiser attendees to leave when they could. (About a third did.) By the next morning, the day scheduled as the conference's official end, a severe drop in the temperature added a deep freeze to the participants' worries. They had good reason to be concerned: nobody was going anywhere. When lake-effect activity picked up again, this time it meant business. Those who had decided to remain until the conference's official end would

221

not be able to leave the Port City and its wintry grip until February 6, adding two full days to what was turning out to be a very uncomfortable visit. But without a doubt, Bob Sykes was in his glory.

He wasn't about to let a little bit of snow – well, maybe, a lot of snow – get in the way of his hosting a successful conference. In fact, Bob decided to use it to his advantage. Noting the particulars of this specific lake-effect event, he offered the opportunity for meteorologists and weather enthusiasts unfamiliar with such phenomenon an opportunity to immerse themselves in it. Though city streets remained unplowed and Bob's forecast would have cautioned people to stay inside, the exuberant conference host led a cautious group of meteorologists out into the storm.

Bob's neighbor, Ken Peterson, also happened to be out in the weather, providing assistance like many in Oswego had learned to do during The Blizzard of '66. Ken was using his snowmobile to make deliveries of essentials like prescription drugs to those in need. Though the bridge over the Oswego River was closed to vehicular traffic, Ken was able to easily make several runs across it, and on one trip, he noticed a gathering of about 40 people at the middle of the bridge. "They were facing northwest, looking out over Lake Ontario. And there in the center of the crowd was Bob Sykes. He was leading a lecture and discussion on lake-effect snow as it was occurring right on top of them."

The irony of a snowed-in snow conference was not lost on media outlets across the nation. WEATHERMEN MEET IN STORM!, heralded *The Rochester Times-Union's* February 4 edition. Terry Dillman, the reporter covering the ESC event for *The Times-Union,* called his editor to inform him that he was "stuck in the snow capital of New York State."

Oswego's daily paper, *The Palladium-Times*, bragged: OSWEGO STRUGGLES OUT FROM UNDER SNOWFALL OF 56 INCHES COMING DURING 50 HOUR STORM." The paper covered the conference's unfortunate timing and unfolding saga over the next several days.* But ESC's and Oswego's biggest claim to fame came on Friday, February 4, when the conference drew national and international media coverage from Walter Cronkite, who interrupted his normal *CBS Evening News* broadcast to announce the story of the snow-trapped weathermen.

Months after the conference, once attendees had a chance to warm up back home, the decision was made to give Bob an award called "The Sno-Foo" in honor of his work during the event.+

* *The Palladium-Times* did, however, miss one day of reporting when the storm's intensity prevented the paper from going to press. It was only the third time in the paper's more than 100-year history that they were unable to publish their daily; the other two were a result of The Blizzard of '66.

+Sykes would receive an unprecedented second Sno-Foo after the 1988 Eastern Snow Conference, where he gave a presentation commemorating the 100th anniversary of The New York City Blizzard.

Bob's Sno-Foo generated a lot of good humor amongst the conference attendees, but the ESC planning committee had learned its lesson. Beginning in 1973, the conference would only be held in spring or summer months. And it would take twenty years for the group to make a return trip to Oswego.

By the early '90s, Bob's contributions to the Eastern Snow Conference - groundbreaking, informative *and* sometimes challenging - would earn him permanent membership in the association. He was only the third person in ESC's history to be so honored.

The 1972 conference debacle would earn a place on Bob's "Happiest Moments" list. Adding a note to this entry, he recalled a special "forecast" he gave to ESC's executive director in June of 1971 - a full seven months before the first guests arrived for their snowy stay in Oswego. "Your people will be able to get in," Sykes predicted, "but they will not be able to get out!"

Chapter 19

A Weatherman to the End

Long after his career as a teacher and daily forecaster had ended, Bob Sykes' enjoyment in presenting weather-related programs for audiences continued. He became a frequent guest speaker, especially at commemorative anniversaries of significant snow events, where this well-schooled weatherman could share his eyewitness interpretations of those powerful storms. He took particular pleasure in his involvement with the 1988 New York City/Long Island Chapter of the American Meteorological Society's 100th anniversary of that area's infamous Blizzard of 1888. Bob was asked to present a paper at the conference, which he aptly titled "The Also-Legend Late January 1966 Blizzard Over Central New York – Maturity, Too."*

---

*Bob's sense of humor often found its way into presentation titles and scholarly essays. When the Central North Carolina Chapter of the AMS invited Bob as a guest speaker at their February 1997 conference, he titled his program "Let It Snow, Let It Snow, Let It Lake-Effect Snow."

The New York City conference was sponsored by a number of Meteorological Societies and Academies of Science from around the northeastern United States. Mark Kramer was the chairman of AMS's NYC/LI Chapter, and when the time came to plan the anniversary event, he remembered Bob from their work together for Niagara Mohawk in the late 1970s. Mark's admiration for Bob's work and the acclaim he received from the '66 blizzard made Sykes a good choice for this special anniversary event.

Along with several presentations about the impact of the 1888 storm on New York City*, there were programs on recent advances in lake-effect snow science and forecasting. But other than a recap of the 1888 storm, Bob's '66 program would be the only historically-based presentation. Mark well remembers Bob, who was in his 70s when the event was held, and his excitement with being at the conference. "He knew some of the presenters and those in attendance," Mark says. "Many were very influential people deeply involved with meteorology, and Bob was in seventh heaven with all those snow fanatics."

Conferences also gave Bob the opportunity to reunite with former students, often reestablishing opportunities for them to work together. In 1995, one of those students, Tom Moore, attended the annual Great Lakes Conference.+ Tom hadn't seen Bob since his early 1970s' college days. Since then, Tom had become a coordinating meteorologist for *The Weather Channel* and it was at

------

*The storm paralyzed the largely-unprepared Northeastern shoreline for days, dumping several feet of snow brought inland on blizzard winds. Over 400 people would perish in the storm, 200 in New York City alone.

+Formerly known as The Great Lakes Weather Workshop, the conference rotated to a different major city around the Great Lakes in Michigan, Ohio and New York State, and drew people from weather reporting venues, college campuses and research centers.

the conference that Bob learned of his former student's rise to such an important position.

"After the conference," Tom explains, "he would call with observations of Oswego snow events and suggest that forecasters could broadcast them on the air. I always made a big deal out of it, saying things like: 'Professor Sykes from SUNY Oswego has called in with this report on lake-effect snow that we are seeing on the radar.' I think Bob liked that his observations could go beyond what he was doing on WSGO."

Bob Maxon, the Oswego-born meteorologist whose parents were friends with the Sykes, had the opportunity to see his mentor at his best during a March 1998 conference in Vermont. Maxon hadn't read Bob's name on the agenda and was surprised to see his childhood hero when he entered the banquet room. Despite the fact that less than a year after this reunion Sykes would pass away, Maxon found him to be as precise as ever. "At these conferences there are hundreds of people," Maxon points out. "When I got within a few feet of where Bob was sitting, he said, 'You've got to be Grace Maxon's son.' There were no nametags, but he looked at me and he knew."

Maxon made sure to attend Bob's presentation, and along with the other younger generation of meteorologists in attendance, he got to experience a Bob Sykes' slideshow. ("He wasn't going to use anything like PowerPoint," Maxon decisively points out.) The program featured details such as his every-five-minute handwritten observations from one of Oswego's big storms and Maxon explains the audience's reaction to Bob's work:

"On ledgers of weather observations, if you see a plus sign after the letter S, which stands for snow, that indicates that you are really starting to get a lot of accumulation. Well, there were these gasps and maybe some sarcastic giggles in the room because, on Bob's sheets, he had as many as six or seven plus signs after some S's.

"There were whispers in the audience, like 'Crazy old man,

what is he doing?' Then Bob said, 'During these times, I couldn't see my birdfeeder, which was about six or eight feet from the house.' And there was dead silence in the room because his visibility calculations were so low – lower than anybody in that room had probably ever experienced. Many in the audience were people from outside of the Northeast and they just didn't understand what it was like to observe intense lake-effect. It was such a cool experience to go from [speakers who did more traditional] weather forecasting to the polar opposite. He was like a cowboy in the weather world: calm, cool and collected – just stating how he had done it."

Sykes didn't just shine at conferences. Wherever Bob met someone willing to talk about the weather and listen to his stories, he found a friend. Greg Mills was the branch manager of Columbia Bank in Oswego, where Bob managed his finances. Mills was used to people coming into the bank ready to talk about options for their financial resources, but that wasn't the case when he met Sykes.

"He loved sharing about what he had done and some of the amazing things he had experienced with the weather," Greg says. "I was new to the community and wanted to learn about the people and Oswego, and Bob was always willing to talk about the weather I could expect here. At first I thought he was making things up, but I soon learned he wasn't."

Elementary-aged children were among his favorite audiences. A photograph in Oswego's *Palladium-Times* shows Bob teaching a class of Hannibal, New York's fifth grade students, the caption below stating that he'd been invited to compliment the teachers' science unit on weather. Another showed him at Oswego's Fitzhugh Park School fifth grade enrichment class; he was also a frequent visitor of Oswego teacher Sharon Komanecky's fourth graders. After visiting so many classrooms, Bob decided that his ideal target audience was sixth graders, who were "aggressive and without planning, and eager to learn."

Children would write to him after his visits and Bob saved their letters along with his career paperwork. One student asked: "How do you know when it is going to snow?" Without any record of whether or not Sykes wrote back to the child, one can only imagine how this weatherman would have crafted his answer.

Chapter 20

No One Knew

What makes his accomplishments all the more remarkable are the challenges that Bob and his family faced throughout his more than two decades of teaching and forecasting the weather. These challenges did not surface immediately, though. In fact, upon moving to Oswego, home life for the Sykes began with a relative normalcy, something Bob and Marie had not yet experienced in their marriage.

During his many absences while in the military, Bob maintained a frequent and richly-warm correspondence with Marie – scores of their letters and cards were saved in scrapbooks – and that was finally able to mature into a more traditional married life in Oswego. The couple learned, as son Fred relates, how to best function as a two-parent household:

"This was before the time of internet and radar and my mother accepted the fact that Dad was a weatherman who needed to go out to sites to observe and gather information. She had more organization, more sense with money than my father, and as a Home Economics teacher, she was concerned about our family home."

Another concern for both parents was their children's assimilation into the Oswego schools and social life. It wasn't an easy transition, as Barbara remembers: "When we moved to Oswego in '61, we had just come back from three years in Germany, so none of us Sykes children were typical. We had been in an Army base school in Germany and most of the children in Oswego schools had never been farther away from their homes than Syracuse, many had never been out of Oswego County, and many did not even know where Germany was."

Things eventually improved. Before long, the children's teachers knew of their unique life and their father's affinity for the weather, and their schoolwork reflected it. In a classroom project written and illustrated by eight-year-old Cindy, she wrote: "There are no two snowflakes alike. Tiny bits of sand, ashes and dust always float in the air. Air is trapped in each snowflake. Snowflakes have many designs. A snow blanket keeps fields warm. Snow has fallen on all 50 states at some time. The snow packs hard. Sometimes the snow brings trouble. It must be cleared from city streets. Sometimes snow brings help."

The youngest Sykes child had clearly been paying attention to her father's work.

As the Sykes children grew into their independence, Marie was also able to once again pursue her career. She was thrilled to return to college for her master's degree at Cornell, noted as the finest school for her subject area. She resumed her teaching career, first in Pulaski, New York and then at the Oswego High School, quickly becoming known as a dedicated teacher who poured much creative energy into the work she did with her students. Some of them, as her colleague Charles Young remembers, "were not always the most academically talented. But Marie would reach out to them and attend to their needs. She made them think positively about themselves, which many young people lack."

Barbara remembers the dedication her mother brought to the job of a Home Economics teacher, watching her spend hours on extracurricular activities, such as sewing uniforms for the Oswego High School cheerleaders. She also heard Marie's candid opinion that others in her chosen profession did not always live up to their responsibilities. "When I first took Home Ec., my teacher was showing us how to sew a circle skirt, which really doesn't have any shaping to it; it's just four pieces of material and a waistband. Mom taught sewing, and she'd taught me to sew. She said, 'This isn't teaching you anything.' She was very upset that students weren't doing something that would give them any real skill."

The Oswego High School faculty often participated in social occasions, and over time, the Sykes and Charles Young and his wife, Ruth, became friends. Ruth taught Latin and Spanish at the high school and one of the highlights of the year for Latin class was the Roman banquet. "We would all get decked out in our togas and olive leaves," Charles remembers. "Since Marie was a fixture at the banquet, Bob also attended, and his big moment during the event was to give the weather forecast for the gathering. Each year, it was the same forecast: 'Hail, Caesar!' "

As the four Sykes children matured and began excelling in school and extracurricular activities, the Brown Drive homestead was an energized environment. All four graduated high school and selected colleges to explore their interests, with each completing their post-high school educations except Cindy. The youngest Sykes child, who had developed health problems early in her life, ended up with many of her goals cruelly challenged. Trouble began when she reached her teen years.

In October 1967, after Cindy began experiencing what appeared to be lingering symptoms of a common cold, Bob and

Marie decided it best to take her for a checkup. Not overly concerned, the doctor released her to return home, but the next morning, Bob found Cindy in a coma. After she remained in that unconscious state for four days at the Oswego Hospital and after thorough tests, her doctors diagnosed her sudden illness as juvenile diabetes. 13-year-old Cindy was told that she would be dependent on insulin shots for the rest of her life.

It was an adjustment for the family, but the Sykes carried on, still maintaining a semblance of routine in their home life. But in the early 1970s, Marie began to experience some health concerns of her own. It started with her feeling tired a good deal of the time, beyond what an active, middle-aged woman should be experiencing. After seeking medical advice, tests revealed that her fluctuating energy levels were a result of pleurisy and emphysema. When the doctor recommended adjustments to her life, at the top of his list was a strong directive: quit smoking.

A habit acquired in her young adulthood, smoking had been a point of disagreement for Marie and Bob for years. He'd voiced his disapproval of it from their relationship's beginning, and his strong opinion resulting from a bad experience he'd had with tobacco while in college.

"I was selected to be the lead actor in my church play, *Fiat Lux*," Bob reflected. "The role required me to smoke a cigar and then faint from doing so. Having never smoked before, I relied on a friend who was home on leave from the service to teach me." It was an unpleasant experience for Bob, but he endured it to fulfill his obligation. Beyond that, his only other encounters with smoking were a result of a few occasions while in the service, especially in Greenland. But this was only to bond with his fellow servicemen in their isolated conditions, and he concluded that "I never took to it much."

When their relationship became serious, Bob more strongly shared his opinion of cigarettes with his future wife: "We went on kind of a date down to Jones Beach on Long Island in July of '41.

234

We were in the car, talking about smoking and I remember saying that each cigarette was a 'nail in the coffin.' Of course," Bob later lamented in his autobiographical notes, "it turned out to be kind of prophetic."

Marie did give up smoking after doctors discovered her health problems, but, by that point, her lungs were scarred and damaged. After a summer 1975 train trip across Canada with Bob, Marie resumed teaching, but she only grew more and more exhausted. On a return visit to her doctor, evidence of liver cancer was detected. Chemotherapy treatments at the Roswell Park Cancer Institute in Buffalo caused internal bleeding and they were discontinued. Shortly after the 1975 holiday season, Marie and Bob shared the news of her declining health with their children.

After formally resigning from teaching, faculty and students were stunned that Marie would be permanently absent from the day-to-day life at the high school. She tried her best to rest at home and enjoy time with family, but she continued to weaken. The long winter in Oswego seemed to cast a darkness over the Sykes home. When an unusually warm Bermuda High brought some relief to the region, spirits brightened. But this was short-lived. On February 26, 1976, Marie Sykes succumbed to cancer. She was 56 years old.

Through their 31-year marriage, nearly half of it spent separated by thousands of miles, Bob had often been denied his wife's companionship. Distraught with the sudden reality of their cruelly-shortened relationship, he first focused on what he saw as his inadequacies in their partnership. In the introspective writings made near the end of his life, Sykes confided: "I was most fortunate in my marriage to Marie. She was more pragmatic with respect to life's regular problems and had some personal capabilities, too, including a cool head and patience. I cannot let these notes go without expressing my deepest thanks to Marie for her understanding of my foibles, idiosyncrasies, and characteristics. She overlooked the negatives and accepted the positives."

Among Bob's career and personal papers was the poem, "Should You Go First," by A.K. Roswell, which began:
"Should you go first, and I remain
To walk the road alone,
I'll live in memory's garden dear
With happy days we've known..."

A memorial service was held on March 3 at The Church of Resurrection in Oswego. Several people in attendance talked of Marie's strength as she dealt with her illness, and her family mentioned this remembrance by Marie's Aunt Maria Mayjes: "It isn't life that matters – it is the courage you bring to it. While passing our way, we thank Marie for her courage, and always, her love." Bob and his children chose appropriate readings, poems and music to celebrate Marie, including Beethoven's Ninth Symphony, which featured these words from Schiller's "Ode to Joy":

"Joy is drawn by every creature
From the breast of Nature;
All men good and all men evil
Walk upon her rose-strewn path."

Though not a highly ceremonial person, after much consideration, Bob found an unassuming, but poignant expression of his love for Marie. In September 1977, he sent out invitations to family and friends, asking them to join him in a dedication for what he called "Marie's Pool Area." In their Brown Drive patio, Bob designed a series of beautiful paving stones and colorful marble into a pathway to honor his wife. Plants and shrubbery lined the path, also selected for their remembrance of Marie. In his invitation, Bob noted the symbolism of the project which he labored on alone, dedicating its meaning to his wife.

Others would seek to honor Marie and her work. Fellow teachers, students and parents of the Oswego High School created an annual commemorative award for a young person who aspired to Maries' goals and ideals in Home Economics. By June 1981, the school district's scholarship committee had selected the first winner of the Marie Lips Sykes Memorial Scholarship.

Attempting to carry on, Bob vehemently returned to his work both at the college and at home. On Brown Drive he had an addition built to his home, including a spiral staircase which led to the second floor observation area. When student Les Austin visited Bob shortly after it was built, he thought it resembled "a turret, with a room that was glassed in so you could look out in any direction. Because it was above the other houses, you could see quite a distance."

But enhancements to his work weren't enough to carry Bob through his grief. Within months of Marie's death, Sykes had requested a much-needed sabbatical from his teaching and committee responsibilities. He envisioned a trip that would take him to several countries, including a stop in New Zealand, where he could observe an October 1976 total solar eclipse. Perhaps viewing the spectacle could help him regain perspective and focus for what lay ahead. When the request was denied, his department head suggested he find faculty to cover his classes and carry out his travel plans. Fortunately, Bob did so, because soon after his return to teaching and other work commitments, Sykes was faced with another medical dilemma: Cindy's illness had worsened.

Upon Marie's death, Bob learned to shoulder the concerns for Cindy's ongoing compromised health as a single parent. His worry for her well-being, though, extended beyond her physical afflictions. Perhaps it was an ill-fated outcome of her poor health, but early in her adulthood, Cindy began making decisions that were not always in her best interests, including the way she formed and maintained relationships. In 1976, at 22 years old, she married. The union lasted only a matter of weeks.

To help his youngest child establish her independence, Bob offered to help Cindy financially. Since she had worked in food service for many years, father and daughter agreed that restaurant management could offer her a fulfilling career. The two formed a partnership in the late 1970s, and to raise capital for a restaurant's purchase, Bob remortgaged his Brown Drive home. Cindy worked diligently to create and test recipes, eventually developing a breakfast and lunch menu, and in March 1978, Lake Effects Restaurant opened.

Located on Bridge Street, Oswego's main thoroughfare, the establishment began to develop a loyal clientele. Father and daughter were pleased with the business' promising start, and Bob was also happy with one particular patron who began frequenting Lake Effects.

Gerda Haggerty was a student in one of Bob's classes. German-born and married when she came to the United States, Gerda had raised three children and divorced by the time she returned to college and took her first class from Bob. After seeing each other off and on at the Sykes' new restaurant, a friendship developed and grew romantic. Soon, the two were traveling together, sometimes in connection with Bob's work and sometimes just to experience other cultures together.

Gerda Haggerty

On June 26, 1982, their marriage was blessed at The Church of Resurrection. An original piece of music was composed by the church's organist to accompany a passage from the Bible. Called "Hymn of a Grateful Heart," it was dedicated by Bob in his marriage to Gerda. Even the drizzle of rain falling from overcast skies could not dampen the joy that had once again brightened Bob's life.

The following year, 66-year-old Bob retired from SUNY Oswego, looking forward to spending more time "in the company of a lovely woman," one he described as "extremely thoughtful, very understanding; a thoroughly wonderful person." He felt blessed to have a second opportunity to share love in a marriage, even making a point of noting the unique qualities that each of his wives had. Noting that Marie's background in home economics and finances meant she could handle "any reasonable related problem," Sykes described Gerda, on the other hand, as "treating such matters very lightly; she was deeply interested in the arts."

Bob's children were happy he had found love and companionship again. They saw Gerda, as son Fred would say, as someone who "understood my father and some of his foibles. She was very good for him." In fact, Gerda was not afraid to take on the continuing battle with Bob's tendencies toward clutter and crowding in his home. She worked with him, as Marie had also tried, to create some semblance of household order. Student Greg Stumpf noticed that, when visiting Bob at home after his marriage to Gerda, she was trying to get him to better manage his accumulated paperwork and related materials. "Eventually, all his data was moved out of the living room," Greg recalls. "He moved a lot of it down to the basement and he also had some of it in the tower."

Along with his newfound joy, it appeared that Bob was also finding some order in his life, and the trials of his last five years seemed less burdensome to him. But shortly after he and his new bride had settled into married life, those all-too-familiar worries resurfaced. It started when Gerda began experiencing trouble walking. When the spells got worse and she began stumbling, Bob found himself once again in a doctor's office, searching for answers. What he learned was not what he hoped. Tests revealed a large, inoperable brain tumor that doctors estimated had been growing in Gerda for 20 years.

Preferring to first try non-traditional healing methods to reduce and stop the tumor's growth, Gerda may have lost what little time she had to treat it. When she finally agreed to an operation, her condition had deteriorated and she fell into a coma, passing away a few days later. After three years of marriage, Bob Sykes was again alone. In the span of a decade, he had twice become a widower.

One the day of her death, June 10, 1985, a rare tornado watch had been posted for the Oswego area, and its swirling winds managed to carry away an early summer heatwave. Wispy cirrus clouds floated above the city. There was a sense of letting go what could not be controlled.

After his second loss, it would have been understandable if Bob had retreated into a life of quiet reflection. But this was not to be. When Cindy's physical condition began preventing her from successfully managing Lake Effect Restaurant, Bob tried to intervene. But his daughter was also still struggling with her relationships – both in friendships and those romantically-inclined – which contributed to her development of weight control issues. This put even more stress on her already weak body, eventually causing her kidneys to function poorly. Her health worsened to such a point that doctors named her as an eligible candidate for a kidney transplant. While on the wait list, too weak to take care of herself, Cindy lived at times with Bob, and at other times with her sister, Barbara.

Lake Effects Restaurant closed in 1980. Cindy, still weak, but desiring to move on, went to live with a friend in Elbridge, New York, and she attempted to open a second restaurant, Porky's Place. It operated from 1985 until 1987, only meeting with minimal success. But with her health rapidly deteriorating, Cindy and her father had bigger concerns. A transplant was performed successfully, but the kidney proved an unsuitable match, causing much suffering in her attempt to adjust to it. Searching, she went through a series of doctors, each who prescribed different medicines, causing her more physical and emotional stress. Eventually, Cindy slipped into a coma.

In time, her doctors determined that she was "in a persistent vegetative state," but it would take weeks before Bob could agree to take her off life support. On March 20, 1989, her 35th birthday, Cindy was released from her struggles to live.

Bob had now lost a third important woman in his life. Each passing brought its own distinct hurt, and with Cindy's, it meant the death of someone Bob thought he might be able to depend on in his final years. After losing two spouses and with his other children busy with their own families, Bob and Cindy had learned to rely on each other. Now that, too, was lost, and those who knew him best saw how terribly this aged him. Some, in fact, maintained that Bob Sykes was never the same.

A month after Cindy's passing, Bob retired from WSGO radio. For 23 years, he had faithfully and enthusiastically offered his listeners a daily forecast and he was ready to give it up, though he would never forego his continual weather observations. He adopted a puppy. He got to know his grandchildren: Barbara's boys, Christopher and Andrew Wall; Bruce's children, Rachel, Sarah, Robbie and Kathleen; and Fred's girls, Beth, Katy and Bekah.

Over time, he learned to become a more attentive grandfather. "When his grandchildren were babies," Fred reflects, "he didn't have a lot of interest in them. But over the years, he began to really enjoy them and their time together. He grew and matured toward his grandchildren."

Three generations of Robert Sykes: grandfather Robert B., son Robert Bruce and grandson Robby. (Photo courtesy of Busath Photography)

And they have cherished memories of their grandfather, with stories that add an interesting perspective to Bob's unique personality. Sarah Sorensen certainly saw her grandfather's tendency to collect things: "Grandpa had a lot of stuff in his house," Sarah tells, "and people accused him of being a hoarder. But I don't remember it being like that." In particular, Sarah remembers one item not normally associated with a weatherman or a grandfather:

"When I was about nine, I saw this coffee table book at his house about the 25th anniversary of the TV soap opera, *Days of Our Lives,* and I thought, *What?* A friend and I had watched the show one summer and he would talk to us about it: the different characters and their personalities. He had watched it, perhaps, just to have something to talk with us about."

Sarah also noticed how he said "the funniest things to people. One 4th of July," she remembers, "we were at a parade and Grandpa walked through the crowds telling people, 'Happy Holidays.' And he'd tell telemarketers when their conversation was ending: 'Rest in peace' or, if he was angry, 'Rest in agony.' "

Beth Sykes Collins admired how her grandpa maintained connection with the people he met when traveling. Beth grew up in Canton, New York and remembers a woman who owned a little gallery downtown. When Bob visited Beth's family, he always made a trip down to see this woman. "He would usually buy something," Beth explains, "and always had a long chat. Later in his life when he was not able to walk, he would send me or my sister down to the store to buy some notecards from her. It was not about the notecards, but about his connection to this storeowner."

Now alone in his life, Bob worked to maintain his connections with students and faculty after retiring from SUNY Oswego, such as his science department colleague, Ray Schneider. One time, out of the blue, Ray got a call from Bob. " 'Ray,' he said," Schneider recalls, 'I want you to come over and I'll cook you dinner.' It was just he and I, and he cooked a number of his special foods. At that point, his second wife had died and he got very depressed there for a while. We had a nice elaborate dinner and had just chit chat about the years passed."

Bob continued his association with a group of retired male teachers from both SUNY Oswego and the city school district. Charles Young recalls his friend's involvement with the group and how Bob once hosted a lunch at his Brown Drive home after Marie and Gerda had passed. "Bob would announce that the lunch would begin at noon. If you arrived earlier than that, you had to wait outside until the noon hour when you were summoned. This was because Bob had hired a chef to create a very elaborate spread and he wanted to sneak the chef out the back door before people could come in for the meal."

Others can attest to similar peculiarities when he planned more formal dinner parties. Chrystal Cardinali describes what attending a Sykes party could be like: "He'd be hosting a dinner for maybe 40 people and he'd issue an invitation by calling and saying, 'I'm having a party and I expect you to come at the time I tell you.' So maybe it would be six o'clock, but for someone else it would be 6:30 or 7:00 p.m. And when you'd arrive at the party, he'd tell you when everybody else was due to arrive. Then he'd say, 'When it gets too crowded in here, then it's time for you to go home.' "

Later in Bob's life, Chrystal saw his behavior became more erratic: "With several parties, you would never see him. He'd get all of us together, and he might come to the door and let you in. He'd say, 'There's food and drink down in the family room' and then he'd disappear."

Occasions like his dinner parties cast an unflattering light on Bob's awkward social etiquette, and he would have been the first to admit that such occasions were never a strong suit of his. But now he was without a companion to help soften and balance his shortcomings, making this behavior seem all the more odd – and lonely. Though he maintained strong relationships with family and friends, Bob needed something to carry him through the stretches of time when he couldn't be with them. And he needed something to help him forget the aspects of life which he had been cruelly denied.

Reaching back to his childhood, Bob Sykes found what he was looking for, spending his remaining years engaged in the interests that had set in motion his extraordinary life.

Chapter 21

Not Just Hobbies, But Avocations

It's not that the interests that enthralled young Bob Sykes ever completely left him; his enchantment with astronomy, pursuit of the perfect eclipse, and meticulously organized stamp collection remained important to him. But it was difficult finding time to enjoy these activities while engaged in three busy careers and a full family life. After he'd retired, though, and his house echoed from the loss of beloved family members, time again became available, and along with reinvigorating his earliest interests, Bob discovered a few other new passions: the collection of and work with exotic wood, a deep appreciation for classical music, and an eye for a good photograph.

It was those avocations – hobbies seems too trivial a word for how Bob embraced them – that somehow helped him carry on following Cindy's death. He lived another ten years beyond her passing, and when he wasn't talking weather with a good friend or visiting his children and their families, he was engrossed in his projects. Some were logical outgrowths of his immersion in weather study, and others, such as woodworking and classical music, emerged from the wonder he found in his surroundings. All propelled him in his desire to appreciate and better understand the world and his intrigue with exotic wood, perhaps, was the most indicative of this.

An interest in unusual wood varieties began in 1966 for Bob, right in the middle of that infamous January blizzard. During the most intense part of the storm, a couple building a house on Brown Drive had been stranded there during the heavy snows and they ended up staying with Bob and Marie until the weather cleared. As a thank you, the Sykes were invited to see the interior of the house as it neared completion, and when Bob commented on the unique wood paneling, he learned that it was actually a facsimile of Brazilian rosewood. Noting its beauty even in an artificial reproduction, Bob made a note to search for the real thing.

The motive for exploring unusual wood grains began as part of the Sykes' home improvement plans. Their Brown Drive residence was only two years old and Bob had several projects he was considering to give it an attractive finish. He started imagining how this South American wood might complement the steps to the house's basement or the cabinetry on either side of the living room's fireplace. How might it enhance his plans for a new recreation room? Sykes was intrigued, but had no idea where to find such an rare commodity. The answer was much closer than he thought: his college campus.

Sykes knew that local lumberyards didn't stock much in the order of exotic wood, but he'd become friendly with SUNY Oswego Industrial Arts Professor William Boyd. While explaining this new interest to his colleague, Bob learned about a store in Syracuse with a name that seemed promising: Woods of the World. A visit to the business proved serendipitous, as its owner had just returned from Brazil with some of the rosewood Bob was in the market for. He eagerly obtained some excellent cuts and used them to begin his paneling and construction projects.

Like any of the deep callings he pursued, Bob's interest in wood quickly flourished. By 1968, he was adding an addition to the house, including a workshop, study and what he called "a memorial room for instrument, record and wood storage." All would feature an array of exotic wood purchased, as his favorite new store proclaimed, from around the world. Anxious to meet and learn from others with this interest, in the late '60s, Sykes joined The International Wood Collectors Society and remained a member for life. From those devoted woodworkers, Bob obtained samples of scores of interesting wood and learned about other venues for purchasing them throughout the northeastern United States.

Bob enjoying a day of woodworking.
(Photo courtesy of Greg Stumpf)

The Society members also encouraged Bob to attend a woodworkers' conference in California, where he had the opportunity to visit redwood and sequoia areas. Bob greatly admired the "jewel quality," as he called it, of redwood burl and purchased rough cuts of it to finish as tables and other furniture. Some he would give away as gifts, others became part of his home. Guests would admire his desk made of jenisaro; walls covered with Brazilian rosewood, special walnut and birdseye birch; the many shelves of tigerwood; and floors paneled in redwood, cherry and other grains.

But attending one conference wasn't enough. Oswego Industrial Arts Professor Ken Richards remembers that Bob was excited about a woodworking exhibit on their campus, where one vendor "had a board on display with unusual grains of wood," Ken says. "Bob saw it and asked to buy it. The guy didn't want to sell, but Bob kept at him until he finally did." Ray Schneider attended yet another conference with Bob and other faculty in Toronto. "As the program was finishing up," Ray says, "Bob just wandered off. He didn't say a word to the rest of us. Apparently what he was doing was negotiating to buy some rare wood from South America."

But Schneider recognized how important such purchases were to Bob. During one of the meals he and Sykes shared at the Brown Drive home, the passionate woodworker showed Ray one of his finished bowls in order to describe the process he undertook. Ray saw "the incredible amount of work he put into these pieces of wood." Others noticed, too, and soon members of The Wood Collectors Society were encouraging Bob to show some of his finish work.

As with his pursuit of the weather, Bob shared his love of fine wood with his students, including Dave Eichorn. The two men's lifelong friendship endured even when Dave took a weather job in Oklahoma City in the early 1980s. On a visit to his former student's new home, Bob was introduced by Dave to a wood supply store in town and it became a point of destination for the two men whenever Sykes stayed with the Eichorns. On one particular visit, the store was having a sale of East Indian rosewood and tulipwood and both men ended up overspending. "When Bob came out to visit and we would make a trip to the store," Dave comments, "my wife used to say, 'There goes another $100 or $150!' "

Despite the dozens of wood varieties he purchased and stored in his home, Bob never thought of himself as a wood *builder.* Instead, it was finishing the wood that he enjoyed. Those who were able to observe him absorbed in this work commented on the dozens of hours he spent on a single piece of wood; hundreds on larger cuts. Barbara remembers watching those long processes: "He would take a piece of wood, sand it down and polish it until it was like a mirror. This took umpteen sandings and polishings, but he worked them until he brought out the warmth of the wood. Once he was done, there were pieces of wood everywhere. They never were made into anything, though sometimes we would get them as Christmas gifts."

Barbara's brothers agree. "My father liked to show them," Fred mentions, "not in a boastful way; he just wanted people to see all these different types of wood." "I think Dad didn't want to finish these products because he didn't want to give them away or sell them," Bruce adds. "There was a woman who lived up the road from us on Brown Drive and she ran a craft shop. She tried to get Dad to build little boxes to sell, but he wouldn't do it."

Bill Wall remembers watching Bob polish wood "until they were like gems. For instance," Bill points out, "he worked with zebra wood, which had an unusual striped appearance to it. It looked interesting on its own, but when he polished it, it would have a different character. He would polish it until, at times, it looked like the grain was a foot deep."

When Tom Galletta ended up living in Oswego after he graduated from college, he had numerous opportunities to observe Bob's work with wood. After Galletta acquired a home on the Oswego River, he became an avid boater and he invited his former teacher for an occasional river ride. As a thank you, Bob sanded a wooden section of Tom's boat.

"He got it to a really high finish," Tom remembers, "and I told him, 'Bob, I can't fiberglass over this. It's too beautiful.' Another time, I had bought a motorcycle and was having trouble with dogs chasing me. Bob fashioned a club out of rosewood and polished it up. 'Take this and use it to fight off the dogs,' he told me. But, it was a fine piece of wood, with colors running through it. There was no way I was going to take this on a motorcycle; it was too beautiful."

Dave Eichorn has a theory of why both woodworking and meteorology were perfect for Bob's enthusiastic approach to life: "What he could do to bring the luster out of wood was just mindblowing. Looking at the grain of tropical exotic wood is almost like looking at the contours of a weather map and the correlation between the two hit me like a ton of bricks."

Sykes did manage to turn some of his woodworking into furniture or functional products and Chrystal Cardinali recalls a coffee table of Sykes that was completely angulated. "Perhaps it was some exotic tree root," she wagers, "but it was all hand-rubbed." There are also specimens of his fine work still cherished by his family and friends. "There's a table in my parents' house that I love so much," shares Kathleen Sykes. "It was my mom's when she was younger. Once, when my grandpa was visiting, we had set up the table down in the cellar and it was just shredded to bits with things my siblings and I had done to it. Grandpa saw it and refinished it until I thought it was a different table. He magically made it beautiful."

Because his interest in exotic cuts never diminished, there was still an extensive accumulation of unfinished wood when he passed. Dave Eichorn, whose interest in woodworking continues today, acquired some of that wood. Other pieces went to family members. Fred, himself a devoted woodworker, inherited his father's tools. "I think of him all the time when I use them," he explains. "And when people come into our house, they see that wood and I tell them about my father."

It was a fellow student from Brown University who introduced Bob to the art of photography. When Sykes was preparing to enter his Rhodesian stamp collection into a contest for college students, his friend Richard Pease provided the required prints for his portfolio. In Greenland, Bob found the process of picture-taking to be an important tool while building and operating weather stations, using photography as illustrations of the reports sent to military administration back in the States. Photography also helped him more fully express the conditions he and his troops were working under and the unique needs an Arctic environment created for weather professionals.

As he moved into his second and third careers, photography helped Bob share what he was learning about unusual weather through visually-arresting examples of it. Sykes incorporated this aspect of his work into interactions with students and his classes often included slideshow presentations. Slides, in fact, were his preferred method of preserving images. Dave Eichorn began taking pictures on his own once he'd learned the basics from Bob, and at times, the two men would get together with a slide projector to go through them. Eichorn thought of those lessons as a way for him to "share the things that I had observed. Bob would then critique them for me: composition, depth of field, how to force colors, when to set the camera down a step or two."

Tom Galletta also got his start with photography from Bob, buying his first camera soon after meeting him. "I did some flying for Professor Chermack on a research project that involved mapping lake temperature," Tom says. "There were several power plants along Lake Ontario and Bob suggested that I take some pictures of them while I was up there. He had an infrared roll of film and said, 'Take this up and test it out.' He was always trying new things."

"My father was always ready for a good photo opportunity," Fred remembers, describing his dad's three cameras always waiting to be put into action. "They were usually 35 millimeter types, but not expensive name brand cameras; I remember it was the Exakta he seemed to prefer. If we were on the road and he saw a really unusual cloud, we'd stop and go back to get the cameras. He might take a whole 36-roll exposure at one time. Over the years, he accumulated a nearly-full freezer of slides."

Bob would have first been exposed to classical compositions

at quite a young age, listening to the family radio or at church with his parents. But a full appreciation of classical music's majesty wouldn't really take hold until his Introduction to Music class while at Brown University. Thereafter, Bob found solace in his favorite compositions on numerous occasions: while enduring months and years of isolated conditions in Greenland, when closed off in a room for hours looking over weather data, and to fill the emptiness from the loss of his loved ones.

Paul Cardinali once benefited from Bob's awareness of music's healing powers, something that still resonates in him five decades after it happened: "I once lost a friend of mine to an automobile accident and Bob said to me, 'What I want you to do is to go into my office and listen to this music and just relax for a while.' The piece was rather obscure, but it was also reflective and soothing in nature."

Paul's wife, Chrystal, has this memory of how Bob's music was an integral part of those SUNY Oswego days: "The earth science department had an old-fashioned mimeograph machine. He'd come into the office and you'd hear him as he was cranking away on that thing, whistling as loud as he could to 'La donna è mobile,' from Verdi's opera *Rigoletto*."

As Jack Kaplan sees it, there's a correlation between Bob's love of classical music and his love of weather: "Music and weather go together, in a way, because they both can display a lot of power. Bob really liked the power of the brass sections."

Music permeated the Sykes' home life, as well. In his quest to fully appreciate the diversity of music and to satisfy his need to dig for finer details, Bob intensely studied the complex world of classical compositions. Fred is amazed that his father knew every composer as well as which compositions were associated with each. Barbara was certain she only heard classical music growing up, not even realizing there were other kinds of music "until I was 10 or 11. Around that time, when I came home from school, my mom and I would watch Dick Clark's *American Bandstand*. That was my first and really only exposure to modern music until we moved overseas and I had my own little radio."

"When the church organist knew my grandfather was coming into town," Beth Sykes Collins recalls, "she would spend extra time practicing. He loved and would always request 'Ode to Joy.' " "Handel's *Messiah* was probably his favorite piece of music," Barbara continues, "and the 'Halleluiah Chorus' was his favorite part of it. At Christmas, he liked a really good version of 'O Holy Night.' There were a couple of opera singers who did that song and reached all the high notes and it was just stunning. He would play that continuously."

With certainty, Bob Sykes loved to travel, but rarely did he do so for its own sake; he liked when his excursions had a purpose. Along with the extensive traveling required of him while in the military, and to a lesser degree, during his SUNY Oswego career, Bob took frequent trips with family to see and experience different cultures. Then, after Marie and Gerda passed away, there were his children to visit. When Bob traveled to his son Bruce's, in Utah, it was often for extended stays in order to explore that part of the country – sometimes with his son, other times with the whole family. And once in a while, it would be with just his grandchildren.

"We were gone for five days," Sarah Sorenson remembers, referring to a trip to the Grand Canyon with her grandfather for her and her brother, Robbie, both not yet school-aged. "At one point, we were sitting in a Chevron gas station with a map spread out, picking places to go. He took us to Kanab, Bryce Canyon and Zion National Park. Then we headed to the Capital Reef and the north rim of the Grand Canyon. He spoiled us on the trip; museums had those bins with rocks and he bought us tons of them. On the way home, his credit card was declined because he'd completely spent it on the trip."

After his first experience in 1925, the quest to witness a perfect total eclipse was never far from his thoughts. Though his second opportunity for a viewing – this one in New Hampshire in August 1932 – was spoiled by cloud cover, Sykes was not discouraged; it only intensified his enthusiasm. Greenland offered a third chance, but it was thwarted by a conflict in military duties. Would the now-adult Sykes ever be able to again realize the magic of an eclipse he'd experienced as a child?

One of Bob's favorite photos of a total eclipse of the sun.

Indeed he would. Over his life, of Sykes' 13 attempts made to witness a total eclipse, 11 were successful. When the extremely rare opportunity to observe *three* eclipses in nearby Canada over the course of a few years, Bob made sure to be there. Two of those times, his son Fred joined him. The first, in July of 1963, when Fred was 11, required the Sykes to travel to Quebec. As a first eclipse for Fred, it a special occasion for him to share with his father.

But his second opportunity, in March 1970, was even more memorable. The proposed ideal viewing location was Nova Scotia* and Fred remembers the drive through Maine and New Brunswick to get there. Near their destination, they stopped at the Halifax airport so Bob could examine the latest weather maps and consult with airport meteorologists. Noticing cloud cover moving in over the region, the father-and-son team thought conditions looked better

---

*Because he was forecasting the weather on WSGO at the time, Bob found it hard to forego his daily reporting on his trips. He always made sure he called the station to give Oswego weather reports, and then treated listeners to his experiences with the eclipse viewing.

to the south. They hopped in the car.

"I was driving," Fred remembers, "and I was speeding. A Royal Canadian Mounted Police vehicle came up behind us and followed us for about five miles. We figured that he saw our New York plates and got his message across that we were speeding on his roads. I drove more carefully. The clouds started clearing, but my father wanted to keep driving a little further south, finally finding a location where there were no other people.

"We had no more than 20 minutes to set up. My father had several cameras; one with a long range telephoto lens. I had a Questar with a Beseler camera and I started taking pictures with the solar filter on. About a minute before totality, everything quickly turned dark. The sound was noticeable; the birds stopped singing. When totality came, I removed my solar filter and started taking pictures; I took about ten in the two-minute totality. My father took pictures with his cameras. It was absolutely beautiful."

Two years later, North Americans had yet another chance for an eclipse viewing, but this time, Bob headed to Canada alone. Fred, by then, was in Naval ROTC, away on summer training. As time went on and circumstances allowed, Bob traveled greater distances for opportunities to witness his eclipses. There was an October 1976 trip to Australia for a total eclipse of the sun. In February of 1980, it was off to India. Summer of 1983 took Bob and Gerda to Germany to visit her family, and while there, he viewed a total solar eclipse in Asia.

On July 11, 1991, Bob ventured to Mexico for a total eclipse. Hoping for a couple extra seconds of visibility, he drove beyond the suggested best spot for viewing, headed for what he felt would be an even better location. His time was wasted, he would later admit, and he ended up seeing only the tail end of the eclipse. Ray Schneider remembers an earlier, and also misguided opportunity, when he and Bob traveled to Disraeli, Canada for a viewing: "As it got toward the end of the best time to see that eclipse, there were some clouds moving in and Bob said, 'I'm going to move.' I got better pictures than he did because I just stayed in my place. But Bob was like that; he could get real fidgety and jump around a lot."

Bob's last eclipse took place at home in Oswego, in May of 1994. Due to his declining health, an anticipated event in 1999, in Europe, was unattainable. But he would forego it with "no complaints," instead expressing his thankfulness for the many viewings he was able to participate in.

Recalling the devotion his father held for these astral events, Fred mentions a wish Bob had once shared with him about eclipses: "He had hoped to live to 2017 when a solar eclipse was slated to cross over the backyard of our house in Oswego. He would have been 100 years old that year."

PART THREE:

A
WEATHERMAN'S
LEGACY

"I am the (son) of Earth and Water,
And the nursling of the sky;
I passed through the pores of the oceans and shores;
I change, but I cannot die."

-Percy B. Shelley. From Bob's essay,
"Arthur F. Merewether 1902 – 1997."

Chapter 22

A Lifetime of Friends

To fully appreciate the legacy of weatherman Bob Sykes, one must consider his many friendships. The deep regard he held for friends went beyond the simple maintenance of those relationships; they were the foundation that sustained him in work and life. In his career paperwork, he made certain to indicate those who were instrumental in a project's success or which young person accompanied him on his winter-storm expeditions. Friends wove in and out of his autobiographical writings, and he often jumped decades in a single sentence to match a particular occasion with the memory of someone important to him.

Certain names showed up numerous times: neighbors Preston Kodak, his earliest and longest-standing friend, and Billy Browne, who introduced him to stamp collecting, Horace Mann and Brown University. At his first college, there was Richard Pease, who showed him the fine art of photography that helped him win awards. Friends from NYU, the military and on the Oswego campus began as professional associations, but matured into ones more deep and meaningful. Some of those friendships were with fellow weathermen, such as his Oswego counterparts Elmer Loveridge and

Bill Gregway.

Close relationships were formed with weathermen outside the Oswego area, too, one being Horace "Stormy" Meredith, who had a military career similar to Bob's. (Meredith was also involved with the pre-WWII cadet training.) His daughter, Joyce, remembers that "my father and Bob collaborated on weather-research projects, including weather-flying safety and forecasting methods, as well as theories about how to improve forecasting accuracy."

But his most personal and deeply-felt friendships were reserved for those shared between teacher and student. Though by the time Bob became a professor at Oswego State he was 44 years old – a full generation removed from a typical college student – this did not prohibit him from extending his role as teacher to one of friend. Some aptly observed that he was willing to do so because he thoroughly enjoyed the enthusiasm of young people.

But it wasn't just youthfulness that drew Bob to his students; it was their passion for his passion. SUNY Oswego's Meteorology program brought Bob and hundreds of like-minded weather enthusiasts together and many were eager to learn all they could. Traditional class time just wasn't enough, so Bob invited the most avid weather watchers into his home and his life.

At Bob's home with SUNY Oswego colleague Dr. Ron Chaldu (seated) and student Jim LaDue. (Photo courtesy of Greg Stumpf)

It would not have seemed odd or awkward for Bob to have extended such an invitation; he had memories of his parents welcoming teachers into their home. And it wouldn't have been unusual to run into students in more social settings. During his Oswego State teaching career, the legal age of alcohol consumption in New York State was 18. Drinking wasn't especially important to Bob, but gathering with students at a local pub to discuss the many facets of weather made for a pleasant evening for Sykes.

Chrystal Cardinali was among the first students who Bob befriended in 1961. "When I became involved with the group of students that [were] invited to his house, I thought it was a little strange," Chrystal admits. "You don't usually get an instructor who broaches a friendship with their students. Normally, teachers tried to be professional, but, in his instance, by inviting students to his house, Bob was *extending* his professionalism. He didn't invite you just to use the pool; he always managed to get back on the topic of weather again. It was more of a relaxed type of interplay between him and the students, but he was instructing by example."

Those who are ardent about the weather never run out of things to discuss, just as there was always plenty of work to be done on Bob's various weather instruments. A social afternoon with Sykes might begin with climbing up his weather tower because equipment was locked from freezing rain. Bill Wall attests that he was "one of the few stupid enough or not afraid of heights to climb up that thing, chopping ice on my way up and cleaning out the equipment. That was the kind of thing Bob inspired in me."

Doug Stewart agrees. Once he got to know Bob during his freshman year, Sykes asked Doug if I wanted to do some work for him. There were jobs like tower repair, but he also needed help with home improvements like the patio stone around his pool. Doug remembers being paid well and that there was also time for fun, like when Bob challenged him at ping pong: "I may have taken a few of those games, but Bob won just about all of them," Doug admits. "He would just give you that smile of his and say, 'You're not going to win this' and then he'd go ahead and win it. Bob wore black-rimmed glasses and I don't know how he could see out of them – they always needed cleaning – but, despite that, he beat me."

Those friendships often baffled his children, who, as they grew up, saw more and more students welcomed into their home. Barbara: "Dad was very generous to students with his time. They were almost a part of our home, more so after I left Oswego and certainly after my mother died. I can remember being a little jealous because they got so much of his time. But looking back on it, I can see that it was because Dad was attracted to people who had the same interests, and they were attracted to him. They were all very smart people, and if a student exhibited interest, Dad would go out of his way to help that person."

Friendships, some suggested, were what kept Bob alive after Marie, Gerda, and Cindy died. Once the Brown Drive house was his alone, if someone in Bob's class was interested in weather and maybe was having a hard time paying room and board at the school, well, he had an extra room. By the time Jim LaDue started at Oswego in 1982, Bob was a year away from retirement, so he never had Sykes as a teacher. "But we got to know each other, anyway," Jim says. "Invariably, my conversations with Bob led to what the lake would do to our weather. One thing led to another, and eventually he had enough trust in me that he allowed me to live in his house while he went off to Africa for about six weeks."

This is not to say that all the boarders Bob took in became his trusted friends. Because of his willingness to help others, there were a few who took advantage and his children noticed this happening over the years. "After he retired," Fred explains, "the kind of people who stayed with my father changed. One time, he needed work done on the house. My brother Bruce had just had some work done on his home in Utah and the guy who did it ended up going back to Oswego with my father. He lived at the house for several years, working on it and other places in Oswego, and then left. There were other people that really were in need and our family never quite took to them. But maybe my father, because of his background, didn't mind."

It seems that Bob's childhood experiences, including those in New York City, *did* strongly influence his altruistic behavior. "I saw the long lines of people [during the Depression] begging for cigarettes, food, and what have you," Bob wrote in his culminating career and personal notes. "The apple lines, the chestnut lines and a lot of things, these are still in my memory." He also never forgot that his parents were unable to achieve a comfortable financial situation, much of that due to the sacrifices they made in order for Bob to further his education. When Sykes reached the point where he could help others, he did, with little consideration of how it might affect his life. "Grandpa always took people in as if they were his family," Sarah Sorenson recalls. "It gave him joy, no matter how the person was receiving it."

Those students who maintained friendships with Bob saw the unique way he attempted to kept in touch. Chrystal Cardinali remained his friend for decades, and from the very beginning, she saw Bob avoiding correspondence, unless it was very important. While working in his Oswego State office, he'd often ask her to "write a letter to so-and-so and tell them such and such."

"I'd do that," says Chrystal, "and he'd say, 'It's not all that important that they see my signature, so sign my name and send it on.' This was also true at holiday time. He would call and say, 'This is your one and only holiday greeting.' Then we would chat for a while. This went on until the cancer got so bad and he couldn't carry on."

Jim LaDue stayed in touch with Bob until the late 1990s, when Sykes started to get sick. "Our communications dropped after that," Jim admits, "because he really didn't want to talk about his illness. He would be private about the welfare of his family or of himself, but very open about his teaching and interest in the weather."

1998 photo of Bob.

Bob's students who took up careers in meteorology maintained a special connection with him after leaving the Oswego campus. When Tom Niziol graduated in 1977, he quickly found work as a research associate at the Cornell Aeronautical Laboratories in Buffalo. This led to his dream job of becoming a forecaster for the National Weather Service, which he felt fortunate to obtain at such a young age. (He was 23 when first hired by the NWS.) As a new forecaster, Tom was scheduled for rotating shifts, and sometimes while working in the middle of the night to get his forecast out, the phone would ring.

"It would be Bob calling," Tom recalls. "He would start his phone call off by saying, 'How is my erstwhile friend?' Bob had tremendous command of the English language and I just loved the way that he could weave such words into his sentences. He said that because I would be so busy at work and had little time to spend on the phone with him, and I often had to cut him off. So he would use words like 'erstwhile' to gently nudge me and let me know that I was important to him and it was important for us to spend time talking."

In 1983, at the end of Bob's SUNY Oswego career, he

noted that among his "greatest positives" as a teacher were "those few students who responded to my trusting and 'open' approach in teaching, [which resulted in] the development of some superb personal associations. Several students will remain always among my closest personal friends."

He would echo those feelings in the written and audio recordings he made at the end of his life: "I am thankful for the many friends I had from my grammar school days, right up and through my retirement years at Oswego. Without my family and friends, I would have accomplished very little. I extend a deep, meaningful, and genuine thank you to all of those along my journey who have supported me, pushed me at times, and otherwise offered helping hands when I really needed them. Thank you all. And thank you, God, for the gifts that you allowed me to share during the many years, especially the weather years."

Chapter 23

Something Greater Than Himself

Reading that Bob Sykes thanked God for his weather-observing gifts might come as a surprise to some who spent a good deal of time with him. God wouldn't have come up a lot in the many discussions he had with friends about the weather, and certainly in the sciences, where a theory is only a theory until proven, Sykes instilled in his students the importance of avoiding pat answers. He preferred living with the questions, which is what kept him wondering about what the skies held. Jack Kaplan remembers his teacher as a man who held weather as his god. "Bob was a good man," Kaplan assures, "but he wasn't heavy into religion."

But there are also indications that Sykes maintained a strong spirituality, though his exact beliefs are hard to pin down. In fact, Fred surmises that his father's certainty of a specific spiritual presence in his life only came when one of the many young people drifting in and out of Bob's life stayed at his home. "My father had more of a Deist belief. He was never a regular church goer, though he did attend our church when he would come to visit us. He and I had a lot of discussions about religion, on things like creationism and such. We didn't always agree, but those were good conversations. I had always been very interested in his spiritual condition since I became a Christian, and he once told me he was born again. [When] I asked him about that rebirth, he mentioned a student who lived with him and who had shared faith with my father. This led him to be born again."

Barbara remembers her father referring to himself as agnostic. "An Agnostic," she notes, "is not atheism, which has no belief in a higher being. Agnostic is like a Doubting Thomas. He was not a disbeliever, but he was not a believer. He did watch Dr. Robert Schuller* and Dr. Frederick S.K. Price on television every Sunday morning. He never missed them, but I don't know if that's because he liked Dr. Schuller's message that you can make yourself over, or because Dr. Price's was much more religious."

When considering his father's belief in God, Bruce thinks of him "more of a Deist: God is present in the Universe and all human life should be in the existence of God. But even that changed over time," Bruce said. Sarah Sorenson would also recognize the unique approach her grandfather took with things greater than himself: "Grandpa wasn't religious, but he was spiritual. He wanted to go to services, but it didn't matter what the denomination. He didn't always go with us to church unless there was something special going on. His love of all things beautiful was a testament to his faith and knowledge of a Greater Power, and he never said a negative thing about anybody."

Though the specificities of Bob's path to his spiritual beliefs may be unclear, the question of God's existence wove in and out of

---

*In a summary of his career at SUNY Oswego, Bob would list Dr. Schuller's *Peace of Mind through Possibility Thinking* among the books that "most impressed" him.

his life. Beginning with his attendance at his parents' Baptist church and through his diverse childhood neighborhood that offered him opportunities to visit his friends' Roman Catholic, Dutch Reform and Episcopalian churches, Bob listened and considered. Added to these formal religions were his mother's claim of their Egyptian origins and his fascination with what he saw when looking into the heavens. The detail-oriented and fervent observer had much to ponder.

Bob did like it when the divisions of religious denominations blurred and blended. While on a trip to see her parents, Marie and Bob visited a Catholic church in the Vatican Exhibition Hall in New York. There Bob saw a copy of *The Guttenberg Bible,* on loan from St. Bartholomew's Episcopal Church. Sykes noted that he "thought *The Bible,* from the Protestant church loaned to the Catholic exhibit, was a good example of ecumenical spirit. I approve of this," he stated.

Bob's open-mindedness concerning spirituality may have had something to do with each of his children's religious path. Once the Sykes children settled in Oswego, Barbara and her siblings were members of a Lutheran Church in town. In her adulthood, she attended services at Episcopal and Presbyterian Churches. At one point, she even attended a street church for the homeless, offering her help wherever she could. When she moved to Oswego in 1994 to help care for her father, she joined Faith United, a Presbyterian church, where she became active in a variety of support roles. Recently returned to Oswego, Barbara is again a member of that church.

When Bruce was 16, he joined the Church of Jesus Christ of Latter Day Saints (The Mormons). At first, Bob and Marie were troubled by their oldest son's bold and extreme shift in faiths and would not sign the parental permission form required for his attendance. Bruce was determined enough to forge the paperwork, but the missionaries recognized it as such and wouldn't permit it. Eventually, Marie and Bob saw that their son's intentions were clear and serious, and they allowed his entrance into the religion. "I don't think they were happy with me joining the Mormon Church," Bruce tells, "but they warmed up to it. My mom even got a Mormon hymn book."

Bruce's introduction into the Latter Day Saints included a required missionary trip, his fulfilled in Germany from 1969 to 1971. Upon completion of his mission, Bob journeyed from Oswego to Germany to join his son, and together they enjoyed a two-week tour of the area. Later, when they'd returned to the States, Bruce returned to Utah to start law school. Utah remains his home where he practices law and his ties to the church remain strong.

Fred's participation in an evangelistic Bible study while attending Ohio State University resulted in his becoming a Christian in 1972. After graduating from Ohio State in metallurgical engineering, he entered the Navy through the ROTC program. Once his military service had been completed, Fred and his family moved first to Ohio and then to Dallas, Texas, where he completed his Theological Master's program at the Dallas Theological Seminary in 1990. When he and his family settled in Canton, New York, Fred became Pastor of the First Baptist Church.

Bob's path to finding spiritual meaning in the world and in his life was certainly shaped in the years he struggled to understand the passing of three family members. He was also well aware of his own mortality, resulting from the series of close brushes with death that took place during his military years. Three more close calls after he became a civilian brought the idea of a powerful spiritual presence closer. The first of these happened in the winter of 1975-76 when Marie was receiving chemotherapy at Buffalo's Roswell Cancer Treatment Center.

Sykes made several trips over snowy roadways between Oswego and Buffalo and his riding companion was often Jack

Kaplan. Jack has vivid memories of what happened on one of those trips: "Bob was driving and I was in the front seat, sleeping. And, it turns out, Bob was sleeping, too; he'd dozed off while at the wheel. Then something came and shook my shoulder. When I looked over, I saw Bob was sleeping and our car going on the other side into oncoming traffic. I grabbed the wheel and he woke up. That," Kaplan is certain, "was my guardian angel."

A second close call came in 1979 when Bob was driving to Canada with three other people, chasing the opportunity for a solar eclipse observation. The car was moving down the two-lane highway at "67 mph," Bob's precise memory recalled. "All three occupants had fallen asleep and my car crossed to the opposite shoulder through oncoming traffic before I brought it to a stop."

The third near-collision took place in 1980, during a return trip to Oswego on a main highway. Bob's memory of it is eerily specific: "I was behind a dump truck at a place on the road where it was just two lanes, one heading in each direction. The truck was going around fifty miles per hour or so and I had in mind to pass it, so consequently I pulled out slightly to the left. As I did so, maybe half of my car was to the left of the center line.

"I felt on my left shoulder the amount of pressure that you would feel as if a man was shaking the hand of a very gracious lady. You wouldn't put much pressure, obviously, if she had rings on. I felt that amount of pressure on my left shoulder. This was something of a surprise because I had no passengers, but I pulled back behind the truck, and as I did so, a fast-moving vehicle came by going the other direction. It was a good-sized truck, and had I gone out into that lane, there would have been no place for me to go."

Those were the most dramatic of his close calls, but Bob was well aware of the countless times he ventured out into the weather concerned more about the pursuit of his passion than his safety. "During the period approximately 1963 to the mid-'80s," Bob wrote in one summary of his career, "I traveled thousands of miles during the winter months, particularly in connection with lake-effect snowstorms. There were many incidents of 'zero/zero visibility' where I was trying to gain experience with the conditions, geographical information about the extent of some of the patterns, the intensities of snowfall, the particular snow types and other variations of interest. I did experience several incidents of crisis and I'm sure that I missed several by as few as fractions of seconds..."

Chapter 24

The Skies Welcome Him Home

Though Bob Sykes never stopped appreciating the intricacies of weather, declining health would eventually prevent him from following it as passionately as he had for more than 70 years. In May 1998, Bob gave his last weather prediction for a SUNY Oswego graduation ceremony. That August, he was diagnosed with cancer, which led to a series of chemotherapy and radiation treatments. Though hopeful for some improvement in life, he resigned himself to the fact that he wasn't going to make one more Eastern Snow Conference, let alone his 2017 goal of viewing an eclipse in Oswego.

He remained in contact with his weather-loving friends as much as his compromised health allowed. Tom Niziol noted how Bob kept track of his work right up to the end: "I remember our conversations in his last days, still briefing him from my office on the current weather conditions and what was to come. And he was as interested as the first day he got into meteorology."

Greg Stumpf paid him a visit in 1988, and again in 1995. "He was still very much spry and we continued to stay in touch," Stumpf remembers, "but a year or so after the last visit, we never talked much anymore. In '99, my then wife and I were planning a trip back east and I was going to show her Oswego. The plan was to visit Bob. It was just about the time when we started to make those plans that I got the news he had passed away."

In his final years, as his health declined, Bob's children were there to offer support. Barbara and her sons moved into the Brown Drive family home in 1994; she remained there until her father's death. Bruce and his family made several trips back East to spend time with his father. Fred and his family came down from northern New York to also be of help and support. Eventually, they moved Bob to Canton, where Fred, his wife and children could attend to his growing needs. Bob spent the final six months of his life with them.

"Toward the end," Fred remembers, "we had home health care to help us because my father was never going to go into a nursing home; he was going to be with us and he would die with us. When he eventually went into the hospital, he was in very serious condition. His mind was fine, but things in his body were all out of whack and the hospital was trying to get him stabilized."

Fred's daughter, Beth, was away at college when her parents called to tell her that her grandpa was not doing well and she should come home. "We drove right to the hospital," Beth remembers, "and I'll never forget how his face lit up when he saw me; it made my heart stop. I didn't know what to say and we just sat there in silence. I held his hand." More family arrived and joined the vigil.

On January 29, 1999, exactly 33 years from the day a blizzard barreled into Oswego and lifted a self-proclaimed "simple weatherman" into a meteorological icon, Bob Sykes passed away. The thermometer outside the Ogdensburg Hospital, where Bob succumbed, did not break freezing. Back in Oswego, a few inches of snow fed from an overnight lake-effect storm blanketed the area around Brown Drive with a gentle white.

An Oswego sunset as seen from Bob's backyard.

His death would be traced to an inoperable cancer in the upper left lung, but its origins were never confirmed. Bruce thought it might have had something to do with working with wood all those years: "His workshop was filled with sawdust, and after he got sick, I had read some stories that cancer is caused by breathing in fumes of some types of wood." Bob had thought about this consideration himself: "I think, at times, I was not too careful about using masks, and my health problems that developed in the early '80s might possibly be related to this carelessness." But Barbara also remembers her father telling her from his hospital bed that it might have come from exposure to asbestos in the military.

In the end, causality was not important. It wasn't a time to question old habits or irreversible situations; it was a time for those who loved him to gather and reflect on his life, his accomplishments and his many gifts to others.

The memorial service offered on February 3, 1999 was, in fact, called "A Celebration of His Life." Held at The Church of Resurrection in Oswego, the same sanctuary where the Sykes family had gathered for so many other joyous and somber occasions, they again came together with Bob's friends, colleagues and former students to share memories. In his weather journal, Paul Cardinali captured the importance of the day: "Chrys and I drive to Oswego with sunroof open to Bob Sykes' memorial service. So many former students of his, many renowned weather people now. Freddy, Bruce, Barb...so long, but so short a while ago."

The church resounded with Bob's beloved classical music: Beethoven's *Choral Fantasia,* Puccini's *Madame Butterfly,* the Prelude from Dvorak's *New World Symphony* and a Chopin piano etude. There were well-known hymns like "Amazing Grace" and "How Great Thou Art" ("O Lord, my God, when I in awesome wonder, consider all the works Thy hand hath made"). Poems by James Russell Lowell and John Donne offered a thoughtful pause. There were readings from the Scripture, and at the service's end, people walked out into the weather, accompanied by one of Bob's much-loved compositions, Handel's "Hallelujah Chorus."

Per his last will, Bob requested that all weather equipment of value be sold to pay off his debts, and if such a sale was not necessary, this equipment and other weather-related supplies should be offered to his children and friends. Dave Eichorn received Bob's copy of Wilson Bentley's *Snow Crystals;* others would find a home for his most precious and well-used weather instruments.

The 1999 Eastern Snow Conference, held a few months after Bob's passing, was dedicated to one of their most loyal participants. *The Eastern Snow Conference Proceedings,* an annual publication of the conference events, included in its introduction a tribute to Bob written by Dave Eichorn and Tom Niziol. (These reflections on their teacher and friend originally appeared in the June 1999 edition of the *Bulletin of the American Meteorological*

Society.)

Along with a summary of their mentor's greatest meteorological achievements, Eichorn and Niziol spoke for many when they offered: "He was revered as one of the 'grandfathers' of lake-effect snow forecasting around the eastern Great Lakes. As a researcher, he laid the foundation for the understanding of the atmospheric processes responsible for the development of these mesoscale events. As a professor and friend, Bob had the uncanny ability to instill that sense of joy and wonder that observing the weather has to offer."

Chapter 25

Through Meteorology's Modern Lens

T here have been hundreds of weather events since Bob Sykes left this world, and several of them looked and felt a lot like the incredible storms he passionately pursued. There were the heavy snows that zeroed in on his birthplace of New York City in 2006. In his adopted hometown of Oswego, there was the Valentine's Day Storm of February 2007, when the area was blanketed with between five and ten feet of snow, depending on who was counting. (Some things never change.) Many believe Bob would have tracked 2012's Hurricane Sandy every step of the way, starting with its birth in the Western Caribbean Sea. And he would have analyzed and reanalyzed the numbers from the 2013-14's polar vortex, which for many felt like they were being held in the grips of a Greenland winter. With each new powerful weather event, those who worked alongside Bob imagined how he might have interpreted them.

But, most of all, Bob's family and friends could have imagined him sitting alongside the researchers in that "Doppler on Wheels" sent to the Tug Hill Plateau of northern Oswego County from December 2013 through January 2014. Many believe he would have loved to be reviewing the lake-effect snow data modern-day meteorologists were compiling, using sophisticated equipment such as instrumented research aircraft, weather balloon sounding systems or radar wind profiler. The project, called OWLeS – Ontario Winter Lake-effect Systems* – had goals to better understand the atmospheric conditions and controlling mechanisms responsible for extreme snow accumulations across Upstate New York. OWLeS' title and ambitious goals sound like the offspring of Sykes' LOTEL project from the 1960s and '70s. Joining in this most recent endeavor would have been snow heaven for Bob.

With the success of projects like OWLeS in today's meteorology, it's difficult to grasp the extent of what Sykes accomplished with only the primitive technology available to him fifty years ago. Those who use today's most modern weather-tracking tools *and* remember what Bob was able to achieve with much less, love to discuss the dichotomy of it all. "The fact that Bob could project a lake-effect snowstorm on his radio program," Bob Maxon marvels, "whether it be for six, eight or as much as 24 hours into the future, and not only to be able to forecast when it would start and when it would end, but also try to forecast snow amounts to the extent of any accuracy, amazes me to this day. And when you see how thin those snow bands really are on modern Doppler radar, while Bob had no images on computers or TV to back him up, it's even more amazing."

Maxon ventures a guess of what was going on in Bob's mind

---

*OWLeS was a collaboration effort between four universities – one being SUNY Oswego – and The Center for Severe Weather Research. Supported with a grant from the National Science Foundation, Bob would have been especially pleased that the SUNY Oswego Meteorology Department has become a trailblazer in weather research, commanding national attention with programs such as OWLeS.

as he carried out his thinking process: "To me, he had really developed his own computer models in his brain. Today, there are supercomputers that develop [such] models and they take hours and hours to run through all the data. Bob, in his own mind, was figuring all that out and using the information for consistent and accurate forecasts. It boggles the modern weather mind."

Jim LaDue agrees that what was going on in Bob's mind was pretty amazing: "Bob had a synoptic memory: a memory of past-weather events and all its details. He had a vast repertoire to what I would call 'pattern recognition,' which is the ability to match a current pattern to one's memory of past similar patterns in order to derive a forecast. Sometimes, when we don't know all the ingredients that create a current weather event, pattern recognition helps fill in the gaps of knowledge. Bob's great memory of past patterns was probably done by internally creating a composite pattern and then associating his memory of what those patterns did in terms of weather impacts."

Many of Bob's weather-savvy colleagues agree that he would have embraced what modern technology is discovering about the incredible lake-snow "machine" he devoted his life to understanding. He would have welcomed the advancements of science, yes, but he wouldn't have been all that surprised with what they were discovering. After all, Sykes was anticipating these new meteorology principles coming, and Tom Niziol, for one, believes that his teacher would enjoy some of the new technology.

"He understood that there would be the sophisticated computer modeling that goes on these days, and of course, he would embrace that technology," Niziol states. "Well, maybe 'embrace' is too big a word for that; at least he'd *use* that technology. But what I think he'd really, really enjoy are some of the other technologies that are out there: the remote sensing, the satellite technology that lets us observe everything that's happening on the face of the earth from the sky. Even more than that, he'd enjoy the tremendous explosion of webcams and video. These help to explain what is going on weather-wise. The ability to look and see weather *anywhere* is where Bob Sykes would have loved the technology today."

Tom Galletta gets a certain satisfaction when he thinks about how Bob would have, in fact, had some inkling that his early theories would someday be verified by those who came after him in the pursuit of understanding winter weather. Galletta remembers a conversation he had with Tom Niziol when satellites began coming into vogue.

"Niziol started to get pictures from the satellites," Galletta remembers, "and he happened to catch one of Lake Ontario that illustrated this phenomenon that Bob was trying to understand using all the barographs set up along the lakeshore. This would have been ten years after Bob's work. So Tom printed one of those satellite pictures off and sent it to Bob."

Dave Eichorn: "There was a professor I was talking with not too long ago about lake effect. He was trying to discuss with me things that he understood about it – some of these 'new' discoveries. I didn't say anything to him, because that would have been rude, but the things that he was explaining to me were not new. He was discovering things for the first time, and that was okay, but I thought to myself about the foundational work that Bob did, but never published. He should've been more aggressive about publishing in peer review journals, because there are things that people have discovered and written about that are not new; things that he observed but never formally wrote up. But I will tell you this: Bob had fun. He had a blast. He didn't publish these things, but he had a blast doing it – and you can't take that away from somebody!"

Dave Eichorn and Bob Sykes investigating a snowdrift in Barnes Corners, New York.
(photo courtesy of Greg Stumpf)

Bob would have also loved the fact that, as Bill Wall states, "weather is still a very unpredictable and dynamic enterprise. There are major aspects of it that still aren't fully understood." Bob, with his insatiable craving to track down the whys of what has yet to be discovered and confirmed, would be quick to settle in and get started.

Bob Sykes' legacy is not only evident because of his ability to predict computer-generated weather models. A more significant aspect of his legacy, especially as seen by his former students, comes much more humbly. Dave Eichorn acknowledges the details of what Bob accomplished in meteorology, but that's not what stands out about his mentor's work. "He had a bridge to the natural world," Eichorn says, "and you don't see that a lot today, particularly as we have gotten more technological. In fact, you rarely find it. But, it's really special and Bob was there 100%, all the way."

Others agree that the study of weather seems to be moving further and further from that bridge Eichorn speaks of. Paul Cardinali admits that how he tracks the weather has changed a lot since first starting back in high school: "I don't have to keep going out and tapping on my maximum/minimum reading thermometer and resetting it, like I used to. But I have to keep kicking myself because the more technical you begin to get, the more you move away from the actual elements. These days, I'm finding myself looking more at the radar than I am out my window, and at times I have to say to myself: 'Hey c'mon, get out there! Get out in it!' "

The problem for modern meteorology, it seems, starts with the design of today's weather observation worksites. Tom Moore, who has to walk a distance from his work station to get to a window, shares this thought: "Every once in a while, I'll run to the window to see what's happening. And when I'm doing that, I automatically think of Bob. He would have lamented a bit that forecasters aren't absorbing the weather into their own being. They are relying on these cold computer models to make many of their decisions. As a professor, he understood that there would be changes [in weather technology], but he would always have a little soft spot in his heart for those who tried to experience the weather and observe it directly."

Chapter 26

As Close as the Clouds

For those who loved him, he is never far from their thoughts. And for some, his memory can present itself in the smallest of gestures; sometimes with just a word. Because Bob had a love of language, he enjoyed being able to manipulate words to best serve the descriptions of what he was observing in the world. After years of witnessing amazing weather phenomenon that no single word could aptly describe, Bob took it upon himself to coin new ones to fit the bill. He often did this by combining two commonly-used words to express something beyond their individual meanings. A word like "snowcrete," for example, was his way to describe the tightly-packed drifts that result when blizzard winds bash snow crystals into microscopic form and fuse them together. Anyone who has walked on such a condition can feel how precisely right Bob's word is.

Jack Kaplan was working alongside Bob when his teacher created another new term: "snowspout." A snowspout, as Sykes would ably describe, is a winter version of the cyclonic waterspouts that form over a body of water and move toward shore, and Jack and Bob observed just such an event when one came in from Lake Ontario. Kaplan was at Bob's house when a strong Arctic front moved through the area, carrying with it some significant snowfall. Jack estimated that visibility was down to about 100 feet when he and Bob got hit with the full force of the front.

"Naturally, we went out in Bob's backyard to feel the effects," Kaplan explains. "While we were out there, Bob and I heard a loud roaring sound. 'What was that?' I asked. 'I think it's a snowspout!' Bob exclaimed, and just as he did, the thing hit like a ton of bricks. It lasted just seconds, turned his barbeque grill over and moved on.'"

Another term occasionally heard in winter weather reports, "snowburst," is credited to Bob. He used it first when describing a 1958 Oswego storm. Though Sykes wasn't an Oswego resident at the time, he was reviewing weather data from the major storm and found that it dropped almost six feet of snow on the city, 40 inches of it in 24 hours. Since then, snowburst* has been adopted by meteorologists and is often used to describe short periods of heavy snowfall. As an example, Bob suggested "a 10- to 14-hour storm, with snowfall rates of around two inches per hour and greater."

"Blizzardburst," a close cousin to Bob's snowburst, was used by him in the presentation he provided for the American Meteorological Society in 1988. Bob's program on The Blizzard of '66 at the AMS conference gave him plenty of opportunity to use his newly-coined word.

---

*The word has its own Wikipedia entry, and acknowledges Bob as its originator. It describes "snowburst" as any heavy lake-effect snowfall not accompanied by high winds." Wikipedia notes that it has become a commonly-used term in meteorology, favored by established organizations such as the National Weather Service and often referred to on *The Weather Channel.*

He coined the phrase "cloud streets" to help people visual the long bands of lake-effect clouds coming in over land from the water. Bob used "cloud streets" when describing such a winter sight to observers standing on the shores of Lake Ontario. And if it wasn't snowing directly overhead, but could be seen in the distance, Sykes would say that the snow was falling "out there, under the street."

There was "snow fog," "snow dust" and "snow debris"; words that perhaps were not coined by Bob, but brought into meteorological vocabulary after his consistent use of them. Even the term "lake-effect snow," now talked about year-round in Central New York and beyond, was not a well-known phrase before his apt descriptions of it in weather forecasts. Charles Young thinks that the name of the restaurant Bob owned with Cindy, Lake Effect, was more than a cute reference for a wintry town like Oswego. "Though he didn't coin the word," Young assures, "he really brought it to the public's attention during The Blizzard of '66. People got to really understand what lake effect meant during that storm."

It isn't only his aptly-named and often-used words that evoke his memory and inspire Sykes' legacy. His influence looms large in the smallest of things, such as a snowflake. The wonder he found in its crystalized form also captured Tom Niziol's imagination. Years later, his teacher's love of snowflakes and snow crystals "pretty much got into my blood," Tom says. "Today, I photograph snowflakes and maintain a website of them, and there you'll see how Bob's love and interest in understanding snow rubbed off on me."

The memory of an influential teacher can show up in a single experience, one that was performed under their mentor's guidance long ago. Though Doug Stewart's career with meteorology has taken him to points around the country and has him working on complex weather projects using computer models, he still thinks about Bob and his college days "whenever I have to climb a tower or review any radar data."

The inspiration for Bob Maxon to be the best meteorologist possible comes from remembering Sykes as a risk taker, "someone not afraid to go out on a limb, and who was willing to take criticism for it. Modern-day weather forecasters are incredibly conservative because of the public backlash, whether it's severe weather, whether it's snowstorms. Most people in the public don't realize how hard it is to project with any accuracy snowstorm totals or tornado activity.

"When things didn't go right, Bob had the thickest skin in Oswego County," Maxon continues. "He knew that it was an extremely difficult act to forecast lake-effect snow. So I try to tell young meteorologists and forecasters to respond as Bob would, and understand that we will have our share of successes and our share of failures. And I think, because of his failures, perhaps Bob wasn't celebrated as much as he should have been."

Even those who ended up in careers not directly related to Bob's still find him in their work. Greg Stumpf, who tracks severe thunderstorm and tornado warnings, acknowledges that he did not follow Sykes' work involving winter storms. "But it was through Bob's understanding of the little, rapid changes – what we today call micrometeorology – that he was able to explain how snow patterns occurred," Greg says. "And that has rubbed off on a lot of his students, including me."

Jack Kaplan, who has never worked in the meteorology field, still finds ways to share all that Bob taught him with others. Kaplan volunteers his time at colleges, and when he talks with students about what they're going to do when they graduate, he likes to explain to them how he started out: "I talk about how I was going to go into a weather-related field and how Bob gave me the resources and materials and taught me to use them. Though I ended up not working in his field, Bob teaching me how to observe things and feel things really let me become fully engaged in *my* work. I took the passion that I felt for weather study and successfully moved it into different areas."

Jim LaDue has also seen that what Bob taught transfers to other types of work, especially in regards to how he thinks about meteorology today: "I got most of my attitude toward the weather from Bob. He imprinted a lot of his outlook on weather on me, and I incorporated that into how I look at things. He was an observationalist and he remembered everything, including if he did something wrong. I took his philosophy and attention to detail to heart, and today I do my best to teach these things to my students."

For many, Bob's memory is stirred simply by doing what he did all his life: look up. "I think about him all the time when the storms come in," says Chrystal Cardinali. "I'll say to Paul when it's snowing and blowing, 'I miss Bob.' Even though he's passed on, if we get some lake-effect snow, I know that he's up there mixing up a storm."

No matter what triggers a memory of Bob Sykes, all who knew him agree that he was one of a kind. Perhaps Dave Eichorn speaks for many when he says: "The intense dedication to observation that Bob had was rare. Today, when I listen to a person being interviewed on NPR or read a blog by someone that has that same intensity in their study, I say to myself, *I knew somebody like that once...*"

To those who knew him best – his family – Bob's legacy is as complex and far-reaching as their father. For Fred, memories begin when he thinks about what is no longer here: "I miss conversations with my father; just sitting down and talking, bouncing around ideas with him. If I got interested in something, he'd come up and help me. I had several projects I did here in Canton and he'd show up for them." Fred's memories are also stirred by the gifts he cherishes from his father, some that stretch back to Bob's early life: "We have pictures of snowflakes that he gave us from the Wilson Bentley book. We still hang them in the house every Christmas."

For Barbara, she finds her father whenever she looks up: "Any time I see a cloud, I think of Dad. He loved all kinds of clouds: cirrus, cumulus, cumulonimbus, ice crystal clouds. I'll see these unique formations and I still say, 'Oh, Dad, look.' When I first got a cellphone, I would call him and tell him. And I'm still doing that, telepathically, up to heaven."

Bruce's thoughts of his father take him back to Brown Drive and the way the Sykes' family home sometimes seemed more like a weather station: " We had built an addition, a long room with a long table, and I can see him hunched over this big table and his papers with all kinds of data spread out." That image, and a conversation he once had with his dad, keeps Bob's spirit alive for Bruce: "He told me he had this gift of being able to look at the sky and tell people what was going to happen. He called it a gift from God. And I got to see him work with that gift."

Epilogue

Rendezvous at SUNY Oswego

January 24, 2014. I pull onto the SUNY Oswego campus, parking within a stone's throw of Lake Ontario. The clouds have taken over the morning sky; not single formations, really, but a moving mass of gray and black. Exiting my car, I feel that stiff wind coming in over the waters. Students walking across campus seem oblivious to what looks and feels like a major storm moving in. Paying no attention to the science of it all, they're just looking to get out of the weather. I smile to think that such a day 40 years ago would have been perfect for Bob and his class to head to the top of Piez Hall.

But Piez is gone. It's been replaced by the ultramodern Richard S. Shineman Center for Science, Engineering and Innovation.* And it's the Shineman Center that is my destination.

---

*Richard Shineman was hired by Foster Brown a year after Bob, and was as influential a professor in the development of Oswego's chemistry curriculum as Sykes was in meteorology. After his death in 2010, he left a bequest which became the Shineman Foundation and included funding for the construction of this new building. It opened in fall of 2013.

I'd scheduled a meeting with Dr. Al Stamm, a professor of meteorology for the college's science department. Dr. Stamm started his career at the college in 1977 and worked alongside Bob until Sykes' retirement from the college. Now in his 38th year with the department, Dr. Stamm has seen plenty of changes in how weather is studied and taught, and some of those changes involved Bob Sykes.

Sitting in his new office, Dr. Stamm and I have a spirited discussion about the evolution of meteorology he has witnessed. He reminisces about his former colleague's teaching style and interactions with students, echoing what others I have interviewed suggested about Bob. Stamm agrees that, as a professor, Sykes was not highly theoretical, acknowledging that he had learned his version of meteorology the hard way.

Like others who worked with Bob, Stamm understood that he found happiness not in a scholarly paper, but in his quest for the perfect weather forecast. Weather, he notes, was always the center of Bob's conversation. Sykes could not imagine that others were not as interested as he in the questions that appeared when looking skyward. As we conclude our discussion, I ask Dr. Stamm what he thinks Bob Sykes' legacy is. After pondering this a while, he offers: "His ability to transfer his excitement for the weather to his students was Bob's greatest gift."

As we conclude our conversation, Stamm offers me a tour through the Shineman Center. His enthusiasm for the learning that is just beginning in the state-of-the-art classrooms and laboratories is evident. He identifies the branch of science that will be studied in each room and points out the recent acquisition of each piece of equipment.

Climbing to the very top floor of the building, Dr. Stamm brings me into the glass-walled observatory, which gives students a 360 degree meteorological view. Here, Stamm explains, students of weather have "the best seat in the house" for witnessing it rolling in from over the waters. The view is breathtaking and I get a closer look at those I-mean-business clouds approaching from the west. What would Bob say if he could be here to see this sight? Better yet, what would he ask his students to look for as they stood beside him?

Later on the tour, Dr. Stamm opens the door to a new research lab, which is home to his prize piece of equipment: a wind tunnel. His excitement in the learning potential of this newest educational tool is a pleasure for me to hear, as I picture the brightest of today's meteorology students latching onto their professor's enthusiasm.

But I am struggling to keep up with the technical science of it all, which I why I feel relieved when Stamm directs me to a storeroom where the department keeps outdated or rarely-used equipment. He picks up a barograph, my first look at one of the dozens of machines that once could be found along Lake Ontario for Bob's "Lee of the Lake" studies.

Dr. Stamm places the barograph in my hands and I feel the cold metal of a machine that's been in storage much too long. But I also feel its history. Rusty and primitive-looking, it's certainly humble in comparison to the wind tunnel a few feet away. But the cylinder still turns and the needle that recorded the miles and miles of data Bob once studied is intact. You can almost see it rising and falling as the barometric pressure has its way with our weather. And standing over it, his own wheels keenly turning, is Bob Sykes.

APPENDIX

Ode to Our Faithful Weather Watchers

"Greetings from the land of ice and snow,
where blizzards rage and fierce winds blow,
where temperatures may drop below zero –
perhaps the weatherman is a local hero!"

That's an excerpt from a poem by Chrystal (Laird) Cardinali entitled "Endurance (Ode to Winter)." As an Earth Science major at SUNY Oswego (where she was a student of and ended up working for Bob Sykes), and from her marriage to another weather enthusiast, Paul Cardinali, Chrystal has closely observed winter weather long enough to know what she's talking about when she writes a poem like "Endurance."

Along with accurately depicting our local snowy conditions, for me her words capture the influence and importance weathermen and women have on our busy lives. My day can't start until I've checked in with our local forecaster to hear about what I'll find when I head out the door. For a person that most of us will probably never meet, isn't it funny how we turn to the weatherman like a valued family member?

Writing a book about weather, even one that relies heavily on people's personal stories of an individual weatherman, is probably best served by an author who at least has a rudimentary understanding of how that science works. From the moment I was offered the opportunity to write the story of Bob's life, I was well aware that deciphering meteorology would be my biggest challenge. True confession here: I squeaked by earth science, biology and chemistry in high school; by college, I satisfied science requirements by taking the most basic courses. (It also helped to have a housemate who double-majored in math and science.) By adulthood, my relationship with the study of weather was as cold as an Arctic storm.

Before I could begin writing this biography of Bob Sykes, I had a lot of catching up to do.

Thankfully, I found the best teachers possible. In my research for this book and its companion volume, *"Voices in the Storm: Stories From The Blizzard of '66,"* I was fortunate to talk with some of today's top meteorologists and weather observers, and they gave me a crash course on weather in general, and winter storms in particular. While I wanted to be precious with their time, it turns out that they loved explaining the facts and figures behind lake-effect snow and unusual weather events like the '66 storm. Much of the reason for this, I found out, is because weathermen who are true weather *observers* aren't necessarily a result of their education and training; most, in fact, are born to the breed.

Once I learned that many weathermen find their way to their work innately, I got curious about their common characteristics and life experiences. How does someone know they want to spend their life watching the weather? This led me to wonder how the whole business of weather observing started. Who *was* the first weatherman, and how did he even know where to start?

Properly answering those questions is quite a challenge since evidence of mankind's intrigue with the weather falling from the skies reaches back pretty far; as far back as India, 3,000 years before the birth of Christ. It's here that the earliest indications of mankind's observations of cloud and seasonal changes can be found. Things got more serious over time. By 350 BC, weather knowledge had become important enough for Aristotle to coin the word meteorology (meteor: things above the earth, and logy: the study of). Gradually, the science of weather advanced, and the accumulation of its facts and figures piled up higher than a lake-effect snowdrift. But that's just information, which seems as aloof as those courses I struggled through in college. What about the flesh-and-blood person who could take all that information and let us weather-challenged folks know what to expect in our own backyard? In that sense, who can we say was really the first?

That person was most probably John Campanius Holm, the Swedish-born chaplain also fondly remembered as one of the first people to help establish a settlement in North America. Known as "New Sweden," the colony in the Delaware area was where John, without the benefit of any instrumentation, made his first weather observations in 1644.

People liked what Holm was doing – using observations to make predictions – and soon many weather enthusiasts, including some people who were pretty important to the successful advancement of the United States, began maintaining records. Thomas Jefferson kept an almost unbroken record of weather observations between 1776 and 1816. George Washington remained faithful to the science by taking his last weather observation just a few days before he died. With the respect our nation felt for these early leaders, common folk began emulating their keen observations of the weather.

Another president, Ulysses S. Grant, furthered the evolution of weathermen when he created the National Weather Bureau (a precursor to the National Weather Service) and ordered the establishment of observation stations on our country's Army bases. But it wasn't until devastating storms like 1888's New York City blizzard and 1900's Galveston hurricane that people truly saw the importance of forecasting weather. Soon, the Weather Bureau shifted their focus to issuing bulletins and more comprehensive forecasts. By 1951, the Severe Weather Warning Center — forerunner of the National Severe Storms Center — began operating out of Tinker Air Force Base in Oklahoma. The '60s brought great advancements in communication technology, and soon Americans were getting their weather news from local forecasters on radio and TV broadcasts. Since then, the weatherman has been a mainstay in our lives.

Once I realized that most of today's meteorologists have had a hankering for the weather since they first took notice of it, I couldn't resist asking where it all started for them. During my discussions with weathermen and women about Bob Sykes or The Blizzard of '66, I took a moment to hear their memories of meeting up with the weather. Their love of it ran as deeply as their admiration for professors like Sykes and was as powerful to who they were as those famous blizzard events, so it just didn't seem right to leave the early-childhood memories of these meteorologists and weather observers out of this book – especially when considering how the allure of a snowy day sent seven-year-old Bob Sykes on his weatherman's journey.

"I've always been interested in snow," Fultonian Paul Cardinali confides to me in his interview. "I fell in love with it as a kid and I remember patiently watching the snow falling outside, thinking I had a pretty good idea how much snow would have fallen in a given amount of time. When I was about seven or eight, I was riding with my dad on a gray October day and asked, 'Dad, can it snow in October?' "

That curiosity led high-schooler Cardinali to start keeping

track of Fulton's weather in 1957. After some time away at college and the first years of his marriage, Paul returned to Fulton in 1971, where he has been keeping weather records ever since. Included in Paul's records are his notes about the '66 blizzard. "The forecast called for a nor'easter that became the blizzard, and I had noted in my journal about three days in advance: 'Forecast of another nor'easter coming up.' I'd said 'another' because there had been several nor'easters predicted that year. Then I wrote down, 'But, it'll probably miss us.' Someone like me is always looking for snow."

Back when Paul was in college and studying under Bob Sykes, he met other students caught up in their teacher's enthusiasm for the weather. One of them, Chrystal Laird, took her weather observing and recording seriously, and Paul noted it. Soon, the two found themselves spending a lot of time together tracking weather under Bob's guidance. They began dating and were married in 1966. In all those years since, Paul and Chrystal have been keeping their eye on Fulton skies, and in a 2007 *Post-Standard* profile of the Cardinalis, Sean Kirst would call them Central New York's "first couple of weather."

For Chrystal, her path to appreciating the weather began in her earliest years. At that time, she and her family were living on an Oswego street that would one day run right past SUNY Oswego's science building, Piez Hall, where she studied and worked closely with Bob Sykes. That street in the still-rural area of Chrystal's childhood led to the shores of Lake Ontario, where she learned to be an observer of weather.

"My father found it was kind of difficult to make ends meet in his job as a maintenance man at Niagara Mohawk's steam plant," Chrystal explains, "so he decided it would be good to raise a few vegetables. Thus began his life as a gentleman farmer, and from there, we added a flock of chickens, a milk cow and a sow. Since my father had been raised on a farm, he was quite weather-wise and he passed the same learning on to me. 'My knees tell me that it is going to storm,' he would say. 'Would you please keep an eye on the chickens? I don't want them to be out in the thunder and lightning.'

"From the time I was six or seven years old, I was taught to look at the sky. 'See the clouds over the lake,' Dad would say. 'Those are storm clouds.' So, I was taught to observe and I was taught the feeling that went with it. I developed a strong bound with my father because of the work we did together and I could sense his apprehension when we saw these things. I could see him tensing his body and I knew that there was a connection between how he was speaking, how he was feeling and the black cloud coming in from over the lake. It just transferred to me. It's like any other skill that is taught, but it wasn't a lesson in a formal sense. It was the same thing I would experience later with Bob Sykes. Like my father, Bob would get excited about the weather, and because of that, I bonded to him just like I did to my father."

As an Oswego kid in the '70s, Bob Maxon never thought of himself as a weather lover. But he trained himself to be a good observer, starting at 10 years old, when he became a huge fan of birdwatching after seeing his brother-in-law deftly identify birds at places like the Montezuma National Refuge. Later in his youth, during Oswego's long winters, Bob tapped into those observation skills when looking out his picture window. "There wasn't a lot else to do when it snowed so hard," Maxon shares. Soon, he began developing some of the same weather observation techniques that his childhood idol, Bob Sykes, possessed. "When you couldn't see the east side of Oswego," says Maxon, "you knew it was starting to come down a little bit. At night, if you couldn't see the streetlights across the river, then that was some real snow."

Maxon started to take notes and make conjectures about snow-related events, like when the plows were going to be able to clear streets. "I would use that information to be able to plan my shoveling the three feet of new snow the plow would leave at the end of our driveway," Bob explains. When his parents saw how their son's observations tied in with the sciences, they started talking to him about meteorology. As his senior year of high school approached, they looked for universities that offered programs in meteorology – but not Oswego: "My parents wanted me to see the world. I ended up at Cornell University, which was the most difficult course of study I ever could have taken, but I got through by the skin of my teeth."

While in his junior year at Cornell, Maxon tried a broadcasting class on television and that led to his successful career today with *NBC Connecticut News Today.* Bob traces his motivation for doing a good job back to Bob Sykes on WSGO radio. "He made me realize the importance of forecasting. No matter how you get to the job of meteorology, you have to realize that it is a huge responsibility and Bob took it as that. You can tell by the care he put into his forecasts."

Other future meteorologists were listening into those WSGO broadcasts by Bob. Oswego native, Les Austin, also discovered his love of the weather through an early influence from Sykes. "I was always interested in science and math," says Les, "and I liked what Bob explained about storms on those radio shows. In fact, once I was old enough to drive, I would drive around to find out where the snow was. It was probably a foolish thing to do, but I really was amazed by it."

Austin attended SUNY Oswego from 1973 through '76, took some time off to serve in the military and then returned to Oswego in 1980, graduating with a degree in meteorology in 1981. But he ended up using that science in his career in aviation. While serving in the military, Les racked up a lot of miles as a pilot and then added to that total in his civilian career, where he worked as a corporate pilot. "As a manager in aviation, I spend a lot of time

307

looking at the weather because I was responsible for the flight department's operation." After 38 years in the aviation business, Les still relies on the skills he first discovered while listening to a Bob Sykes' broadcast during a snowstorm.

It's a long way from Wappingers Falls, New York, where Jim LaDue grew up, to Norman, Oklahoma, his present-day hometown and job site. But LaDue sees a connection between the teaching he does at the National Weather Service's Weather Forecast Office and his childhood, noting that he has been "interested in all kinds of weather as far back as I can remember." LaDue also speaks for a lot of dedicated weather watchers when he says that, growing up, he never would have been considered a normal kid:

"I was not a popular-culture kind of guy. I had an interest in sports, music and things like that, but it wasn't a total devotion where I knew all the stats and such. I focused on understanding the natural world, a cross between geology and geography and meteorology. I did lots of science fair projects and did well at them. It was in junior high, in ninth grade, when it really solidified, where I knew this was what I was going to do."

It was at a high school career fair that LaDue met a representative from the FleetWeather Group, a professional weather consulting service, who talked with Jim and her parents about work in weather. "Why don't you come by sometime and volunteer?" the rep offered Jim. There he met other people with a shared interest, "which wasn't something you'd find every day where I grew up," Jim tells.

Jim also benefited from having a friend who was as interested in the science of weather as him. Greg Stumpf grew up about a mile away from Jim and, as LaDue puts it, "we kind of fed off each other." Greg echoes Jim's thoughts on their friendship by adding: "We met in 9th grade, in earth science class of all places. We were randomly seated together and happened to notice that we were both drawing weather maps and it was there that we discovered our mutual interest in meteorology."

Stumpf's curiosity, however, led him to tracking extreme weather conditions like storms, and he can trace his fascination with such phenomenon back to its origins. "I grew up with the fear of thunderstorms. It was like a fear of the unknown. Even in Wappingers Falls, which doesn't see a lot of severe weather, there was always the fear that a rumble of thunder you heard could turn into something bigger. For me, the fear translated into a desire to understand."

Both Greg and Jim were determined to learn more about the weather and that took them to the same college, Oswego State, where they studied under Bob Sykes. And though their career paths have not been particularly similar, today Greg also works in weather study in Norman, Oklahoma, as a University of Oklahoma employee. As could be expected, Stumpf is heavily involved in hazardous weather testing and evaluating, especially those following severe thunderstorms and tornadoes, just like the ones he learned to respect as a child.

It was while on a sailboat that Doug Stewart realized his fascination with the weather. After the Stewart family settled in a little town called Burnt Hills, north of Schenectady, New York, Doug became friends with a guy in high school who had a sailboat. "It was a 14-foot two-person dingy," Doug remembers. "His father acted as his 'crew' and he was often harsh and critical to my friend, so I replaced him. We sailed on Sarasota Lake in the summer and it was my involvement in sailboat racing that got me interested in wind shifts and weather, etc. From there, my interest in meteorology grew."

Doug attended SUNY Oswego from 1971 until '75 and he took several classes from Bob Sykes. He also worked on several of Bob's weather-related projects, including helping his professor with his home weather station. The hands-on experience he received helped Stewart tremendously.

Doug went on to earn his master's degree in MIT in 1977 and then his Ph.D. at the University in Miami. He's always worked in meteorology, but in really unique ways. "Since 1992, I've been working for a company of a fellow college student who started a fog project for a paper mill in Tennessee. Today, I'm working with weather in computer software that I develop." That's quite a far-reaching career for Doug driven by the winds in a boat's sail.

Jack Kaplan means what he says when he comments, "I can't remember a time that I didn't love the weather." Born and raised in Syracuse, Jack was only two or three when he made a phone call to his grandmother, who lived in Ithaca. "While on the phone with her, I said, 'Grandma, it's snowing here in Syracuse, what's it doing in Ithaca?' I always had questions about why it was raining and why the clouds formed like they did. People worship their own form of God, in whatever way they believe. I believe in power and I think that weather is power. Things like tornadoes, hurricanes, lake-effect snow – all those things have always intrigued me.

"When I graduated high school, I attended college to pursue a career in weather, starting my meteorology degree at the University of Missouri in 1970. But I got a little homesick and came back, and that's when I found out that Oswego State had started the meteorology program. So in my junior year of college I started at Oswego, and that's where I met Bob Sykes."

Once graduated, Jack did not end up working in the meteorology field, although he's had a successful management career in industry and business. And he still studies the weather: "I don't forecast and make money from it, I just forecast on my own. I teach people all the time about the weather. Though I ended up not working in the area that Bob did, his teaching how to observe things and feel things really let me become fully engaged in my work."

Tom Moore grew up in Rome, New York and remembers Hurricane Hazel coming through when he was in kindergarten. "My parents and people their age still talk about that storm and how unique it was." By the time he was seven years old, Tom had developed a keen interest in both the weather and baseball, and thinks that since both are statistically oriented, they held his interest.

In second grade, Moore's teacher challenged the class to create a newsletter and Tom was assigned to cover the weather. "I remember getting really into it, with observations and writing about the weather every day. That led to me buying a weather book or two. For Christmas I got *The Golden Book of Weather* – and the rest is history."

That interest continued throughout his elementary and high school education and led him to SUNY Oswego and Bob Sykes. Tom used his training in the college to launch a successful career as a coordinating meteorologist with *The Weather Channel,* just as that mainstay in television forecasting was launching in 1982.

Dave Eichorn is another student of Bob Sykes who's had a longstanding and successful weather career, serving as a chief meteorologist for Syracuse's NewsChannel 9 Storm Team since 1990. (Dave took several years off from television broadcasting to complete his master's degree in environmental science.) Eichorn traces his commitment to the study of weather "as far back as I can remember. I think it stems from my love for snow. I wanted to know as much about conditions leading up to snowfall events as possible. My poor mother: I remember when I was seven or eight years old, she would be preparing dinner while I sat with her in the kitchen going on and on about an approaching front or the mention of snow in the forecast.

"My father and older brother had quite an interest in the weather, too," Eichorn continues, "so I guess it ran in the family. The Blizzard of '66 pretty much set me on my way. When I heard in high school about the intense snowfalls that occurred downwind of Lake Ontario, I knew that was my ground zero. That's where I had to be."

How does a person become known as the Winter Weather Expert on television's most trusted meteorology program, *The Weather Channel?* Such a prestigious position is only afforded after years of training and study, which is how the opportunity came to Tom Niziol. Just as he was ending a 32-year career as the Meteorologist-In-Charge at the National Weather Service's Buffalo headquarters, Tom got a call inviting him to join *The Weather Channel* staff. Prior to that, his inspiration for studying the weather was strongly influenced by Bob Sykes' unique approach to meteorology. But Tom traces the roots of his interest in weather back even further:

"I found a love of Mother Nature very early in life. As a young boy, I was curious about everything from insects to watching cumulus clouds produce powerful thunderstorms. I studied nature whenever I could, including car rides in the country on Sunday afternoons. Money was always in short supply for my family, so as an inexpensive form of entertainment, my dad would load the car with the neighborhood kids and drive us to the Buffalo airport to watch the planes take off and land. Next to that airport was a National Weather Service office, and instead of watching the planes in flight, I was watching weathermen send up balloons to capture what was going on in the atmosphere above us."

A high school science teacher helped Niziol focus his inherent interests on meteorology, and by the time he'd graduated, Tom was anxious to dig into that science on the college level. He found the perfect mentor in Sykes, who used experiments like launching weather balloons to inspire the curiosity of his students. Because of his guidance turning Niziol's childhood fascination of Mother Nature into a venue where he today reaches people worldwide, Tom credits Bob Sykes with his phenomenally successful career.

Of course, not all our trusted weathermen and woman were taught by Bob Sykes, though it seems that anyone from Central New York working in the field during Bob's years in Oswego knew him. That would include Bill Gregway, who has been Oswego's Cooperative Observer for the National Weather Service since 1968. From the minute I walked into Bill's kitchen for our interview about Sykes and The Blizzard of '66, I knew I was in the presence of a true weatherman. Evidence of that fact has taken over Gregway's kitchen table, which is situated beneath a picture window and gives him a great view of all the weather happening outside.

What Gregway observes is transcribed to numerous charts and report forms, all of it detailed in pencil or pen. (Bill never learned to use a computer.) There are also piles of newspaper clippings, many faded from years of rereading, all with headlines about winter snow statistics, blizzards and mammoth Oswego County storms. There's a digital weather forecaster that records the time, temperature, humidity and even gives a forecast. A common hand-held calculator is ready to figure out the day's numbers. The most recent edition of Oswego's *Palladium-Times* has its few inches of column space devoted to the forecasts circled in pen.

"My uncle was a weather observer in the Army Air Corps in World War II, stationed in China. When he came home, he brought his field manuals from the Army and he was instrumental in my interest in the weather. I also remember looking out the window at the storm of 1947 when I was 13. Then, in my high school earth science class, my teacher, Tony Mirabito, was very encouraging to me."

Gregway is a retired draftsman, and at 80 years old, he's never made a living as a meteorologist, but it certainly has been a driving force in his life. As one of the National Weather Service's 12,000 weather observers, Gregway provides the organization with the vital service of measuring and recording Oswego's weather. He's also a wealth of knowledge when someone comes knocking on his door looking for information on local meteorology. If it has to do with Central New York weather, you can bet that Bill will have the answer.

Maybe Carol Yerdon is the exception when considering today's passionate weather observers who started young. For Carol, it didn't begin until she hit adulthood, but she sure has made up for lost time. Quick to point out that she hasn't ever had a career in meteorology – Carol is a special education aide at a local elementary school – nor has she ever taken a class in it, Yerdon says she falls into that category of people who stumbled onto weather observation by chance. She managed to land in the right place, though. Carol makes her home and observes the weather in one of snowiest areas in the world: Redfield, New York, due east of Lake Ontario in the Tug Hill Plateau.

"When I moved to Redfield, where my husband's family has lived for generations, I was able to spend more time outside," Carol explains. "I found myself with more time to observe things and Redfield's weather and heavy snow were interesting to me. One day, I saw an article in the Syracuse newspapers that they were looking for weather observers. I knew that all the towns up here were known for their snow and it seemed that measuring it was kind of silly, but I thought, *OK, I could do that.* I remember my husband's father saying: 'Measure it? Why?' "

Carol got the okay from the newspapers and started using the standard measuring tools of a yardstick and snowboard. She made sure she kept her observation area away from the wind, just like her instructions stated, and she started measuring. And, boy, did those numbers add up. "Pretty soon, the guys at the Syracuse TV stations like Dave Longley and Dave Eichorn picked up on my numbers listed in the newspaper and got in touch with me," Carol says. "They were wondering if I would send in reports to them. Things started spinning out of control because, little did I know, I was sitting in the spot where lake effect dumps.

"I started comparing my numbers to local towns like Williamstown and Parish and mine were often way out of whack. Finally, Dave Eichorn explained why. It seems that the wind that blows the lake-effect snow from over Oswego and up the Tug Hill, ends up dumping that snow 'straight down on Carol Yerdon's house,' as Dave tells it. And you can see that he's right. If you drive up here in the winter – let's say you are coming up through Lacona and Boylston – you'll start seeing the difference in the size of the snowbanks. As you travel up the Tug Hill or, as people say around here, 'head up the hill,' the snowbanks go up and up and up. This also correlates with the difference in elevation: when you leave the Sandy Creek area the elevation is around 400 feet, but by the time you get to where I live, the elevation is just under 1300 feet.

"I really thought that, after I started out, someone would come along and say, 'Look, I already do this.' Or, 'We've been doing this for years.' I thought someone who was a meteorologist or from the TV stations would say, 'You need to change how you are keeping track of your records. You're doing it wrong.' But that's not what happened. In fact, up until me, as far as I know, no one has ever gathered daily snow measurements in our area – not even in Lacona or Sandy Creek.

"My in-laws have lived up here their whole life, as a lot of people around here have, and if you ask them after a storm how much snow fell, they'll say: 'We got a lot.' And if you ask them how much, they'll say: 'A lot. *A lot!*' But nobody had been measuring with numbers – they measure by the telephone poles: 'It's almost to the top of the telephone poles.' To this day, my father-in-law still kids with me. He'll say, 'How much did you get, because it looks like there is six inches on my truck.' And he'll be pretty close, just measuring with his eyes."

Though Carol makes it clear she doesn't have any meteorology credentials, she sure has made a name for herself with some who have. This includes her involvement with what she calls some exciting events: "In Feb '07, The National Weather Service had predicted some heavy lake-effect over an extended period of time in my area. After the fact, they considered it three different snow events, but, in my world, from January 31 until February 12, which is 13 consecutive days, we had 183 inches of snow. And that brought out the big guns from CBS and CNN and *The New York Times* to report and film.

"They were saying that this was a record-breaking snowfall for 10 days. So, reporters showed up in town and called our house: 'This is so and so from CBS and we'd like to interview you.' No warning. I thought it was *Candid Camera*. But it turned out to be Katie Couric's sidekick, Kelly Wallace. It was so unreal. I did a live satellite on the morning show. They were here for the entire day and it was such a thrill...It was like paparazzi."

More recently, Carol found herself invited to a pretty important weather study taking place right in her backyard. "I was lucky to interact with meteorologists who came up from SUNY Oswego to do some weather tests here over the winter of 2013-14. (Yerdon is referring to the OWLeS – Ontario Winter Lake-effect Systems – project mentioned in Chapter 25 of this book.) It was really cool – I went over to visit them, thinking I was glad to meet them, but that I really wouldn't mix with this crowd. I mean, they were geniuses!

"But they were a great group of guys and were really excited about me measuring snow with them. I was hesitant about if I would know what to do – I saw all their fancy equipment – but when I got there, they handed me a ruler. So I guess I'm not that far behind. Of course they had computers and all, and were doing some amazing experiments with technology, but they still really had an interest in my simple numbers."

Carol shared with me some of those "simple numbers" she's gathered in her years keeping measurements and they are impressive enough to catch the interest of any weather enthusiast:

- Highest yearly snow total: 420 inches in the winter of '96 – '97.
- Lowest yearly snow total: 149 inches in the winter of '11 – '12.
- Earliest measureable snow: October 2, 2003.
- Latest measurable snow: May 12, Mother's Day, 1996.
- Carol made special note of the 2013-14 winter: 386 inches. "This was our third heaviest since I've been keeping records. We tied for third, actually, and I was thinking, we might as well go for first. But everybody was hissing at me by then: 'OK, Carol, we've had enough. We don't need any more snow.' But we were so close!"

Spoken like a true weatherman.

Acknowledgements

When I decided to write a book about the legendary Blizzard of '66's impact on Central New York, I knew that I wanted Bob Sykes to be a part of the story. I was ten when the storm hit, just a few years older than Bob was when weather first stirred his curiosity. With my family's radio tuned to WSGO, as it always was during Central New York's winter months, I heard the voice of a well-spoken man trying to help us make sense of what was happening to our world.

Though his broadcast had a few words I was unfamiliar with, there was something in this weatherman's voice that caught my attention. While all the other adults in my life were bemoaning the storm shutting down their world, this grownup was sharing his amazement in it all. His passionate telling of that storm's story seemed to match the intensity of the raging blizzard filling the view from my family's picture window, and this memory of Bob Sykes made including him in my book imperative.

I knew that I had my work cut out for me to track down the details of Bob's involvement in the blizzard, having heard of his passing over 15 years ago. But I didn't realize that, though Bob was no longer with us on this side of storm clouds, his passion for weather was still playing out as vigorously as a lake-effect storm. His legacy had been picked up and nudged forward by a long line of weather enthusiasts, including his former students and colleagues.

Following this chain, I found my way to what I was looking for: Bob's three surviving children, Bruce Sykes, Fred Sykes and

Barbara Sykes Wall, who were willing to share their own cherished memories of their father's contributions to that '66 storm's claim on Central New York. As they explained their father's involvement with it, stories of the rest of Bob's life surfaced, and they were as rich and important to the study of weather as was his role in that blizzard. There was a bigger story to tell about Bob Sykes, and with his family's approval and support, the idea for his biography was born.

Researching the life of a man I had never met seemed daunting at the onset, but that was before I was aware that Bob's excitement for a stormy winter day would be matched by his fervent attention to detail. Everything he noticed, it seemed, he recorded, including the details of his life. Shortly before his passing, when Bob received his diagnosis of cancer that he would not recover from, he started compiling his life's stories. Some of this was prompted by his children, but some was done with a genuine interest to "lay his life out" in much the same way he had preserved his careful notes about the study of weather.

Through the generosity of his children, I was given the opportunity to read this manuscript of Bob's life. His son Fred, who was there when Bob compiled it all, told me that his father did not have to rely on any notes when he recorded his story. Anecdote upon anecdote showed that Bob hadn't lost his knack for detail and specificity, even as his body was losing its abilities.

I learned so much about Bob's life from those notes, but not all of it. There were aspects of his personality that even a keen observer like Bob could not have been aware of. Those included the impressions Sykes left on his students and colleagues. Through my interviews with many of those that knew him at the State University at Oswego, insights were revealed about his convictions, his zest, his robustness and, yes, his shortcomings. My inklings about what drove the passionate voice I heard on WSGO were confirmed time and again.

Sitting with Bob's life narrative in one ear, and his family and friends' recollections echoing in the other, I embarked on the journey of writing this biography. What a joy to see the details fall into place, as surely as snowflakes. It is with much gratitude that I acknowledge those who helped me along the way:

Joe Abbate
Donna Atkins
Les Austin
Pat Brennan
Busath Photography, Salt Lake City, Utah
Paul Cardinali
Frank Castelli
Bernadette Crisafulli
Tom Daniels
Lisa Davis
Nick D'Innocenzo
Kerry Dorsey
Dave Eichorn
Tom Frawley
The Fulton Public Library staff
Tom Galletta
Rick Gessner
Bill Gregway
Cliff "Fritz" and Janet Harris
Dr. Luciano (Lou) Iorizzo
John J. Jansen
Jack Kaplan
George and Cheryl Knopp
Mark Kramer
Karen Krause
Chrystal (Laird) Cardinali
Jim LaDue
Phil Markert
Betty Mauté
Norbert Mauté

Bob Maxon
Mark McClave
Mike McCrobie
Peg McKinstry
Joyce Meredith
Tom Moore
Tom Niziol
Ken Peterson
Francis Quirk
Ken Richards
the river's end bookstore
Al Roker
Robert Schell
Dr. Ray Schneider
Dave Sheltra
Laura Smith
Diane Sokolowski
Dr. Al Stamm
Doug Stewart
Steve Chirello Advertising
Greg Stumpf
SUNY Oswego Office for Development and Alumni Relations
Barbara (Sykes) Wall
Beth (Sykes) Collins
Bruce Sykes
Fred Sykes
Kathleen Sykes
Sandy Sykes
Sarah (Sykes) Sorenson
Bill Symons
Clarke Warner-Long
Bill Wall
Rod Wood
Charles Young

Resources

Azarian, Mary and Martin, Jacqueline Briggs. *Snowflake Bentley.* Boston, MA: Houghton Mifflin Company, 1998.

Balchen, Bernt Balchen; Ford, Corey; LaFarge, Oliver. *War Below Zero: The Battle for Greenland.* Boston, MA: Houghton Mifflin / Riverside Press,1944.

Brown, Andrew H. "Americans Stand Guard in Greenland." *National Geographic,* October 1946.

Eichorn, D. N. and Sykes, Robert B., Jr. "Early October 1974 Snow Debacle Near Oswego." *Weatherwise,* Dec. 1974.

Ferlito, J. and Sykes, Robert B., Jr. "The February 1972 Eastern Snow Conference Weather Experience at Oswego, New York." Proceedings of the 1992 Eastern Snow Conference, publication date unknown.

Fuller, John F. *Thor's Legions: Weather Support to the U.S. Air Force and Army, 1937 - 1987.* The American Meteorological Society. Boston, MA, 1990.

Grogan, Mike. "Joys of Forecasting." *Syracuse Post-Standard,* date unknown.

Hardy, Janet and Taylor, Susan Taylor, Editors. "Eastern Snow Conference, Proceedings of the 1999 Annual Meeting." Publication information unknown.

Haynes, C.V., Major General, USAF. *Greenland in Brief..* Publication information unknown. June 1948.

Howarth, David. *Sledge Patrol.* New York, NY: The Macmillan Company, 1957.

"In the Know About Snow." No author noted. *Syracuse Herald-American.* January 2, 1966.

Judd, John H., Research Scientist and Sykes, Robert B., Jr. Director. "Lake Ontario Environmental Laboratory (LOTEL) State University College, Oswego, New York, A Brief Introduction And Commentary." February 23, 1970.

Kirst, Sean Kirst. "Oswego's Foul-Weather Friend." *Syracuse Post-Standard.* November 27, 1988.

Livingston, Lansing; Falconer, Raymond, and Sykes, Robert B., Jr. "Studies of Weather Phenomena to the Lee of Eastern Great Lakes." *Weatherwise.* Vol. 17, No. 6. Dec 1964.

Mandeville, Richard Mandeville. *"Sykes Retiring From Teaching."* *Oswego County Messenger.* Friday, May 20, 1983.

"Major Sykes Decorated With Danish Cross." No author noted. *Yonkers New York Herald Statesman.* Dec 17, 1947.

"Major Sykes Tells of Escape From Icebergs Off Greenland." No author noted. *Yonkers New York Herald Statesman.* 1944.

"Oswego Weather Is Project Of Detailed Scientific Study." No author noted. *Watertown Daily News.* April 24, 1965.

Pack, A. Boyd, State Climatologist, National Weather Service, NOAA; Loveridge, Elmer, Retired at Oswego and Sykes, Robert B., Jr., LOTEL, SUCO. "The Climate And Snow Climatology Of Oswego, N.Y." June 1971.

Peace, Jr., R.L. and Sykes, Robert. B., Jr. "Mesoscale Study of a Lake Effect Snow Storm." *Monthly Weather Review.* Vol. 94, Issue 8. August 1966.

Report on Greenland 1949. Author and publication information not noted. From the collection of Fred Sykes.

"Robert Sykes Made Major." No author noted. *Yonkers New York Herald Statesman.* August 11, 1943.

Smith, Andrew Smith. "Lineage Led To Interest in Weather." *Syracuse*

Post-Standard. August 6, 1992.

Sykes, Robert B., Jr. "Oswego's Tardy, Tough Winter of 71-72." *Weatherwise.* Vol. 25, No. 6. Dec 1972.

---------. "The Blizzard of '66 in Central New York State—Legend in its Time." *Weatherwise.* Vol. 19, No. 6. Dec 1966.

---------. "Weather and Life in the Artic." *Oceanography and Meteorology.* The New York Academy of Sciences. Vol. 16, Issue 1, Series II. Nov. 1953.

---------. "Arthur F. Merewether, 1902-1997." *Bulletin of the American Meteorological Society.* Vol. 78, Issue 10. October 1997.

---------. "Some Historical Remarks On Meteorology And Miscellaneous Comments Regarding The Weather In The Oswego Area." Oswego County Historical Society. May 20th, 1969.

---------. "On The Blizzard of '72 in Oswego, New York." Proceedings of the 1972 Annual Meeting. Oswego, N.Y. 3, 4 (& 5) February 1972.

---------. "1971/1972 Winter at Oswego, N.Y.: A Short Commentary." Proceedings of the 1972 Annual Meeting. Oswego, N.Y. 3, 4 (& 5) February 1972.

---------. "A Career at the State University College Oswego, New York (Fall of 1961 through January of 1983 – Reflections and Reconsiderations." February 1983.

---------. "Wind Speed Estimation Means." August 1976.

---------. Taped Interview by Bruce Sykes. Saturday, September 12, 1998.

"Volunteer Weather Observers Study Lake Ontario Storms." No author noted. *Lakeshore News.* Wolcott, NY. March 12, 1964.

Walker, Paula Walker. "Blame It On the Snow." *Syracuse Post-Standard,* Empire magazine. January 13, 1980.

web:Oswego.edu/news/index.php/site/news_story/shineman_philanthropy.

ABOUT THE AUTHOR

Jim Farfaglia is a writer, teacher and life coach based in Upstate New York. In 2011, after a fulfilling career directing a children's camp and advocating for youth, Farfaglia transitioned to focusing more time on his lifelong interest in writing. Along with his poetry, which is featured in his hometown of Fulton's newspaper, *the Valley News,* Jim enjoys researching and writing about local history. Visit his website at www.jimfarfaglia.com.